MISS SHIRLEY
BASSEY

MISS SHIRLEY
BASSEY

JOHN L. WILLIAMS

Quercus

First published in Great Britain in 2010 by
Quercus
21 Bloomsbury Square
London
WC1A 2NS

A CIP catalogue record for this book is available
from the British Library

ISBN 978 1 84724 974 6 (HB)
ISBN 978 0 85738 098 2 (TPB)

Typeset by Ellipsis Books Limited, Glasgow
Plates designed by Helen Ewing

Printed and bound in Great Britain by Clays Ltd, St Ives plc

For Owen

Being Shirley Bassey is a tough way to run a life.
SHIRLEY BASSEY, 1964

CONTENTS

INTRODUCTION	FOR ONE NIGHT ONLY	1
PROLOGUE	THE GAMBLER	6
ONE	MOTHER AND FATHER	10
TWO	IN TIGER BAY BEFORE THE WAR	19
THREE	THE CANADIAN CAFÉ	27
FOUR	LIFE DURING WARTIME	32
FIVE	ON THE STREET WHERE YOU LIVE	41
SIX	THE RAINBOW CLUB	46
SEVEN	DOWN THE DOCKS	58
EIGHT	HOT FROM SPLOTT	71
NINE	STORMY WEATHER	90
TEN	TALK OF THE TOWN	104
ELEVEN	BURN MY CANDLE	123
TWELVE	MY BODY'S MORE IMPORTANT THAN MY MIND	134
THIRTEEN	VIVA LAS VEGAS	151
FOURTEEN	SOPHISTICATED LADY	162

FIFTEEN	CRUEL TO BE KIND	180
SIXTEEN	SHIRLEY THE WEIRDIE	193
SEVENTEEN	SCREEN DREAMS	212
EIGHTEEN	LOVE AND MARRIAGE	225
NINETEEN	I (WHO HAVE NOTHING)	241
TWENTY	A KNIGHT IN SHINING ARMOUR	253
TWENTY-ONE	THE MAN WITH THE MIDAS TOUCH	266
TWENTY-TWO	THE SECOND TIME AROUND	273
TWENTY-THREE	NAPOLEON AND JOSEPHINE	282
EPILOGUE	AFTER THE RAIN	296

DISCOGRAPHY   300

APPENDICES   303
1 A SHORT HISTORY OF TIGER BAY
2 BUTE STREET AND ITS CAFES
3 A SHORT HISTORY OF MAHMOOD MATTAN
   AND THE MURDER OF LILY VOLPERT
4 A SHORT HISTORY OF MINSTREL SHOWS
5 A SHORT HISTORY OF BRITISH STRIPTEASE

NOTES   329

ACKNOWLEDGMENTS   339

PICTURE ACKNOWLEDGMENTS   341

TEXT ACKNOWLEDGMENTS   343

INDEX   345

For One Night Only

November 2009. I'm standing in the Roundhouse, North London, waiting for Shirley Bassey to come on stage. There's a real excitement in the air. The crowd, a cheerful mix of gay and straight, young, old and middle-aged, have left the bars and they're packed into the converted Victorian auditorium waiting to welcome a woman who started her career before most of them were born.

Some of the people here are obviously long-time fans, thrilled to see Dame Shirley again. But there are plenty more who, like me, have never seen her live before; have probably never listened much to her records, beyond the inescapable karaoke classics. But we, all of us, sense that this is something special, that we are about to be in the presence of an actual star. A 'star' from a time when the word meant something.

For young people growing up in South Wales in the 1960s and 1970s, Shirley Bassey was inescapable. She was in the singles charts when I was born, in 1961. She was on TV in the 1970s, when I was growing up. I never thought very much about her: she was just there on the telly, like *Coronation Street* or cigarette advertisements. Her music was not the music of my generation. Her great brassy voice was as far removed as can be imagined from the punk rock whine of the bands I favoured at sixteen. The TV shows she

1

appeared on were the kind of thing my grandmother would watch when she babysat for us on a Saturday night: light entertainment.

If I thought about Shirley Bassey at all, it was because she came from my hometown of Cardiff. Wales being a small place, we're always hungry for heroes and heroines, and in the 1970s we didn't have many to choose from. We were always ridiculously proud if someone Welsh appeared on a quiz show or in an episode of *Crossroads*. Our handful of genuine big names were cherished regardless of whether we actually liked what they did: Richard Burton, Stanley Baker and the young Anthony Hopkins in the world of acting; John Toshack in football; Tommy Cooper in comedy. And in music there was Tom Jones and Shirley Bassey. They were our principality's representatives in the big, wide world.

I didn't know much about Shirley Bassey, just that she was born in Cardiff, in some dockland neighbourhood called Tiger Bay that didn't appear to exist in the actual Cardiff I knew, at least not under that name. She didn't live there any longer, of course; she had become glamorous and lived somewhere appropriate: London or Switzerland or Monte Carlo, somewhere James Bond-ish. I don't recall her racial background as impinging on me at all. She certainly didn't seem 'black' in the way that Bob Marley, say, or even Diana Ross was: that's to say recognisably belonging to a black culture. Shirley Bassey's culture seemed to be that of international showbiz, and her natural skin tone not that far different from the permatan of a Sacha Distel or Cliff Richard.

As I grew up and moved out of Wales I came across her less often, but throughout the next couple of decades her name would flicker into the national consciousness from time to time. A court case covered in the papers; a TV special glimpsed in a pub; a breakfast time TV interview lying on a bed with Paula Yates; launching the Rugby World Cup wearing a dress made out of the Welsh flag.

Somewhere along the way she'd become part of Welsh heritage: a national monument, the girl from Tiger Bay.

But even so, I took her existence for granted. It was a chance viewing of a TV show that made me stop and reconsider. The programme was a fairly basic run-through of Dame Shirley's career, but right at the beginning there was a piece of very early live footage. She was eighteen or so, belting out a song I'd never heard before called 'Burn My Candle', in front of a very staid 1950s TV orchestra. Everything about it was as cheesy as you might expect, yet the young Shirley was a revelation. She had her natural Afro hair cut short and she had a direct sexuality that seemed completely alien to everything I thought I knew about the austerity Britain of the 1950s.

Afterwards, when I started thinking more about the Bassey career, and reading up some basic biographical information, it struck me for the first time just how extraordinary her achievement was. Break it down to its bare essentials: in 1954 she was a seventeen-year-old black single mother living in Splott, Cardiff. Ten years later, when she recorded 'Goldfinger', she was an international star and seemed to come from the planet Glamour, which is a long way from Splott – and I speak as someone who lived there for a short while.

And the more I researched the more remarkable her story seemed. From the Tiger Bay of the 1930s, to the variety theatres of the early 1950s, to the Soho clubs of the late 1950s, Shirley Bassey's life had been lived in a series of now vanished worlds, each of them a strange mix of the glamorous and the grim. So I resolved to write about her life, not the whole of it but the decades that shaped her. I would end the story in 1967, when she was thirty years old and an established star. For me it's always the route to the top that fascinates, not life at the top, with its endless round of TV specials, profiles in *Hello*, and albums of Andrew Lloyd Webber songs.

3

The more I learnt about the young Shirley Bassey, the more she fascinated me. Very different from the diva stereotype: a deeply insecure and troubled, but remarkably brave, young woman. One who'd found herself thrust into a stardom she'd never anticipated or even particularly wanted, and was oscillating between having the time of her life and feeling desperately lost and alone. That said, she was also, and remains, a born survivor.

So where did it come from, the strength that allowed the young Shirley to win through in a world that routinely ate up starlets and spat them out again? The answer, I think, has to be 'from her mother'. For if Shirley Bassey's story is a remarkable one of triumph against the odds, her mother Eliza Jane's is hardly less extraordinary and in many ways surprisingly similar. Both mother and daughter knew what it was like to have children out of wedlock when they were young, to leave the place they grew up in and make a new life on their own in a new city; both had their lives dogged by scandal – both even had lovers pull guns on them.

It must have been her mother's example that gave Shirley Bassey the strength to live the life she has. When she was born, in the late 1930s, to be a mixed-race child brought up by a white mother in Britain was highly unusual. Today, in the major cities at least, it's commonplace. What's extraordinary about Dame Shirley is that she managed to make it seem unremarkable at the time, hardly worth commenting on. For a long period, during the radicalism of the 1960s and 1970s, her stance seemed out of place. When black Britons were fighting against racism, and for a distinct black British identity, Shirley Bassey was busy flirting with Prince Charles in a see-through blouse, and sipping cocktails with Joan Collins, almost as if denying there was such a thing as racism to worry about.

Today we can look back and see that, in fact, she was playing the long game. Throughout her career she was anticipating a time when all the old prejudices would be seen as simply out of date, stupid. For, in retrospect, Shirley Bassey seems to have been a pioneer who rejected all the identities society likes to put on people, a woman who refused to acknowledge the restrictions of race or class or gender. Shirley Bassey's is a strangely modern life, then, or at least one with lessons for the generations that came after her.

And that's why, that evening at the Roundhouse, what we were waiting for was not a nostalgia act, but someone who we all sensed had something to tell us about what it is to be British today. Someone whose past we could hardly dream of, bringing us lessons for the present.

And that's the story I hope to tell here.

The Gambler

Kenneth had no idea what time it was, whether it was light or dark behind the curtains. He called out for the nurse but there was no reply – blokey must have slipped off down the pub. Maybe he would call Sheila for a chat – or had he called her earlier? He wasn't sure. He had taken a sleeping pill, what . . . a few hours ago? He'd take another one soon. After all, if he was awake it must be time for another one, mustn't it?

First, though, he would have a little think, a little think and a little drink, if nursey hadn't found the cognac under the pillow. No, it was still there. Good.

So where were we? Oh yes, up shit creek all right, but still paddling. Hah, maybe that's what he'd call his autobiography. He was going to have to tell Shirley something. He'd promised so much. Your musical will open in September, dear. On the West End stage. Josephine, starring Miss Shirley Bassey as the Empress of France.

She could stop all the touring, stay home with her girls, starring in the West End six nights a week plus two matinees. Then it would transfer to Broadway and then at last, at last there would be a film. Josephine in CinemaScope, followed by endless walks down the red carpets: Cannes, the Oscars. She longed to be a movie star. And all he wanted was to make it happen. And make a few bob as well, obviously.

But as usual he'd got ahead of himself, let his mouth run away with things. Announced in all the press, front page everywhere: Josephine will open in September. Broadway blah, Hollywood blah. Show would cost £110,000; he would be promoting it himself.

Oh, why was he such a bullshitter? A hundred and ten grand. Jesus, where was he going to get that from? He was down to his last ten. He'd been unlucky, of course. Everyone has one of those runs. The cards, the roulette. Well, especially the roulette. Maybe he should have one more shot. Pop down to Les Ambassadeurs and see what happens. Seize the day or go down in a blaze of glory. Sort of thing people will talk about for years: you remember the night Kenny Hume lost the lot at Les A? Should have seen his face.

Yes, soon as he felt better that's what he'd do. Wasn't like he could carry on the way things were. He was dying, he was sure of it. The pneumonia, the insomnia, the emphysema and the pleurisy: he was so weak the next thing that came along was bound to blow him away. Weak and tired too. So tired. Tired of all the graft. Shirley was going to find out sooner or later that all the money had gone. And she wasn't going to be pleased. Three seasons in Las Vegas and the money all gone. Have to sell the house in Chester Square if something didn't turn up.

Still, Shirley would be all right, she could always earn some more. She was starting at the Talk of the Town next week. 'A Farewell to Cabaret', he'd told them to call it. Might have to change that: 'A Hello Again to Cabaret' season. Or maybe 'A more and more cabaret till manager and ex-husband Kenneth Hume Esq. stops losing it all in the casino' season. Didn't have much of a ring to it, that. No.

Six years they'd been together now. Two years of happily married life – well, in their funny way – and yah boo to all those people who'd said he'd only done it for the money, little queer like him, marrying a sexy girl like that! Love's not all me Tarzan you Jane, you know.

7

Shirley had had enough of all that. She'd wanted a man who could teach her stuff about art and books and interior decoration. And whatever they say about the money, he loved her too, she was funnier and a million times smarter than she thought she was, and they had a laugh, it had even been all right in the other ways too. If only he'd been able to keep it buttoned up around the boys, they'd still be husband and wife.

But they'd got over all that, hadn't they? Just her manager now, but that was fine. Things were going well. He had, if he said it himself, done a good job. Taken her to the States: the Las Vegas deal, the American record deal, the Dean Martin Show, *the* Andy Williams Show, *the* Danny Kaye Show, *the TV special* Bassey Meets Basie. *Done all of that, with a little help from Leslie, of course. Where was Leslie, anyway? And there was the new record, too. Best one in years. That song he found for her, 'Big Spender', that was a hit if ever he'd heard one. He'd done good. It was just a shame about the musical and the films, a shame he couldn't answer all her dreams.*

'Cause they still loved each other, you know. Of course, she had her fellers, he had his fellers, but any time they needed someone to talk to they'd be right on the phone. Day or middle of the night. Best friends. Which was why he couldn't bear the situation. He'd let her down, he knew that. He wasn't well. Pneumonia and now this . . . this awful bloody depression.

And this time nothing was working. Dr Ratner and his pills weren't working. The trick cyclist Ratner sent round wasn't doing the job either. Convinced it was something to do with him being a homosexual. That wasn't it at all. He wasn't one of those tortured fucking queers, he'd always accepted himself for what he was. Even after the business with Lord Montagu and the Boy Scouts. Kenneth knew who he was. No, he wasn't depressed about that. It was just the way he was. Churchill's black dog, well, that was a hound he was familiar with. And this time nothing was working. One more sleeping pill, maybe another little drink, make it through till morning. Call Shirley then, just tell her the whole thing. Have to postpone the play, just for a few months. It'll work out in the end, you'll see. Don't worry, you'll see. Just one more little pill and he could get some sleep and it would be all right. In the morning.

And as he drifted off Kenneth remembered an old, old idea. Maybe, if Josephine didn't after all come off, they could revive it. It was a simple plan, obvious too, like all the best ideas. They would make a film together of Shirley's life, Shirley's extraordinary life – from the time he first met her back in '55, when he directed her first TV appearance, just a gauche little kid with big eyes and attitude. Right up to now: international cabaret queen and true st-a-a-a-ar. There'd be flashbacks too – all that old Tiger Bay stuff, tell the truth about all of that. And even further back, back before that. Because if you wanted to understand Shirley, you needed to know about her mother. Yes, that would be the way to start. With the mother.

ONE

Mother and Father

So yes, let's start with her mother, Shirley Bassey's mother Eliza Jane Start, and the place she came from. That place was New Marske, an ironstone mining village in Cleveland that had been built no more than forty years before Eliza Jane was born there on 29 March 1901.

A century earlier this place, where the North Yorkshire Moors meet the sea and the marsh banks of the River Tees, had been a forgotten corner of England. There were a handful of fishing villages along the coast, Coatham and Staithes and Marske-by-the-Sea, but you had to travel as far as the fishing-town-turned-coal-exporting-port of Whitby for any sign of prosperity. Then came the Industrial Revolution, coal and iron and a new port at Middlesbrough. Ironstone mines were built, new towns were constructed by their owners, and the rush was on for the workless of Yorkshire and its surrounding counties to find new jobs and new lives. By 1870 there were around a hundred blast furnaces lining the River Tees to process the ironstone from the mines and Middlesbrough was known across the Empire as 'Ironopolis'.

The mining village of New Marske takes its name from the ancient fishing village a mile or so down the hill. Among the first inhabitants of this new village, these half-dozen streets thrown up to house the three thousand workers needed by the pit, were the Barber family.

Shirley Bassey's maternal grandparents were Eliza Jane Barber, who was born in Arthur Terrace, New Marske, in 1871, and David Start, a miner. After they married, they lived together in the same two-up two-down terraced house that Eliza Barber had grown up in. In 1901 their daughter, also called Eliza Jane, was born.

So Eliza Jane Start, Shirley Bassey's mother, spent her first years in this tiny house in this tiny village attached to a fearful mine in which men worked and died. To walk out of the front door of number 60 Arthur Terrace was to be confronted by the Industrial Revolution in all its smog-ridden glory. Walk out of the back door, though, into the little allotment garden there, and you were confronted by something else entirely. Arthur Terrace is on the very edge of the village, and if you looked out from its garden you had an unbroken view over the fields to the old village of Marske-by-the-Sea, and beyond that you could see the sea, see the ships heading to Redcar and to Middlesbrough and to Stockton. And you could see them leaving too, see them heading to all those great ports of empire, to lands unimaginable, to Kingston and Georgetown, to Aden and Bombay, to Cape Town and Calabar.

Born in the same house her mother was born in, given the same name her mother was given, watching the boats go by, the young Eliza Jane's thoughts must have turned to escape. And escape she did. By 1910 Eliza Jane, her siblings and parents, had moved from New Marske to Staithes.

Staithes was a fishing village ten miles to the east. At the time there were eighty boats going out to sea from Staithes. There was also a potash mine and, most likely, that's where David Start would have worked.

Apart from its fishing, the other thing Staithes was famous for

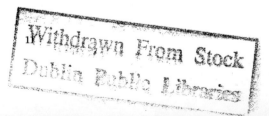

was singing. A boom in choral singing was one of the less predictable side effects of the Industrial Revolution. In the mining towns and iron town and fishing towns and port towns alike, on Sunday the men and the women went to church and the men would sing. Each mining town had its miners' choir, each fishing town its fishermen's choir. Staithes still boasts one of the last of the great fishermen's choirs. One of its oldest members, Tom Hall, remembers how the singing was in the village in the early 1920s, not long after Eliza Jane and her parents lived there:

> The fishermen all foregathered on the staith on a Sunday evening, in front of the Cod and Lobster, and they marched up the street singing at the tops of their voices . . . and then as they come to the various chapels, which of course they all had their own ones, they peeled off still singing, and went into it. And it was then that if you come down at this village on a Sunday evening you'd practically hear them lifting the roofs off.[1]

The Starts didn't stay in Staithes for long, though. They went next to South Bank, Middlesbrough, a sprawling working-class settlement built on the Teesside marshland and caught between the river and the slag heaps thrown up by the ironstone mines to the immediate south. Locals called the place Slaggy Island. The family lived at number 65 North Street.

They were respectable working-class folk, David and Eliza Start. In the 1950s the local paper ran a brief article celebrating the couple's sixtieth wedding anniversary. Their daughter Eliza Jane, however, was a less conventional sort. In 1919, at the age of eighteen, while still unmarried, she gave birth to her first child, a girl called Doris. No father was named on the birth certificate.

A year later on 20th November 1920 Eliza Jane married Alfred

Metcalfe, a labourer from West Hartlepool, another fishing-village-turned-booming-port-town only a few miles north of Middlesbrough. Metcalfe was the father of Eliza's second child – another girl, Florence, born just a few months after the wedding.

Like many a shotgun marriage, the relationship between Eliza and Alfred failed to last. Just two and a half years after Florence was born, Eliza gave birth again, to a girl she called Ella, and once more there was no father listed on the birth certificate. A cursory glance at Ella's skin colour would have confirmed that, whoever her father was, he was not a labourer from Hartlepool, but a black man, no doubt one of the sailors who'd called into the already fading town they once called Ironopolis.

It would be hard to overstate how shocking this must have been at the time: a married woman with two young children giving birth to a black baby in the all-white town of Middlesbrough. Most young women in her position would have given up the baby for adoption immediately, tried as best they could to hush up the whole affair. Not Eliza Jane. She was determined to keep her baby, at whatever cost.

And the cost was considerable. To keep Ella, she had to give up everything. The story passed down through the Start family is that Eliza's relations, the older folk a few miles away in New Marske, were so horrified by her carrying on with a black man that they gave her an ultimatum – ditch the man and get rid of the baby or leave town. Eliza made her choice. She left her oldest daughter, Doris, with her parents. She left Florence with Alfred Metcalfe. And she took baby Ella with her to find a place where they could live without shame.

Eliza did keep in contact with her mother and Doris over the years to come. Florence and Alfred, on the other hand, seem to have broken off contact completely.

In the 1920s there were only a handful of places in Britain where a white woman could bring up a mixed-race child without being the object of scorn. The best-known of these was Cardiff's Tiger Bay. Perhaps she was told as much by the father of her child, perhaps she just heard it on the wind, but the next time Eliza Jane Metcalfe appears on the public record it's September 1926 and she is living at number 15 Fitzhamon Embankment, Cardiff; another port town, another Victorian boomtown, but one with a well established multiracial dockland community.

It was there that she gave birth to her fourth child, Iris. Once again the child was of mixed race. On her birth certificate her first name is given as Iris and her middle name as Johnson. The baptism record makes sense of this oddity: there Iris's father's name is given as Samuel Johnson.

Thus by the end of 1926 Eliza Jane Metcalfe had established herself in Cardiff, on a street full of boarding houses looking over the filthy waters of the river Taff, along with her two mixed-race daughters. She was already a long way from the respectable life. There's no sense, however, that she was ashamed of the choices she made. And she clearly came to some kind of peace with her parents. The magician Paul Daniels is also from South Bank and he told me that his mother recalls Eliza coming to visit her parents there, accompanied by a black man and two black children, a most unusual sight at the time. Most likely the children were Ella and Iris. The black man may have been Samuel Johnson. It's also conceivable that he might have been someone else: the man who would become Eliza Jane's second husband, Henry Bassey.

*   *   *

Henry Bassey was a thirty-year-old merchant seaman from Calabar in Nigeria. Calabar was an older port than either Cardiff or Middlesbrough. In the sixteenth century they traded in palm oil out of Calabar, there on the Niger Delta on the border between what is now Nigeria and Cameroon. Later the British came, and they traded in human cargo: slaves.

The slave ships out of Liverpool and Bristol would stop off in Calabar, purchase a slave cohort of mostly Igbo origin (the people of Calabar themselves being largely Efik in origin) and take them on the Atlantic crossing. Records suggest that the number of slaves trafficked via Old Calabar, between 1720 and the trade's end in 1830, was around the million mark.

The slaves came from inland villages. Efik raiding parties went into the interior to capture them. Chiefs in the villages first sent out all their criminals, debtors and rivals. Others were taken by force. Men, women and children were shackled together and taken downriver in boats to Calabar. They would be traded with the ships' captains for goods . . . copper rods and manillas, beads and cowrie shells, guns and gunpowder, brass pans, cloth, rum and whisky, gin and tobacco. The Calabar locals were as happy with the trade as the slavemasters back in Britain. The chiefs of Old Calabar, so the legend goes, would take albino girls downriver to sacrifice them to the deity 'Ndem Efik' in order to keep the traders coming.

After the slave trade ended Calabar continued to do business. Palm oil still, as well as ivory, timber and beeswax, but around the turn of the century, not long after Henry Bassey's birth in 1895, its importance began to wane, eclipsed by Port Harcourt, the terminus of the new railroad.

As a result the sailors of Calabar joined the merchant navy and travelled the world. They were given new westernised names when they joined up, often following the pattern of a western-style first name and then a surname that is in effect more of a clan or tribal name – Bassey is one such name. Thus Henry Bassey was just one of a number of unrelated Basseys from the Calabar region to serve in the merchant navy.

Many of these West African sailors put in at the great coal port of Cardiff, with its famous Tiger Bay. More than a few of them stayed. Some stayed just for a while, in between stints at sea. Others put down roots. Typically they would buy or rent a house in the docklands and set it up as a legal, or more often illegal boarding house, catering to their fellow sailors. Henry Bassey was one of those who stayed.

He arrived in Cardiff in 1919, the year the city exploded into a series of race riots. Whether he was there for the riots themselves is unknown, but he must have been aware of them and their legacy: the sense that Tiger Bay was an embattled island in a city and a country that had little use for, or understanding of, black people. Over the next twenty years he lived at a bewildering number of addresses in Cardiff but all of them were either in Tiger Bay itself, or the community to the immediate south, known simply as the Docks, and generally seen as a slight step up from Tiger Bay.

What eventually anchored him in Cardiff was what anchored many of his fellow seamen: starting a family. Plus the fact that his job at sea was as a fireman or, more commonly, stoker. This was pretty much the worst job on the ship. Stokers worked in the boiling engine room shovelling coal into the boiler, gruellingly hard physical labour with a constant danger of suffering severe burns. It was not a job anyone would do for longer than they had to. Much of the time though, it was the only job an African sailor could get, the one no one else was prepared to do.

This is the kind of journey Henry Bassey made. On 19 July 1926 he signed on as a fireman and trimmer with a ship called the *Trevarrack* sailing out of Cardiff. A look at the crew list confirms that the engine room was indeed the province of the Africans: alongside Bassey was a Kofee Brown from Sierra Leone, another

Sierra Leonean by the name of Tucker, and a man from Lagos with an unreadable signature. Two and a half weeks after setting sail they arrived in Philadelphia and spent five days on shore, in its deceptively named Quaker City sailortown. Four weeks later they were in the old slave-trading hub of Rio de Janeiro where they spent a week, no doubt investigating the delights of Vasco de Gama, the street where, as the sailor-turned-writer Stan Hugill has it, 'Latin and Negro *putas* hung out of every doorway . . . catering for every form of sex perversion. It was a common sight to see little Negro and mulatto girls of ten and twelve offering themselves to foreign seamen. By the First World War the sailor quarter of the port also had a dirty film joint to add to its already doubtful pleasures.'[2]

Another week's sailing and Bassey was in the river port of Rosario de Santa Fe on the Rio Parana in Argentina, famed for the quality of the Russian whores in its *casas de putas*. Four days there and a short sail to Buenos Aires where he spent ten days in La Boca, the dockland community with its pubs, cafés, dance halls and brothels, the Liverpool Bar and the Flags of All Nations, its crimpers and beachcombers, its flourishing trade in pornography, and its balconies boasting their all-female 'German orchestras', full of what the sailors called 'silent pipers'. And after that a full month spent sailing back across the Atlantic, before reaching his final destination, Amsterdam, on 10 November.

By the time he returned home from that trip Henry Bassey was a father. On 29 October 1926, Eliza gave birth to their first child together, and her fifth: another girl, this one named Edith Grace, though known always by her middle name. The birth certificate reports that the child's father was Henry Bassey, a 'mercantile marine fireman', and that he lived with her mother Eliza Jane Metcalfe at number 40 Loudoun Square, the once grand, now fading heart of Tiger Bay.

Five months later, Henry and Eliza Jane were married. Henry Bassey's father's name was given as John Bassey (deceased). Intriguingly, Eliza gave her father's name as Alfred Metcalfe, which was actually the name of her first husband, and she claimed that he too was deceased. One can only presume that she was never divorced from Metcalfe and, to avoid the suspicion of bigamy, passed off Metcalfe as her maiden name rather than her married name, thus turning her husband into her father.

The couple had moved from Loudoun Square to number 164 Bute Street. Bute Street was the effective high street of Tiger Bay, at the time amongst the most notorious neighbourhoods not just in Cardiff, or indeed in Britain, but across the whole seafaring world, where it was known and treasured as one of the true sailor-towns, a Celtic cousin to La Boca or Quaker City. And it was on Bute Street, Tiger Bay, that Eliza Jane and Henry would remain for the next decade and Eliza would give birth to five more children, the last of whom would be a girl called Shirley Veronica Bassey.

TWO

In Tiger Bay Before the War

This world-renowned sailortown in which the Basseys lived was not, in fact, the original Tiger Bay. In the memories of sailors there are three Tiger Bays. The first Tiger Bay was actually in London, in the Dickensian East End centred around Ratcliffe Highway in Limehouse. The sailor-turned-folksinger-and-writer Stan Hugill paints a vivid picture of that Tiger Bay's inhabitants back in the 1840s:

Coming up from the docks one would meet dock-labourers, dirtied with the type of cargo they had been working; bewildered emigrants, with their bags and bundles; gaugers with their 'spears' dripping with rum or wine, and men with faces dyed blue from working indigo out of the holds of Indian traders. All types of seamen would be rolling by – tall, blond Scandinavians from the timber ships; black-faced Blackball-hatted Negroes; bland Orientals in half-masted, blue dungaree trousers and quilted jackets; and in their tarpaulin hats and black neckerchiefs, sunburnt East Indiamen. As they strolled along the Highway the Ratcliffe harpies would be out in force to meet them, taking no umbrage apart from a flippant Irish curse, at being brushed aside. The whole area teemed with brothels and prostitutes, foreign sluts as well as emigrant Irish girls . . . Other habitués of the Highway were the Negro street singers, the sellers of broadsides, and the 'chaunters' who, playing their fiddles, sang of recent fires, murders, crimes and executions.[1]

The other Tiger Bays, the one in Georgetown, Guyana and the one in Cardiff, Wales, both got their names in recognition of the degree to which they measured up to this lawless prototype. The reputation of the Cardiff version began to overtake that of the original as the nineteenth century wore on. Hardly surprising, as this was the period when Cardiff came from nowhere to become one of the great ports of the Victorian age; the one that provided the coal on which the world's shipping ran.

When Henry Bassey arrived in Tiger Bay soon after the end of the first World War, it was a place under siege. The race riots of 1919 had made it clear that the multiracial settlers had better stay in their own dockland isthmus and not venture into the centre of town. And gradually what had begun with mob violence became enshrined in official policy. What soon became known as the 'colour bar' came down to deal with black immigration. Industry was almost entirely closed to blacks, and seafaring jobs were made ever harder to obtain by cynical manipulation of nationality laws. The slump of 1929 simply saw economic matters go from bad to worse. Tough times for families like the Basseys.

In that year a paper presented to the Conference on the Health and Welfare of Merchant Seamen reported that:

In Cardiff, and to a certain extent in Manchester, difficulties are increasing in connection with the association of coloured seamen with white women and the subsequent growth of a half-caste population, alien in sentiment and habits to the native white inhabitants. The Chief Constable of Cardiff has reported to the Watch Committee and suggested the desirability of bringing into existence legislation similar to that found necessary in South Africa to check this demoralising development.[2]

Thankfully Wales did not take this advice. It never introduced its own officially sanctioned version of apartheid, but the unofficial version was oppressive enough. Trapped as they were between the bigots and the murky green sea, the people who'd settled in Butetown, men like Henry Bassey, had to construct their own economy, based on catering to the traditional desires of men who have spent the last few months on the ocean wave. As time went by, Henry would go to sea less and less, and instead concentrate on subletting rooms to new arrivals and putting on rent parties – ad hoc gatherings with booze and women and dancing to live music.

One of Cardiff's pioneering black musicians was the singer Don Johnson, who was actually brought up in the neighbouring dockland community of Grangetown. Talking to the historian Val Wilmer, he remembered Tiger Bay as it was in the early years of the century:

I first went to Tiger Bay when my father was still alive though he forbade us to ever go there. I used to sneak down with my brother Bully – we'd heard it was a wild place with lots of black people there. So one Sunday we went off and we got to Bute Road, a long road with a series of shops and cafés and almost every one was a brothel though we didn't know what a brothel was. There'd be these girls would be sitting outside on chairs with their legs crossed, they'd say come here darling and they used to rub our heads for luck and give us some coppers. Once we discovered we could get money going down there, this became a regular thing on Sunday mornings. If my father had known![3]

As it happened Johnson's father died while his son was still a teenager and so missed out on seeing him become a leading light on the Bay's music scene:

> Later on after my father died I used to go to the Deniz house regularly. Their father played the Quattro and was teaching Frank, and Joe could play the ukulele so I started to bring the mandolin over. All we could play at first were calypsos, 'Sly Mongoose', 'The Bargee'.* After about twelve months in the front room of Mrs Deniz's house we became quite good. It was like a music shop in there, we were collecting all these instruments.
>
> After a year or so we got a sort of reputation as a calypso group. We would play at house dances for when the seamen came back. We'd play from ten at night till five or six in the morning, non-stop. There'd be a long table with West Indian food, a lot of the men were good cooks or they'd teach their wives. The dances would be attended by all the local ladies of the night and all the West Indians, and after a while we'd be playing three times a week. Mr Riley would say, 'Be at the house on Wednesday, I pay you five shillings.' Calypsos was mainly the music that we heard, these guys would get hold of as many West Indian records as they could.[4]

Henry Bassey, then, was one of these men who threw house dances for the sailors. It's a matter of some regret that the music that was played in the Bay in those years was never recorded, as it seems to have been a pioneering fusion. And while its direct musical influence on the community's most famous daughter may be limited, it still provided a context in which a girl like Shirley Bassey could believe she might have a future in the world of music. So it's worth exploring in a little depth.

*Both quite likely learned from records by pioneering calypsonian Sam Manning.

There was a lot more than just West Indian calypso in the Bay's musical mix. Apart from the different ethnic musics that the sailors brought with them, the fact that Cardiff was a port meant that musical fashions from abroad came there first. In the 1920s the latest fashion was for Hawaiian music. So before long, Johnson and his friends were providing a home-grown Cardiff Hawaiian sound: 'There was George Glossop, the charmer – he used to play Hawaiian guitar, Victor Parker, he used to play a lot of bass, Arthur George he played Quattro. In the summertime we'd go all over the streets playing this Hawaiian music, just because we liked to play.'[5]

When it came to making money, though, a lot of the best gigs were connected, in one way or another, with the area's flourishing prostitution industry.

> There were these two very nice ladies, a Londoner and a Welsh lady, and they were on the game. They knew about our music from coming to the dances and they figured out this scheme whereby they would get a couple of gents for the evening, and we would come and play, Victor Parker and myself, and we would provide the entertainment before the serious business started later on. We would get pretty good money for that: the punters would be told you'll have to pay these boys if you want to have a dance. It was a good paying gig, these guys were plied with drink, there were Norwegians, Danes, Swedes, and if they wanted a particular tune they had to pay.[6]

This was the world that surrounded the Basseys as they made their home in Bute Street. It was a place full of illicit activities but one in which music offered both an escape from the struggle to get by and also, for the musicians themselves, the chance of a better life. By the 1920s the singers and players of Tiger Bay were starting to make a name for themselves in the wider world.

Some of the most significant players on the Tiger Bay music scene were the aforementioned Deniz family. Antoni Deniz was an African from the Portuguese-owned Cape Verde islands out in the Atlantic. Antoni married a mixed-race Cardiff woman, Gertrude Boston, and they lived in Christina Street in the heart of the Bay. Both parents were musicians, Antoni playing guitar and violin, Gertrude playing the piano, so it was unsurprising that their three sons, Frank, Joe and Laurie, all took up the guitar. Their first influences were the traditional Portuguese folk and fado they would hear at the Cape Verdean get-togethers at the family house.

Those influences were soon augmented by calypso and the Hawaiian boom. The oldest Deniz boy, Frank, followed his father into the seaman's life and spent ten years on the boats, soaking up a wide variety of musical influences, American jazz in particular. Antoni died while working on the boats and the younger brothers, Joe and Laurie, showed little enthusiasm for such a perilous line of work. Joe soon followed his fellow Hawaiians George Glossop and Victor Parker up to London to try his luck there. Frank followed and in due course Laurie too. All of them became stalwarts of the British jazz and dance band scene, working with the likes of Ken 'Snakehips' Johnson and Leslie 'Jiver' Hutchinson.

What their success made clear was that there was at least one way for the mixed race people of Tiger Bay to make it out of Cardiff, and that was through the world of entertainment: through music and, to a certain extent, through films. Every once in a while there would be a British film that required some black people – as extras in films set in Africa, for example. And rather than fly in actual Africans the studios would send someone down to Cardiff to recruit some rather more local black people. This process reached its apotheosis with Alexander Korda's 1935 jungle epic *Sanders Of the River*, a starring vehicle for the great black American singer and activist Paul Robeson, then the toast of London liberal society. The film required no less than 250 black extras and Tiger Bay provided many of them. (Others were African students living in London – among them, remarkably enough, the future Kenyan revolutionary leader Jomo Kenyatta, who was there studying anthropology.)

Butetown native and local historian Neil Sinclair recalls in his book, *The Tiger Bay Story*, the lasting impact the film made on the community:

> Everyone knew the witch doctor dancing wildly in the African village was Mr Graham from Sophia Street. And that was Uncle Willy Needham in the loincloth that he kept for years after. The little black baby Robeson held in his arms was Deara Williams. Deara went on to become an exotic dancer with an act including a boa constrictor. And we all waited for the 'River Boat Song' to begin so we could all join in. 'Iyee a ko, I yi ge de,' we would chant in unison with Paul and all the African boatmen. Some twenty years later you could often see a gang of Bay boys on a separated timber log, singing the 'River Boat Song', rowing across the lake of the timber float, a little south of west Canal Wharf.[7]

The dancer Louise Benjamin, a contemporary of Shirley Bassey's, came from another of the Bay's musical families, and her mother appeared in the film:

> It seems like in Cardiff loads of people went off and did things. I remember my mother saying that for *Sanders Of The River* they came to Cardiff to get black people. It was really good money. She was supposed to be a mother with two children in the African village and then the director called 'Cut' and pointed at one of the children and said, 'He's got wellington boots on!'

My mother and my auntie Alice were there and the director said, 'Can all the light-skinned ones come forward?' They were both mixed race and my mother wasn't sure what to do but Aunt Alice who was very showbiz said, 'I'm going forward, it might be a better part.' She came back later and said, 'Oh God, look what they've done!' and she was covered in burnt cork. They'd put burnt cork on them to make them blacker!

That was 1935. It can hardly be a coincidence that among the children born in Tiger Bay in the next few years there would be a remarkable number of entrants into the world of show business. Where black and mixed-race children elsewhere in Britain could have little expectation of appearing on stage or screen, the children of Tiger Bay were able to see their mothers and fathers, uncles and aunties, up there on the screen, and they wanted to follow suit.

THREE

The Canadian Café

In 1936, the year after the making of *Sanders Of The River*, Eliza and Henry Bassey and their children were living in Bute Street, when a young sociologist called Kenneth Little made a study of Tiger Bay and its people. The study, published as part of a more general book called *Negroes in Britain*, was entitled 'The Coloured Folk Of Cardiff', and was a conscious attempt to counteract the commonplace racism of the British.

It was a bold and unusual subject to take up. At the time, most British leftists were more concerned with the fight against fascism and anti-Semitism. Anti-black racism had a lower profile, though it still existed. In July 1936, for example, the *Daily Express* ran an investigation into life in Tiger Bay which carried the subheading 'Half-caste girl: she presents a city with one of its big problems.' By this time, of course, the Bassey family included five 'half-caste girls', with another one on the way.

Kenneth Little offers a wealth of useful information about the area. He estimates that the population of Butetown would have been around ten thousand, the non-white community making up around six thousand of those. These would have included West Africans, West Indians, Somalis, Indians, Malays and Arabs, with the Arabs being the largest single group. The remainder of the population was made up of 'Greeks, Cypriots, Maltese and Spaniards with a rather smaller number of Portuguese and Italian families', as well as the Welsh, English and Irish.

The heart of what Little calls the 'coloured community' was around Loudoun Square:

> . . . with perhaps eight coloured out of every ten persons . . . In comparison, for example, with similar communities in other seaports of the kingdom, such as Liverpool, London, South Shields, etc., the concentration and segregation of the Cardiff coloured folk is very significant and worthy of emphasis. Indeed, so plentiful are dark skins in comparison with light in Loudoun Square and its satellite streets that a stranger entering the district for the first time might well imagine himself in some oriental town.[1]

The Bassey family had lived for a while in Loudoun Square itself, but by the time Little was writing they were living on Bute Street, the main thoroughfare of the area. This was the road along which the Tiger Bay community interacted with the outside world, whether visiting sailors or their fellow Cardiffians.

It was lined with pubs and cafés catering specifically to sailors on shore leave. These were the establishments that gave the area its dubious reputation. The pubs with their colourful nicknames – the House of Blazes and the Bucket of Blood – were rougher than rough. The so-called cafés meanwhile were actually after-hours drinking dens generally offering prostitution on the side.*[2]

This was the world, then, that the Bassey family inhabited. Theirs was a hard-scrabble life in which people did what they had to do to get by. The family survived by subletting rooms in

---

* For more on Bute Street and its cafés, see the relevant appendix.

the houses in which they lived, and by organising rent parties. The extent to which this was a hand-to-mouth existence can be inferred from the fact that every time the family show up on an official record they have moved house again. This was life lived in perpetual fear of the landlord and with an ever-increasing brood of children.

At the time they got married, in March 1929, the couple had already had their daughter Grace. Plus there were the two older girls, Ella and Iris. Their second child together was a girl called Verona who was born in June 1930, but died of gastro-enteritis just five months later. Two years later, in 1932, Eliza gave birth again, this time to twins: Eileen and Henry junior, her only son. Three more years and Marina Bassey was born. Then, on 8 January 1937, Shirley Veronica Bassey was born.

*　　*　　*

Shirley was Eliza Bassey's tenth child. She was born in a street full of brothels. There was no money, no prospect of money. The community around her was in terminal economic decline and the wider world was starting to gear up for another war. The newspapers were branding girls like her as a social problem. To say that her start in life was inauspicious is to put it mildly.

By this time the Basseys were living at 182 Bute Street, in rooms above one of the street's many 'cafés'. This one was called the Canadian Café and it was run by a Sicilian called Lawrence Mollia. In 1930, when the police were pressurised by the politicians into making a token effort to clean up Tiger Bay, the following report on the Café was drawn up by one of the local coppers:

With regard to the Canadian Café which is occupied by Lawrence Mollia, a Maltese. He is really employed by another Maltese named Louis Fenech. In these premises dancing on a rather large scale takes place nightly.

The main difficulty is that while dancing is in progress the windows are heavily curtained and generally there is someone keeping watch on the front door so that we are unable to ascertain who places the pennies in the automatic piano which is essential to prove the case of public dancing in these places.[2]

The copper was at least able to detail the building's layout and its inhabitants at the time:

The premises consist of a shop with a room behind. In the shop there are two automatic pianos (one of which is an electric piano)* purchased at a cost of about £300. There are also about six tables and eight chairs. This room appears to be used exclusively for dancing. It is frequented by women and foreign seamen. Upstairs there are seven bedrooms – the first is occupied by the keeper, Lawrence Mollia,

---

* This was more than likely an Ampico reproducing piano. These were similar to the more common player pianos, but instead of being wound by hand they were electrically powered so that the rolls could fairly precisely reproduce the playing of a particular pianist. Many of the rolls were of classical performances by the likes of Rachmaninoff but the Ampico specialised in popular performances, thanks to 'a lively band of musical arrangers and "hot" pianists', who gravitated around the Ampico Studios, and not only recorded their versions of the latest hits, but in many cases created musical arrangements that almost no one could have played by hand. Zez Confrey and Ferdie Grofé, who was Paul Whiteman's pianist, were regular Ampico recording artists. The popularity of these pianos was obviously limited; gramophones and radios were the coming thing, but their poor sound quality and feeble amplification rendered them unsuitable for dancing, so through the 1920s and into the early 1930s it was the electric automatic pianos that ruled the dance floor when a live band was unavailable.

the second by Beryl Davies, the third by Mary Ford, the fourth by Elizabeth Crook. The other three rooms are empty.[3]

Lawrence Mollia is described as a Maltese, fifty-one years old, who had previously held similar licences on other premises in the city. Beryl Davies and Mary Ford ('or Lanchester') are described as 'servants'. Beryl Davies is twenty-two and from the Valleys. Mary Ford, 'who manages the residential part of the business, and who cohabits with Mollia, is now in custody on a charge of wounding, the result of an affray in the dancing room.'[4]

This was not, by any stretch of the imagination, a respectable address. It certainly provides grounds for speculation as to just what kind of activities Henry and Eliza were engaged in when it came to earning a living. Whatever they may have been, though, they were about to change for the good. Because, just a year after Shirley's birth, a hidden secret was about to blow the family apart.

FOUR

Life During Wartime

On 3 February 1938 Henry Bassey was arrested, and in the Cardiff police archive it is recorded that he was charged with 'Defilement of a girl under sixteen years.'

Little more than a month later, on 4 March, the case came to trial at the Glamorgan Assizes. The records of what happened are still there in the archives. The charges against Henry Bassey are neatly written out by the clerk to the court, one Illtyd Allan. The first of them sets the tone:

> Henry Bassey is charged with the following offence: Carnal knowledge of a girl under thirteen, contrary to Sect. 4 of the Criminal Amendment Act 1885. Particulars of the offence: Henry Bassey on a day unknown between 1st January 1932 and the 31st October 1932 in the county of Glamorgan had carnal knowledge of [name deleted], a girl of the age of nine years.[1]

Further more or less identical charges follow; only the dates are changed. The accusation is simple: that Henry Bassey repeatedly raped a young girl over a period of nearly six years, from the time she was nine till the time he was finally charged, when she was fifteen years old.

At the trial Bassey pleaded his innocence, forcing the girl to testify against him in open court. She was brave enough to go through with it. She told the court that 'this sort of thing had been going on since she was nine'.[2]

The court believed her testimony and on 11 March Henry Bassey was sentenced to eight years' penal servitude with a recommendation for deportation to Nigeria to follow. Two weeks later he sought leave to appeal but the judge refused, citing the compelling testimony from the girl. In the end Bassey would serve five years in prison before being deported back to Nigeria in 1943. He is reported, not necessarily reliably, to have died there some time in the 1950s. The girl involved in the case died more recently.

It would be hard to exaggerate how terrible this must have been for Eliza and her children. The affair scandalised the whole community. Scandalised them and shamed them too. Child abuse was far from unknown in the 1930s; a brief trawl through the court records of the time reveals that the Bassey case was hardly isolated. However, the other cases involved families in the chapel-dominated South Wales valleys. Bassey's was the only case of the time to occur in Butetown and it was doubly upsetting in its implications. First, the crime itself is one that is most unusual amongst West Africans in Britain and as such a shocking blow to the community's self-image. Secondly, the people of Tiger Bay were all too well aware of the low regard in which the outside world held them. For one of their own to disgrace himself in this fashion was inevitably to bring disgrace to the community as a whole.

The case made the local paper under the headline, 'Eight Years For Coloured Man'. It offered a chance for outsiders to tut and point and say, 'Well, what do you expect?' as they read the brief article, which informed readers that:

> A coloured seaman convicted of six indictments alleging serious offences against a young girl in Cardiff was sentenced to a total of eight years in prison. He was Henry Bassey, aged 42, a West African, whose correct name was stated to be Okun Apauso.* What were described as 'horrible details' were given in the case.[3]

The paper did not, of course, elaborate on the horrible details, but the damage was done as far as the community was concerned. An already bad reputation had been further undermined.

Just how shameful the community believed this story to be can be gauged from the way in which it has been a jealously guarded secret ever since. It was a story that was soon forgotten by the wider world, but in the close-knit docklands it has lived on, all the more so when one of Bassey's children became the famous Shirley Bassey, the girl from Tiger Bay. Even now, when I talked to members of the older generation of Docks people about the Basseys, I saw how guarded they became. Some would change the subject; others would try to gauge what I had learnt – 'You know about her father?' No one volunteered the information I found in the archives. And, remarkably enough, in the fifty years that Shirley has been famous, no one from the community she came out of has ever told the papers about the shame and scandal that surrounded her family at the time of her birth.

That said, while close-knit communities may be good at shielding information from outsiders, they also tend to be rife with gossip. This is certainly true of Tiger Bay/Butetown. The story of Henry Bassey's awful transgression made its way around the area in no time and has been passed down through the generations. And while

---

* This would seem to be an approximation of the Efik name that Bassey was born with. Okun may well be correct. Apauso, however, doesn't appear to be an authentic Efik name.

such gossip might not have had much effect on Bassey himself, off in prison and then deported, it must have been unbearable for Eliza, as she tried to protect her younger children from the knowledge of what had happened. Evidently she soon realised that unless she wanted to spend the rest of her life listening out for people talking behind her back she would have to move out of Tiger Bay, the one place where she had finally felt at home.

It was a cruel decision to be forced to make. But it's always been the – deeply unfair – case that sexual abuse is a crime in which some kind of guilt by association seems to stick to everyone connected to the perpetrator. Thus Eliza, who had already been forced to leave her hometown, was now obliged to move again in order to escape the gossips.

The family left Tiger Bay. They didn't go far, just a mile or so east to the neighbouring dockland settlement of Splott. Splott was no smarter than Butetown. In fact, in many ways it was a step down. Where Butetown had its fine houses built for the ships' captains, Splott was no more than a collection of two-up two-down terraces, built to house the labourers who'd flooded in to work in the steelworks, the docks and the iron foundries. But where Butetown was multicultural and cosmopolitan, Splott was mostly, though not entirely, white, with a strong Irish community.

From Eliza's point of view, however, Splott was a place where her neighbours didn't know her, her family, or their recent history. The family lived in Portmanmoor Road, in a terraced house over the road from the steelworks. They didn't have too much trouble fitting into what was in the end just another rough-and-tumble working-class community. And it wasn't long before there were plenty of other families around with absent fathers. War was on the way. When I found the copy of the *South Wales Echo* from March 1938 that carried the report of Bassey's conviction, I didn't at first notice what the main headline of the day was. Checking it over a few days later, I was struck to see that it read, 'Hitler Explains Why He Invaded Austria', and went on to report a Goebbels radio broadcast. This was the moment that the Second World War went from being a probability to an inevitability.

Cardiff suffered considerably during the war. Through 1939 and into 1940 the city prepared itself, issuing gas masks to children and distributing corrugated-iron Anderson shelters for people to put up in their gardens. Life carried on in something approximating normal fashion during this phoney-war period. Then, in May 1940, Hitler invaded France and it became clear just what Britain was up against. Now the Luftwaffe had bases in France, and Cardiff, like most of the rest of Britain, came within range of the German bombers.

The first bombs fell on Cardiff in June 1940 and continued to fall sporadically through the rest of the year. Then, on 2 January 1941, the Blitz came to Cardiff. The day before, Britain had mounted a major new year bombing raid on the dockyards of Bremen in Germany. Now Germany launched a savage reprisal. Around a hundred aircraft were involved in the bombing. They began by dropping flares and incendiaries; high explosives and the deadly parachute mines followed. The death toll was highest near the River Taff; in Riverside, where sixty people died; in Bute Street where nearly twenty people were killed, including three Norwegian seamen.

Inevitably it was a night that made a powerful impression on the young Shirley Bassey, then just coming up to her fourth birthday: 'Mother always used to lock our bedroom door when we were safely asleep,' she reminisced in the pages of the *Empire News* in 1957. 'But during the big air raid on Cardiff Docks a bomb blew the windows in. Grace and Eileen had their faces cut by flying glass and started to scream blue murder. When my mother unlocked the bedroom door, they all scrambled out, leaving me behind, yelling.'[4]

The final death toll for Cardiff was 165. Six days afterwards there was a mass burial of the victims in Cathays Cemetery. The *South Wales Echo* observed that 'High and low, young and old, mingled around the communal graves while they tearfully but silently honoured the dead. It was a scene that those who witnessed it will forever have indelibly printed on their minds.'

The bombing raids carried on over the next two years, but never again with quite the same ferocity and loss of life. There was plenty of loss of life, of course, amongst those Cardiffians serving in the armed forces. And worst hit of all were those who served in the merchant navy.

There were around 145,000 people serving in the merchant navy during the war. More than 32,000 of them died, a higher casualty rate than in any of the armed services. The South Wales merchant seamen were particularly hard hit: 164 ships sailed out of the South Wales ports, and, of these, three-quarters were sunk by enemy action. The Cardiff firm of Reardon Smith, for example, lost 33 out of its 41 vessels.

Ironically, being in prison may well have saved Henry Bassey's life. He remained under lock and key till his deportation back to Nigeria in 1943. The ship he sailed on was a requisitioned liner called the SS *Stuyvesant*, administered by the Elder Dempster line, specialists in travel between Britain and West Africa, who had by this time lost all their own ships to enemy action.

The fact that so many children lost their fathers during the war may have made life a little easier for the effectively fatherless Shirley, or at least made her experience seem more normal. Of course, the chaos of war was playing all kinds of havoc with family life. Shortly after the Blitz there was a drive to evacuate children from the Cardiff Docklands, as Shirley remembered: 'My sisters and brother were evacuated up in the valleys, leaving me at home with my mother. I missed them but as long as I had my mother I was all right.'[5]

Indeed, Shirley would remain close to her mother until Eliza's death in 1982. However, in keeping with her general policy of saying as little as possible about her family in interviews, the following brief tribute is the closest she's come to putting on record her childhood memories of her mother: 'She was quite Victorian in many ways. She was a quiet, Northern woman with beautiful, very white skin who didn't give much away about herself and was a great cook. I remember her egg and bacon tarts. And her Yorkshire puddings. We also had a lot of offal because offal was cheap, but I hated that.'[6]

Elsewhere she would add a little gloss to this portrait. 'You don't know how pretty she was when I was small. Why, she had such beautiful long hair she could sit on it,' she told the *TV Mirror* in 1959. And 'My mother was a very lively, happy-go-lucky person who loved to dance,' she told *Reveille* in 1972.

Children being children, growing up during wartime was not all offal trauma. One of Shirley's friends and contemporaries, Louise Benjamin, told me about her own experiences of the war as experienced by a child in the Cardiff docklands:

> There were these raids and I had a gas mask and it was a thing of going to the shelter every evening then coming home and going to bed and then getting up in the morning and finding shrapnel. It was quite exciting really. We would look out over the Channel to Bristol, watch the ack-ack guns firing, you could see it all in the sky. We'd go down by the Esplanade and watch. For my mother, with my father at sea, it must have been horrific, but as a child, that was what my life was. After a while my mother got very blasé and we went under the stairs. I can remember one night we went under the stairs and

my mother had hold of my hair and every time there was a blast she would pull and I was screaming. It must have been horrible for the adults. A lot of children's fathers died in the war, they were mostly merchant seamen. They got torpedoed. It got a little better after '43.

In fact things were never as bad again in Cardiff itself after the night of the Blitz. In 1941 the German army foundered in Russia and the Americans joined the fight. In the summer of 1942 the Americans arrived in Cardiff. The city already had its share of displaced persons – exiled Belgians, French and Poles, but where they were running from terrible defeats, the Americans arrived oozing confidence. They had money – paid five times as much as British soldiers – and they had style. There were also, for the first time in an American army, a substantial number of black GIs.

Across Britain this led to a certain amount of trouble. White GIs did not take kindly to black GIs fraternising with the locals, especially the local girls. The local girls, for their part, were particularly interested in the black GIs. Before long there were serious incidents involving shootings and even killings between black and white GIs, in places as far-flung as Launceston in Cornwall and Bamber Bridge in Lancashire. To deal with this, de facto segregation was brought in. Black troops would be bussed to one pub, their white comrades to another. In many cases the locals took the side of the black soldiers, not necessarily out of profound anti-racist spirit but rather because, as *Time* magazine observed, 'Great Britain . . . had never faced the "race problem" at home. Ninety per cent of Britain's citizens had never actually seen or talked to a black-skinned human being before. America's polite, liquid-voiced, smartly uniformed Negro soldiers were a surprise, a pleasure, and a happy opportunity for them to thumb the nose of moral self-righteousness at the US.'

The decision was made to house the black American soldiers as far as possible in places which had some experience of black people. Cardiff was an obvious choice and before long there was a substantial population of black GIs in the city, including 700 stationed at Maindy barracks. The barracks soon became a considerable attraction for local girls and stories circulated about all manner of sexual activity in the nearby bushes, about mothers and daughters both found entertaining the troops in the barracks themselves, and so forth.

It didn't take the black GIs long to find their way to Butetown. They were generally delighted to find themselves in a genuinely multiracial community and word soon spread so that black GIs, wherever they were stationed in Britain, tended to make their way to Butetown for their R&R. The Bay girls were more than happy about this too, so much so that, at the end of the war, there were seventy-two Bay girls who became GI brides. One of these was Shirley's older sister Grace. She met a soldier called Victor Biami and soon after the war they were married. Grace went to live with him in Milwaukee.

It must at the time have seemed an impossibly glamorous fate. And one that the young Shirley must have envied, because the life of the Bassey household was a hard one. The war may have been over in 1945. Shirley's school would have provided its pupils with a Victory Tea ('one buttered roll, one sausage roll, one iced cake, and one trifle per child'), but overall, life in the Bassey household wasn't getting any easier.

FIVE

On the Street Where You Live

The Basseys were poor. Poor even by Cardiff standards. Their Splott home was a basic little terraced house, with no bathroom and just an outside toilet for Eliza and her seven children. Shirley slept in a bed with Marina and Eileen, the three of them fighting for the best spot, the middle. Shirley, the baby of the family, generally won out. All they had to live on was what little Eliza could earn, though things did improve a little from 1948 onward, when the new Labour government passed the National Assistance Act, replacing the old poor laws with their attendant humiliations. From 1948 on, Eliza received £2.10s. in National Assistance.

They were not poor the way we know it now, poor with central heating and a DVD player and living on takeaways, poor that has enough to eat but suffers an impoverishment of the spirit. This was *poor* poor, hand-me-down clothes, even hand-me-down underwear for Shirley. Poor living on a staple diet of foo-foo, a vegetable mush popular in West Africa, and offal. Poor in the ration book years, poor through the winter of 1947, the coldest of the century. Poor living opposite a giant steelworks belching fire and black smoke into the air so nothing was ever really clean, least of all the air they breathed. Poor so all the children left school the moment they could to work. Poor so that dreams were nothing but ridiculous.

And yet, growing up amidst all this deprivation, Shirley always had ambitions: 'I wanted to be an air hostess, every year I had a different ambition. I wanted to be a model, wear all those lovely clothes, because I always had to wear my sisters' hand-me-downs, and I was really getting fed up that I only had new things at Easter or Christmas.'[1]

She went to school in Splott. First Walker Road Infants, just round the corner from their house, then Moorland Road Primary School, on the far side of Splott, over by the railway line. After that she went to the hulking great board school, Splott Secondary Modern, on Splott Road.

Primary school is where Shirley first encountered racism. Ifor Harry, the barber who lived and worked two doors down from the Basseys, is quoted as saying that 'You know it was an all-white school and we know that children can be cruel. Mrs Bassey tried her best, but I think it was a nasty shock to the little girl. I watched her grow up and I could tell.'[2]

It may be unwise to make too much of this. Looking back forty-odd years later, Shirley simply commented that: 'The odd kid at school would call me names, but not for long, boy. There was a fighter at the time called Kid Bassey and people used to think we were related!'[3]

And while it's true that Splott was no Tiger Bay, the Basseys were not the only black people to live there at the time. Portmanmoor Road's electoral roll alone reveals that there were people with Arab and African names – Allis and Mensahs – living in the same street as the Basseys.

In fact it's the poverty rather than the racism of her childhood that appears to have stuck in Shirley's memory. It's what she mentions in interviews, and no wonder. Racist remarks may have been an occasional annoyance but it was the grinding poverty of her upbringing that made life a terrible struggle, as she later remembered:

There was only one other coloured family but not being among one's own kind did not bother me particularly. There was obviously the odd incident – you know what children are like. When they cannot beat you they think of the worst thing they can say to hurt you. No, being coloured was never my problem, never has been. In Cardiff our problem was more basic: it was a four letter word – food.[4]

I had as much love from my mother as she could possibly give to the youngest of eight children and not having my father around . . . So it wasn't an easy life, you know. We were living from day to day and of course this got into my heart, my soul, and, being the youngest, I had all the hand-me-downs. That was really bitter. It wasn't really a happy childhood.[5]

Her sentiments are echoed by another old classmate, Pat Durrant, writing to the BBC:

I remember Shirley from Moorland Road School. I was bumped up two classes so I could take the eleven-plus (or whatever it was called back then) and was in Mrs Lewis's scholarship class with Dame Bassey and my older sis Shirley. And for those who criticise her for not embracing her Splott background – don't judge – you have no idea what life was like for all of us then.[6]

One positive effect of the move to Splott was that it brought a degree of stability to the lives of Eliza Bassey and her children. Back in Tiger Bay they had been constantly on the move. Once they'd arrived in Portmanmoor Road* they had finally been able to settle.

* Exactly where the family lived between 1939, when they left Bute Street, and 1943, is a matter for conjecture. One early interview with Shirley suggests they may have lived for a time in Adeline Street in Splott; other accounts suggest they may have moved directly to Portmanmoor Road in 1939.

*   *   *

By the time of the 1945 electoral roll (the first for six years, thanks to the war) Eliza Bassey is registered as living at Portmanmoor Road, along with her seven children, the eldest of whom, Ella, is registered under her married name, so presumably she was living there with her husband. Intriguingly, the next-door neighbour is a man called Sam Johnson, the name of Iris's father.

In 1948 the roll shows a change in the household line-up: Ella has moved out and Eliza's surname is now given as Mendi. Presumably her new partner, Joseph 'Bobo' Mendi, was also living there. Grace, meanwhile, is listed under her married name of Biami, so was just awaiting the arrival of her green card.

By 1949 the household has settled into the set-up that would last until Shirley left home – Eliza and Bobo Mendi; Iris and her new husband Bill Denning; the twins, Henry and Eileen; Marina and Shirley. Even this, though, may well be a simplification of some fairly ad hoc domestic arrangements. A mesh of possibly faulty memories from friends and acquaintances suggest that Shirley and/or Marina may have lived with friends in Butetown at least part of the time during their teenage years.

The most significant change in the household, from Shirley's point of view, must have been the arrival of Mr Mendi. He was another West African sailor, this time from Sierra Leone. He was a donkey-man, the ship's engine-room job that was one step up from being a simple fireman like Henry Bassey, and he was still making regular trips to sea, which helped with the family income to a limited degree, as Shirley remembers: 'My father [i.e. Mr Mendi] was in the merchant navy and my mother's allowance which always came by registered letter was often late. I can recall weeks going by waiting for this envelope to arrive and then inevitably things going into pawn.'[7]

It's likely that Eliza had known Bobo Mendi for some while. He had lived just round the corner from the Basseys when they were in Bute Street, a decade or so earlier. He was a quiet man by all accounts. The kind of man who liked to sit in the corner of the living room reading the paper and minding his own business. Just when he came on the scene remains unclear. A newspaper report suggests he married Eliza in 1941. However, the electoral roll – and Shirley's own reminiscences – suggests the date is more likely to have been around 1947.

Either way, he was clearly an important presence in the young Shirley's life. It's often Joe 'Bobo' Mendi that she seems to be referring to in interviews, as above, when she's asked about her father. For instance, when she wrote about her life for the *Empire News* in 1956 she combines Joe Mendi with Henry Bassey to form a composite father. 'My father Joseph Bassey was a big West African who worked as a ship's donkeyman. I don't remember much about my father. He was just a big stranger who would occasionally appear out of nowhere and pick me up and try to kiss me.'[8]

And by the time Bobo Mendi came to live with the Basseys it was already becoming clear that the youngest girl, Shirley, had a definite talent.

SIX

The Rainbow Club

Over the next few years, from the ages of ten to fifteen, Shirley would move from childhood to adolescence, would change from being a sport-loving tomboy to a teenager known for her sex appeal and her singing.

At the age of ten Shirley Bassey had a long-standing love of singing coupled with an unusually strong voice for a child, something her family were all too well aware of, as Shirley later recalled in a TV interview:

> When I started to sing, bedtime, my sisters were: 'Mum, can you tell her to shut up, we're trying to sleep.' So how I became a singer I really don't know, 'cause everyone told me to shut up. Even in the school choir the teacher kept telling me to back off till I was singing in the corridor![1]

Her classmate Pat Durrant was struck by Shirley's singing while still at primary school. 'I have a distinct memory of her singing "Can't help lovin' that man of mine" from *Showboat*,' she told the BBC. 'Even then she sang with such feeling that she made our teacher uncomfortable.'[2]

Just where this talent for singing came from remains mysterious.

Eliza Bassey, interviewed in 1970, did her best to come up with an explanation:

> Even when she was a little girl she was always singing. She used to come home from school at lunchtime to sweep the hall and the stairs and all her friends would stand around outside the open front door listening to her singing while she swept. I think she must take after her father who was always putting on the gramophone and fooling around with the kids when he came home from sea.[3]

Here Eliza is presumably referring to Bobo Mendi rather than Henry Bassey, who had disappeared out of Shirley's life before he could have passed on his love of music. Shirley herself has generally professed herself baffled as to the origins of her own talent, but once, when interviewed by a US tabloid, she credited her mother, rather than her biological father or Bobo Mendi, as her primary influence.

> The myth about blacks being born musicians always seemed funny to me. My dad can't even carry a tune. Mum taught me to sing before I went to school. There were six kids and I was the youngest, so she had me home alone a few years and got me started on music to keep me out of mischief. She was so gay, always singing and I guess I take after her. She says that even as a baby I was always singing the songs I heard on the wireless, though I can't recall it. What I wanted to be was a dancer. My sister Gracie was a wonderful dancer and I'd toddle along behind, trying to imitate her steps.[4]

By 1948 Shirley's love of song and dance was undeniable and Eliza decided to send her over to Butetown for some after-school dance lessons at the Big Apple, a Saturday night dance hall off Sophia

Street, in the heart of Tiger Bay. The area was familiar to the young Shirley; it's only a mile or so from Splott, but was one she had mixed feelings about, as she told Wyn Calvin a few years later in a radio interview:

> We used to go back frequently. At that age I don't suppose it meant anything except the place I was born. It seemed to be the only place in the world [where black people lived] – until I left home when I was sixteen and found there were other places. I remember as a child when I went back there, there was always some fight on a street corner. It was a bit frightening to me as a child. When I was about seven we were walking back home after visiting my aunt and there was a crowd outside this club and, being young and inquisitive, I had to see what it was all about. I saw this brutal fight, this man on the floor and another man kicked him right in the face. It was horrible. I ran away and I couldn't find my mother and sister anywhere. In the end I found them at the bus stop, my mother looking frantic, and she said, 'This'll teach you to be so nosey.'[5]

The dancing school Shirley went to was run by a West African, Walter French, a pillar of the Butetown community, universally known as Frenchie, and it was the launching pad for a whole generation of mostly female, mostly mixed-race, talent to emerge from the Cardiff docklands. A generation of Bay girls, inspired no doubt by the showbiz experiences of their mothers and aunties, saw singing and dancing as their route out of poverty. Shirley Bassey was by far the most successful of them, but she was not the only one to have a good career in show business.

One alumnus of Frenchie's and the Rainbow Club (another after-school facility for Bay kids) was Irene Spettie, who took the stage name Lorne Lesley and had a long career in international cabaret before getting married to her manager David Dickinson, future host of the BBC's *Bargain Hunt* et al. Similarly singer Patti Flynn toured the world in cabaret before becoming a broadcaster and writer. Many others, as we shall see, had more fleeting encounters with the bright lights. These include two of Shirley's contemporaries, dancers Louise Benjamin (now Freeman) and Maureen Jemmett (now Ombull).

Today Louise Benjamin lives in a nice house in a peaceful part of West London. In her early seventies, she still looks like the professional dancer she was in her late teens and twenties. Subsequently she married another Tiger Bay legend, the rugby league player Johnny Freeman, and relocated to Halifax, Yorkshire, where she lived for a long while, working for an engineering firm and bringing up her children, before coming to London to share a house with her youngest daughter who works in the music business. These days Louise takes the occasional TV acting job, most recently in the NHS comedy *Getting On*.

Back in the days of the Big Apple, Louise – or Lulu, as she was known – was seen as the girl most likely to succeed. She did well at school and came from a family who were seen as rather a cut above. Louise remembers her upbringing:

We had a kitchen with a corrugated-iron roof and the rain used to come through but I loved it, I never thought we were poor and we weren't as poor as some, we had a piano in the front room and my mother was a pianist. Our piano always went into the street on these party days, my mother would play, Louie Benjamin, her name was. Then my father came back from the war and he was not right, you know he was ill and my mother really kept the household going playing the piano. She had a dance band and she played in a couple of clubs and at the dancing school. She kept us going financially. It was lucky, really, as she wasn't the kind of person who could have gone into Curran's factory. She was very ladylike, my mother.

Unsurprisingly, given her mother's example, Louise was one of those Bay girls who was bent on a show business career from the start:

I went to dancing school, learnt ballet and tap. I started there when I was about eight. Afterwards my mother became the pianist for the dancing school and the ballet exams and that. My whole life was in the dancing school; that's all I ever wanted to do, be a dancer.

She remembers Frenchie's very well:

Frenchie was an African man and he had a dancing school and he also had a nightclub. It was just off Sophia Street and there was the annexe at the colonial club, they had a lot of dances there and when the Americans came they used to go there. A lot of the kids went to the dancing school there. Thinking about it now, the health and safety! It was down an alleyway upstairs and if there'd been a fire . . .

If Louise Benjamin represented the aspirational side of the Tiger Bay community, Maureen Ombull represents its more rambunctious side. Maureen, another very bright and funny seventy-something, lives on a Peabody Estate off Ladbroke Grove, close to the railway line that runs from Paddington to Cardiff. She likes modern jazz and barley wine and has no time for the pieties some of her contemporaries resort to when they talk about life in old Tiger Bay.

Her own mother was a white woman who had one child with an African called Ombull, more children with a West Indian called Jemmett, and then Maureen with Ombull again. The similarities to Eliza Bassey are obvious. Maureen was a couple of years older than Shirley, and friendly with her sister Marina. She was a talented dancer who went to the same lessons as Louise Benjamin and, again, she saw showbiz as a way out: 'We formed a little trio: Beryl Freeman, Lulu and me. Me and Beryl used to wear black top hats, tails and dickey bows and Lulu would be in the middle in a white satin outfit, and we'd sing "Stepping Out With My Baby" and we'd win the talent competition every year.'

Like Louise and Maureen, Shirley Bassey was initially much keener on dance than singing, for all her evident talent at the latter. She loved her dance lessons, and was less than pleased when Frenchie started to single her out to appear in shows the children put on, not for her dancing ability but for her voice. 'I was furious – my mother was paying for the dancing lessons and they made me sing!'[6]

It clearly hadn't taken Frenchie long to realise that this same voice that drove Shirley's family crazy was actually a remarkable natural instrument. And he quickly tried to steer Shirley away from dancing and into singing, giving her the lead vocal parts in the shows the kids would put on. Shirley wasn't convinced, though, and after a couple of years she gave up going to the dance classes. She didn't stop singing, though. She sang at home, she sang at school. It was part of who she was, but not something she saw as in any way remarkable: 'Well, I was always singing, I suppose, though I do not recall being very musical or even wanting to own a radio. Nor did I ever learn to read music or play any instrument. My brother was the musical one of the family. He liked to imitate Al Jolson.'[7]

Her regular haunt was the Rainbow Club on Bute Street, an after-school club for the neighbourhood kids run by a good-hearted couple, the Capeners. Mrs Capener, in particular, encouraged Shirley's singing, but mostly Shirley just got on with being a kid:

I was always a skinny little creature, and my thin face seemed to be all eyes and black curly topknot. In fact I was typical of the children you'll see playing any day in Cardiff's dockland. I was left to run wild. Terrible tomboy. Always climbing trees. Maybe I didn't feel feminine enough to be with the girls. And then, in my late teens, I learnt to become more feminine as a way of controlling men. Girls can't help but flirt.[8]

Even then she was a contradictory personality, a girl who enjoyed being the centre of attention, while being an essentially solitary soul: 'I was a loner. I didn't really need friends. I could be among people and still be alone in my own little world. I was a peculiar child.'[9]

Everyone knew her: she was that kind of girl. You can see it in the school photos that survive. Shirley aged eight, smiling and mischievous. Shirley on a school trip to Porthcawl where she would take the talent show by storm with her rendition of 'Over the Rainbow'. Shirley in the baseball* team pulling a face of cartoon aggression, a Splott tomboy.

Her classmate, Shirley Coles, wrote in to the local paper with her memories of Shirley at school:

She was a tomboy and she was always playing netball and was very sporty. She used to sing 'Glow Little Glow Worm' and 'Jezebel' for us in school and when we went away on camp to Porthcawl every summer for a week she would get up on a table and sing for us. Shirley was always the one who started the pillow fights. She was great fun.[10]

---

* That's Cardiff baseball. It's a halfway house between rounders and the American game, played almost exclusively in the port towns of Cardiff, Newport and Liverpool. It's the summer game of working class Cardiff; there are thriving leagues both for men and 'ladies'. In Shirley's day there would have been 'international' matches played between the top of the league teams in Cardiff and Liverpool. These were often held at Curran's sports ground.

Shirley was never a child who was going to do well at school. She was from a family who had no expectations of education and she went to schools that had no expectations of their students. And so, sure enough, when she was fourteen she left Splott Secondary Modern and before long she followed her sisters into Curran's factory.

Curran's was a Cardiff institution, a hulking great factory on the edge of the docks, producing all manner of steel and enamelware. It was set up around the turn of the century by Edward Curran, the son of Irish immigrants. He developed a furnace with a capacity for moulding steel which led to his business being awarded major munitions contracts during the First World War. The factory quickly became a major employer for Cardiff's Irish Catholic community. Curran's boomed again as a munitions factory during the Second World War, but by the time Shirley worked there, in 1951, its speciality was making baths and enamelware and its employment reach had moved beyond the Irish community.

Shirley worked in the packing department, placing chamber pots in cardboard boxes and filling in the space around them with wood shavings ('wrapping pee pots in brown paper', as she later put it to Russell Harty). She sang along to *Music While You Work* and she took part in the recreational activities available at the factory's nearby sports and social club complex on Penarth Road. 'I was happy there. I had a great time. The social life was very good. Every Thursday there was the factory club: archery, darts, dancing . . . I became quite good at archery . . .'*[11]

This was the adult world that Shirley was moving into now. The

---

* Unlikely as it might seem, Dame Shirley continued to take more interest in sporting matters than the average diva. In the 1960s she was the mascot for the Showbiz X1 football team and used to take the kick-off at their charity fixtures. And in 1976 there was a minor scandal when she was expelled from the Lord's dressing rooms after she popped in to visit the England cricket team.

packing department was a female enclave but Curran's was a big factory full of men doing men's work and it didn't take long for the men to take notice of Shirley, or she of them. Fresh from a girls' school and a poverty-stricken home life, her job opened up a new world for Shirley. She had her own money for the first time and she knew what to spend it on: high heels and lipstick and a dress of her own: 'It was tartan, with a big skirt that rustled. I wore it to the factory dance and was in heaven.'[12]

The spur to smarten up came from her first boyfriend, a neighbour boy called Vivian Jones, who dumped the adolescent Shirley for being too much of a tomboy urchin:

> He just didn't want to go out with me any more. He said, 'I can't go out with you any more, you're too dirty.' It upset me and overnight my mother saw a change in me. She and my sister said: 'Look at her. Shirley's combed her hair!' They were amazed at the sudden change. It was really overnight. Bump. From then on I started taking care over the way I looked.[13]

And with the new high heels and the dresses, not to mention the singing, came attention, plenty of attention, from the opposite sex, the young and the not so young.

> Yes. I've always liked boys and even when I was knobbly-kneed and no shape at all they liked me. They've always hung round me like bees round a honeypot. And that's a great temptation. Boys were never catty about me. Girls were. Boys never laughed or jeered at my hand-me-down clothes. They said nice things to me. They let me play cricket with them. That's why I like boys.
>
> I had my first proposal when I was 14. He was much older than me – 21. We used to go for walks together and dance together at the

local youth club. I liked dancing with him. But there was no funny stuff. No kissing or flirting. We used to dance and talk and walk. Then one day when we were walking home he asked me to marry him. I kicked a stone and said I was too young. It was all I could think of saying. Then I shot him a quick glance and saw that he wasn't joking. He looked all serious and sort of sad.

A few days later I was sitting outside our house with my mother when he came along and started chatting. Suddenly he burst out, 'I want to marry your daughter, Mrs Bassey.' I wanted to run off like mad but I didn't dare. I heard my mum say, 'I think Shirley's a little too young.' He flushed and said, 'I'll wait until she leaves school.' Mum just shook her head. She liked that boy and knew he was real serious. But I could see she was worried.[14]

At least, that's the version Shirley told the *People* in 1958. Nearly forty years later she revisited this incident but dropped in a couple of significant details that had gone missing before:

Men have always liked me. When I was quite young, married men would be after me. I remember, once, me and my mother were walking down the road when this married man came out of a pub and said to my mother, 'I love your daughter.' My mother said: 'Go away. Leave her alone.' I was so ashamed. 'But mum, I love him,' I kept crying.[15]

Since the innocent young chap is now a married man coming out of the pub, it's maybe not overcynical to wonder about the absence of 'funny business'. For, while the boys may not have called her names to her face the way the catty girls did, if you talk to any of the old fellers who knocked around Splott and the Docks when Shirley was a teenager, they have their own hurtful names for the kind of girl they all speculated about.

There was a new kind of post-war girl who was causing concern to the national moralists. Girls who didn't necessarily equate sex with marriage. Tiger Bay may have had a fast-and-loose attitude to sexual morality for generations, but most of Britain was still firmly Protestant and proudly buttoned-up. Typical of the general reaction was this horrified gloss on the new females by the sociologists responsible for a 1956 book on coalmining communities:

> Since the war the emphasis on 'sex' rather than 'love' and 'romance' has increased and become more open. Weekly magazines of a certain type are widely read by young women as well as men, and in these 'sex appeal' is very deliberately cultivated. The trend in films and in the increasingly popular American pulp novelette is towards pornography and sex as part of a whole picture of violence. Women are as directly influenced by these developments as their brothers, boyfriends and husbands. A woman who was thirty in 1953 was very different in her attitudes, derived from her reading and film-going experiences, towards sex, and towards men, from her counterpart in adolescence in that year. All this can only tend to make the attitude of mind of girls towards sex approximate to that of the young men in the sense of seeing it more as something in and for itself.[16]

These were not romantic times in a country still struggling to get over the aftershocks of war, a place still poor and rationed, a place of spivs and tarts, a new country in which sex was less the traditional prelude to marriage, or the ecstatic communion of the new idealists, than just another commodity to be traded, a basic need that could turn a shilling or two. Britain after the war was a place, in short, where everything had its price.

Shirley Bassey stayed at Curran's for a year or so, and over that time it became clear that there were two things that she had going for her: she could sing and she had sex appeal. Gradually, if unconsciously, for no one who knew her then ever noticed the remotest hint of careerism in her, she began to feel her way towards allowing these gifts to work for her, to use them in tandem, to become a performer.

SEVEN

Down the Docks

By the beginning of the 1950s, when Shirley first started to sing in public, the Cardiff docklands were much changed from their pre-war incarnation. After a wartime boom they were in terminal decline, as the world's shipping had stopped using coal as fuel. In 1950 imports into Cardiff outstripped exports for the first time. And as the trade declined, so too did Tiger Bay.

Many of the myriad pubs and cafés closed down, though the Canadian Café was one of those that remained in business. Player pianos, whether manual or electric, were also a thing of the past. The new breed of record players were powerful and loud enough to provide dance music. But there was still plenty of demand for the real live stuff. There would be bands playing at the Saturday night dances, and there was regular work to be had for musicians in the many surviving pubs, like the Glendower and the Quebec, and cafés like Eddie Gomez's Casa Blanca. Some of the regular musicians were survivors from the pre-war years. The guitarist Victor 'Narker' Parker was a fixture on the scene. Others, like the Deniz Brothers and Don Johnson, came and went.

The audiences too had changed, with the focus shifting from the transient sailors to the regular visitors from US army bases. In musical terms that was probably a good thing: the GIs were surely a more discriminating audience than the drunken sailors. On the other hand, it meant that the American influence, black American in particular, started to overwhelm the range of world musics that had previously permeated the Bay's music scene. Certainly Shirley's musical heroes were all popular American singers, rather than the calypsonians or Hawaiian dance bands of the previous generation.

If you could characterise the popular sound of the time it would be pitched somewhere between jazz, blues and crooning, all with a distinct American bent, thanks to the records the GIs brought along with them. The biggest musical star in the US at the time was the singer Billy Eckstine. Eckstine had a serious jazz background. His 1944 big band featured a roll-call of the hippest young beboppers of the time: Dizzy Gillespie, Dexter Gordon, Miles Davis, Art Blakey, and even Charlie Parker among them, to say nothing of Sarah Vaughan as Eckstine's co-vocalist. But by the late 1940s he'd crossed over into pop balladry with smooth vocal confections like 'Prisoner of Love' and 'My Foolish Heart', all of which would make him an inspiration for crossover black American vocalists to come in the following decade, from Johnny Mathis to Sam Cooke.

Billy Eckstine was the favourite artiste of Shirley's brother Henry, by this time the sibling she was closest to. Together they would listen to Eckstine's records, and in particular his 1949 duets with Sarah Vaughan, 'Dedicated To You' and 'I Love You', which they would do their best to copy. In later years Shirley would claim that she sang the Billy Eckstine part and Henry the Sarah Vaughan part. Certainly Eckstine, rather than Sarah 'Sassy' Vaughan, was the bigger influence on the young Bassey. Eckstine was elegant and sophisticated, and his singing style was not what we would now think of as 'black'. When he came to the New Theatre, Cardiff, around this time, Shirley went to see him, and generally credits that as being the moment at which the possibility of being a professional singer first entered her mind.

For now, though, such glamour seemed a long way off. Henry and Shirley would sing together in an empty box room, illuminated by a single bare light bulb, where Henry had his record player and his collection of 78s – Frankie Laine, Ella Fitzgerald, Al Jolson, Eckstine, Vaughan and Judy Garland. 'Somewhere Over The Rainbow' was a particular favourite of the Bassey siblings, with its ineffable belief that there had to be a better life out there. These are names that might look oddly assorted now, but they went together easily enough in this time before the critics and the radio programmers had set up a musical apartheid system where Billy Eckstine was 'jazz' and 'black' while fellow balladeer Frankie Laine was 'country' and 'white'.

By the time she started working in Curran's, news of Shirley's singing talent had already spread. Her first performances were for friends and family and, so legend has it, she would start off under the table, too terrified to look her audience in the eye (of course, for all those children who had lived through the Blitz, the space under the table was a place of traditional security). Before long, though, she'd got over her nerves and in her very early teens she could be seen in the pubs of Splott, the pubs over the road from her house, the steelworkers' pubs, the rough men's pubs, the Lord Wimbourne and the Bomb and Dagger, literally singing for her supper. 'She had it tough,' remembers her contemporary and fellow singer, Patti Flynn, 'going into the pub when she was twelve or so to sing a song for a couple of shillings or whatever.'

According to the jazz historian Val Wilmer, Shirley may have made her first more or less formal public performance as early as 1949, when she was just twelve, at Eddie Gomez's Casa Blanca club on Bute Street, just three doors down from the building in which she was born. Gomez was another old-school Tiger Bay character, born in Trinidad, a First World War veteran and a ship's carpenter. By 1930 he was settled in Cardiff and running a Bute Street café.

Gomez was most likely the first man with music business connections to take notice of the young Shirley's nascent talent. Others soon followed, including an African American singer called Eddie Craig who had settled in Cardiff after the war and ran a series of clubs in the Bay. But then again it's true what they say, success has many fathers; there's no shortage of people prepared to take retrospective credit for talent-spotting the young Shirley. Among the most unlikely people to have recognised her nascent gift were two of the most famous radio voices of the post-war era, the poet Dylan Thomas and the commentator John Arlott. According to Arlott's biographer the twosome, both keen drinkers, made an excursion to a club in Tiger Bay, where they 'were struck by the talent and potential of a young girl singer and they told her so. Her name was Shirley Bassey.'[1]

Among Shirley's regular accompanists were a trio featuring the pianist and boxer Mal Innocent, a Tiger Bay product himself, and a young guitarist called George Parry, who had recently arrived in Cardiff from his native Snowdonia. These days George Parry is back in Snowdonia, still playing in the Django Reinhardt tradition and handmaking gypsy-style acoustic guitars:

> I came from this little village and I left in the early fifties to go to college. All the music I had was a couple of records and what I heard on the radio, the occasional song in a film. When I went down to Cardiff I realised straight away that all the music was down the docks.

He soon hooked up with Malcolm Innocent – 'a good pianist and great in a punch-up' – and found himself in a very different world from North Wales:

A hell of a lot of places in the Docks were brothels then. The buses didn't run down Bute Street after nine o' clock so that the upper-deck passengers didn't see into the houses of horizontal refreshment! But I never had any trouble at all – it was safer than walking round Caernarfon – and the people couldn't do enough for you.

It was in the pubs though, rather than the brothels, that George used to play with Shirley, generally in upstairs rooms in places like the Ship & Pilot or the Glamorgan. He remembers accompanying the young Shirley:

We'd be playing, and she must have got the idea from the old Holly-wood films – you know how there'd be a scene in a nightclub and a couple would sit down at a table with a candle, and then the singer walks round the club – and the voice still sounds the same even without the mic! Well, Shirley used to do that. She'd walk around the tables and whenever she did that, all of a sudden she'd change key! I didn't know much about keys, I'd taught myself. So if Shirley changed keys I just changed with her. I think that's why Mal got me in for the gig.

She'd come down there and sing – mostly ballads, things like 'Autumn Leaves' – and then she'd disappear at about half ten. A very respectable gentleman with a homburg hat would pick her up. The first new cars after the war were Rovers; there were two models and he had the expensive one. He was the manager of a big furniture store in town.

Shirley shared her own memories of these first musical adventures with the *Melody Maker* a couple of years later. Already it was something of an edited version:

My brother was an admirer of Ella Fitzgerald and spent all his spare time listening to her records. I sat around and listened and pretty soon started singing the numbers myself. I sang at home and I sang at work. It was while I was singing at my bench in a Cardiff factory one day that a girlfriend of mine said, 'Shirley, why don't you enter the talent competition at the Louis Ballroom next Saturday night? You never know, you might win.' Well, I did win and no one was more surprised than myself.

That started me off singing with a real live band and when I wasn't on the stand at the Louis or some other ballroom I was singing with a small group in a Tiger Bay club. I wasn't earning much but I was having fun – at least until I got into trouble with the police. I was only fifteen at the time and as you know no one below the age of six-teen is allowed to be on the premises when intoxicating drinks are being consumed. So whenever the word went round that there were cops in the vicinity, the boys in the band used to smuggle me out of sight. Then, when the scare had died down, I used to reappear and carry on singing.[2]

One man who saw Shirley singing in a Tiger Bay pub and imme-diately recognised her talent was another radio star of the time, Wyn Calvin. Wyn Calvin had grown up on the smart side of Cardiff and was a member of that generation who had fallen for the showbiz life via a stint in the Army's entertainments corps, ENSA. By the early 1950s he was forging a career as actor, comedian, panto star and radio presenter.

Wyn Calvin still lives in the house he grew up in. He's a very active eighty-something who only recently hung up his frock as Wales's leading pantomime dame and is still involved in charity work and after-dinner speaking. A practised raconteur, he's happy to recall the first time he set eyes on the young Shirley, in a pub on James Street, just off Mount Stuart Square in the commercial heart of the Docks:

> I saw this amazing kid just singing in the Ship and Pilot. I'd been told about her, but when she sang there it was almost spontaneous. There was a feller playing something accompanying her but I can't remember what. I just remember she was tremendous. The docks then were very musical because of the varying nations and types there. Music was much more natural than the rather correct choral singing of the rest of South Wales. What really struck me was her impact on an audience – all the fellers there – there was no presentation and yet her impact on these fellers, who weren't expecting anything at all or even paying attention, was immediate – 'Hey, what's this? This is good. She's all right, in't she?'

Calvin mentioned his new discovery to the formidable BBC radio producer Mai Jones, with whom he was working on a popular variety show. Mai Jones was in her early fifties at the time, a former singer and accordionist in such pre-war groups as the Five Magnets and the Three Janes. She'd been working as a producer for the BBC since the early 1940s, during which time she'd also established herself as a songwriter, responsible for that classic of kitsch Welshness, 'We'll Keep A Welcome In The Hillsides'. As far as Welsh light entertainment went, Mai Jones was the woman you needed to impress:

> I told Mai Jones who was the producer of *Welsh Rarebit* – it wasn't a local programme, it went out to all Britain and had audiences of something like 19 million a week on a Thursday night. Radio was the one means of instantaneous mass communication back then. Anyway, I told Mai about this girl, said she was tremendous, and we arranged an audition.

Wyn Calvin met the young Shirley as she arrived at the BBC offices. Taken out of the world she knew, though, this Shirley Bassey was no longer a teenage man-magnet, but an overawed kid: 'Yes, she was shy, unsure, desperate for reassurance. Going to a BBC studio then was intimidating for a kid, and she was still a kid.'

Shirley duly auditioned, singing 'Stormy Weather', a song made famous by another of her major influences, Lena Horne, and was swiftly turned down, as Calvin remembers: 'I was told afterwards not to waste their time with rubbish like that again. Mai didn't like this kid who was undisciplined, didn't read music . . . etcetera.'

Ah yes, etcetera. This was one of Shirley's first ventures outside the Cardiff docklands and thus one of her first chances to experience genteel racism in action. She had been used to the name-calling of a Splott playground and found her own ways to combat it. She had been the subject of plenty of snide remarks from her fellow teenage girls, but she knew that the Docklands boys, both black and white, were hers to charm. But what to do in the presence of Miss Mai Jones, empress of BBC Wales? Nothing but to slink off home.

Maybe a lesson was learned here. It's certainly the case that women would play precious little part in Shirley's subsequent rise to the top. Partly for simple reasons – women were rarely in such positions of power as Mai Jones occupied – but also surely because the young Shirley was becoming all too well aware of the genteel racism of women – a racism neatly encapsulated in this quote from a contemporary women's magazine:

Many coloured men are fine people, but they do come from a different race, with a very different background and upbringing. Besides, scientists do not yet know if it is wise for two such very different races as whites and blacks to marry, for sometimes the children of mixed marriages seem to inherit the worst characteristics of each race.[3]

That's not to say Mai Jones was guilty of such conscious racism. She simply didn't see Shirley Bassey, or anyone who looked like her, as being properly 'Welsh'. As Calvin points out: 'In fairness to Mai, she was producing a programme which reflected Welsh humour and Welsh music. This was somewhere between African and Caribbean, the style of this kid, not at all the vision of Wales that Mai was meant to be presenting to the rest of Britain.' And there, maybe, is the real lesson that the young Shirley learned from her abortive visit to the BBC – if she was going to make it in show business, as a Welsh woman of colour, it would not be in Wales.

*   *   *

In 1952, then, the messages were starting to come over loud and clear for the fifteen-year-old Shirley: stay in your quarter of the city and keep your head down. But there were other messages too, more positive ones. Especially if, like Shirley, you were a teenage girl.

Many of Shirley's generation of Bay girls were dreaming of escape from their seaside ghetto. Some, like Shirley's sister Gracie and dozens more, took the simplest route: they married GIs and went to the USA. Others, like Shirley and Louise Benjamin and Maureen Jemmett and Patti Flynn and Irene Spettie, looked to take their future into the own hands, looked to make their mark in show business as singers or dancers or both.

What gave these girls from this backwater such ambition? The Rainbow Club and and Frenchie's tap-dancing classes certainly helped. Coming from a place where music was all around you must have been a great part of it. Mostly, though, it was their common experience of childhoods lived amid the grand drama of war, and adolescences lived amid the greyness of rationing, all of which left these Bay girls with an abiding love of glamour.

They weren't alone in this, of course. There were hordes of teenage white girls who would have entertained the same dreams, but just then, just for a brief moment at the dawn of the 1950s in austerity Britain, these coloured girls from Cardiff had just a little bit of a head start.

There was a fashion in the post war years for touring revues. These were basically traditional variety shows – with a comedian or two, a singer or two, a magician or other speciality act, a dance troupe and a chorus line – but all given a theme. Often this would be geographic – Hawaiian or French or Brazilian – basically anywhere that sounded exotic to the glamour-starved Brits – and, of course, provided plenty of excuses for dancing girls to wear skimpy costumes. Another, perhaps surprisingly popular, theme was transvestism. There were a number of successful touring revues entirely made up of men in drag, amongst them the likes of Danny La Rue. These were always billed as 'ex-servicemen's shows' to make sure that everyone understood this was just good healthy manly fun.

And these boys who wanted to be women were not the only social outsiders to find a place in the revues; they also provided opportunities for Britain's still-small black communities. The fashion for exoticism led to a series of revues with a black American jazz theme. The first of these was a show called *Four and Twenty Blackbirds*. Like a lot of the revues, it was based on a pre-war show. However, the economics of the situation plus strict musicians' union rules meant there was no question of importing actual black Americans to perform in the show; instead, the producers went in search of black British singers and dancers. They found some in London, some more in Liverpool, but mostly they found them in Cardiff.

Maureen Jemmett was one of the Cardiff girls recruited to join the chorus line:

> There were five or six of us girls from the Bay: me, Hazel Langford, Marie Actie, Beryl Freeman, Deara Williams, Audrey Beezer, Vera Parker. We came to London to join *Four and Twenty Blackbirds*, which originally in the 1920s was a big all-black American show in the West End. Charlie Woods came down from London to find girls for it. We all used to go down to the play centre in Bute Street, the Rainbow Club. We used to go there twice a week for activities etcetera, and we were all interviewed there for *Four and Twenty Blackbirds*. We all had to do a little dance and they said OK and then they all had to meet our parents and our parents had to sign an agreement and we all left for London. They paid our fare and everything, they met us at Paddington Station and we all lived in digs in Camden Road.

The dancing and singing abilities of the Bay girls were rather less important than their skin colour: 'I think there were only three of us in the show who could dance,' says Maureen, laughing at the memory of the odd assortment of Bay girls she'd gone off on tour with.

The best of the local dance talent, Louise Benjamin, wasn't quite old enough for *Four and Twenty Blackbirds*. Besides, she had her sights set rather higher, what with her piano-teacher mother, her ballet lessons, her talent show domination, her head-girlship at the local school – 'I was a right little wheedler,' she says now. If anyone was going to make it out of the Bay, it would surely be Louise, rather than an untutored kid like Shirley Bassey. So while Louise waited for the right opportunity to show up, she left school and did her bit to integrate Cardiff's secretarial classes:

I went to the labour exchange and they sent me to this place – BTD, the British Transport Docks Board – as a junior learning the switchboards and so on. I got on fine there. I left when I was seventeen and a half. I later found out that when I first went there the boss had said to the rest of the staff, 'We've hired this young girl, she's black – do you mind?' I was really shocked because I hadn't come up against that prejudice in the Bay. But they said all right, she can stay.

While she was working there Louise saw an advert in the *Stage*, placed by the Ben Johnson Ballet company, an all-black ballet troupe. It was the chance she'd been waiting for:

Well, I went to the audition with Ben Johnson. I saw the advertisement in the *Stage* that they were looking for black dancers and I thought, 'Oh, this is me, I'm a black dancer,' so I discussed it with my mother and she said OK and she came with me to the audition and I got the job, which I was thrilled with. We did a few weeks' rehearsal and then we went on tour in *Paris After Dark*, the Paul Raymond revue. We went to places like New Brighton up north, and I thought it was absolutely fantastic to be on the stage getting paid. I didn't mind the grottiness of the digs or the awful food, I thoroughly enjoyed it.

Ironically enough, though, the shows the trained dancers of the Ben Johnson troupe were appearing in were often also the revues that were recruiting Bay girls simply on the basis of skin colour. In 1953 a man called Cliff Gordon, a Welsh actor and producer based in London, returned to Cardiff to recruit for the latest of these revues. It was called *Memories of Jolson* and, as the name suggests, it was based around the songs of the blackface minstrel himself. After seeing Shirley perform at the Old Comrades Club he invited her to audition for the show:

I was singing around the clubs. One night in the Workmen's Club in Paradise Place, off Queen Street, Cardiff I met the director of *Memories of Jolson*, an all-coloured show just going into rehearsal. He asked me to join the show.[4]

Shirley's initial reaction was that this was just another chat-up line, so she told Gordon he'd have to contact her mother and ask her. Shirley thought that would be the end of it, but, sure enough, next morning Gordon showed up at their front door in Splott, and asked Eliza if Shirley could come up to London to audition for the show. Eliza was dubious pointing out that her daughter had never been away from home, but Gordon was insistent and agreed to pay for Shirley's friend Iris to come with her as her chaperone. And so the just barely sixteen-year-old Shirley Bassey made her first venture into show business proper – or, as she put it to a TV interviewer, 'that was the end of my childhood.'

EIGHT

Hot From Splott

The time Shirley Bassey spent in the revues in 1953 and 1954 is perhaps the most confusing period of what was already a pretty confusing life. There are a few things that can be said for certain. She was in two touring revues – *Memories of Jolson* and *Hot From Harlem* – and somewhere between the finish of one and the start of the other she became pregnant.

At the start of her run in *Memories of Jolson*, she was a girl from nowhere with a big, if as yet untrained, voice, precious little experience of show business, and a limited knowledge of life. By the end of *Hot From Harlem*, she was still a girl from nowhere with a big and still untrained voice, but she knew rather more than she wanted to about both show business and life.

So far so good, but the devil is in the detail. They say of the 1960s that, if you can remember them, you weren't there. Well, much the same seems to go for the touring revues of the early 1950s. Neither Shirley herself, nor any of her contemporaries, seem to have anything more than an impressionistic grip on who was in what show doing what, where and when.

Shirley's own accounts of this time tend to conflate the two tours into one (and whenever possible leave out the business of getting pregnant in the midst of it all). Which is quite confusing. More confusing still is that talking to people who were in the shows tends only to make matters murkier, as they contradict each other at every turn. But what follows is pretty close to what happened.

Sometime in 1953, following Cliff Gordon's recruiting trip to Cardiff, a selection of Bay girls, including Shirley Bassey, Iris Freeman and Mahala Davis, were told they were going to be in the show. And then they heard nothing more, as Shirley Bassey recalls in her 1956 *Empire News* account of her early years:

> He (Cliff Gordon) asked me to join the show, but I wasn't interested. Finally I agreed. I left the factory – and immediately regretted it. I was out of work for two months and I didn't seem to be likely to get into the show after all. Then one morning I was lying in bed when my mother came rushing in. 'Get up,' she said. 'There's a woman downstairs to see you. She wants you to go to London.'[1]

It turned out there was another more formal audition stage for Shirley to go through. Her first audition had obviously been impressive enough that she was now up for a solo spot in the revue, and not simply another place on the chorus line:

> I was wanted for an audition, so Mother sat up half the night washing, ironing and packing my clothes. Next day I took the train to London. I was met at Paddington by Joe Eastman, the manager of the show, and Ben Johnson, the choreographer. After lunch we got a taxi to the rehearsal rooms in Windmill Street. I sang 'I Believe' and 'Walking My Baby Back Home', and that was it. I was in – a real professional artist at last.

Back home to Splott, then:

The funny thing is, Mother was much more excited than I was. When I got home she threw a terrific party for all the neighbours. It started in our house and ended up in a hotel across the street. You'd have thought I was a star already![2]

Soon afterwards Shirley returned to London to meet her rather motley bunch of co-stars. *Memories of Jolson* was essentially a minstrel show. For years Cliff Gordon had worked on a successful radio show called *The Kentucky Minstrels*, which finished in 1950. Gordon was convinced that there would be public demand for a theatrical version. He was right, of course, but a little ahead of his time. A decade later *The Black and White Minstrels* would have one of the most successful runs ever seen in the British theatre. *Memories of Jolson*, however, was a distinctly low-rent forerunner, and while *The Black and White Minstrels* featured an all-white cast, *Memories of Jolson* was, in the parlance of the time, an almost all-coloured show.

Shirley's co-stars in this venture were a collection of show business veterans. The headline attraction, Eddie Reindeer, was an old-school singing comic (and coincidentally another Cardiffian, real name Eddie Reinhardt). Roy Hudd, in his book on the lost legends of post-war variety, recalls the man:

> Eddie Reindeer was an old-fashioned patter comic. My happiest memories of him are travelling back from the Continental Chatham by train. He would regale me with tales of variety, digs, stars, eccentrics, has-beens and never-was-es. He really came into the business too late. He was loud, boisterous, unsubtle and totally lovable.[3]

The other main attraction was Ike Hatch, who was in his early sixties by the time of *Memories of Jolson*, and had had an extraordinary career. He was born in New York around 1891 and was a trained classical singer. 'It was claimed that Isaac could sing in Italian, French and "Jewish" and could speak the "Jewish" language fluently,' according to the jazz historian Arthur Badrock. Hatch appeared in vaudeville and in 1919 he played with W. C. Handy, the self-professed 'father of the blues'. In December 1925 Hatch was making a record in London. He clearly found England to his liking, as he remained there for the rest of his life. He owned, ran or fronted a succession of Soho clubs, among them the Shim Sham Club, and made records under the name Ike ('Yowse Suh') Hatch and his Harlem Stompers. From the late 1930s onwards he'd been a star of *The Kentucky Minstrels*, with its mix of parlour ballads, Al Jolson and southern minstrelsy.

Other acts on the bill included another black American, Chris Gill, an acrobatic tap dancer and crooner; and Benny Nightingale, one of the first black comedians to work the British stage. There was a fair bit of showbiz experience on show, then, but not much in the way of a marquee attraction. *Memories of Jolson* was to be a hand-to-mouth operation, as Shirley remembered: 'I'll never forget our opening night. No costumes turned up. We had to go on in our street clothes and one of the girls lent me a frock for my "spot".'[4]

The opening night in question was at the Grand Theatre, Luton, where the troupe were booked in for a week. Added to the bill for these shows were the Ben Johnson ballet troupe, featuring Louise Benjamin. Ben Johnson's wife, Pamela, took charge of the momentarily dispirited Bay girls. She laid out the time-honoured logistics of getting by in showbiz on a pittance. Rather than pay the landlady two pounds a week for an evening meal, taking a huge chunk out of their five pounds a week wages, they would each put ten shillings into a kitty and cook their own food on Pam's Primus stove.

It was at this point that Shirley demonstrated she was not cut out to be a team player. She refused to put her ten bob in the kitty, saying that she'd sort out her own food. This may well have been the characteristic behaviour of the youngest child in a big, poor family – a girl who's learned the hard way that sharing is a nice idea in theory, but the littlest one rarely does well out of it – yet it immediately alienated her from her fellow chorus girls.

Looking back now, Louise Benjamin is puzzled by her memories of Shirley's abiding self-centredness:

> Well, I never fell out with Shirley. She and Pam fell out quite a few times, and others did too. I took her as she was. I knew what she was like, always borrowing your stuff without even asking, so as long as you knew about that . . . I just wondered why she would be like that. Nobody actually liked her and that must have been sad – she felt that – but she did it to herself by her mean-spirited ways. I don't know whether when she got money she changed . . . Her upbringing was poor, and maybe that's why she was like that. If you're lacking in things . . . It was a big family and the pecking order must have made it hard for her.

But if her fellow chorus girls were none too keen on the young Shirley, the male contingent on the tour seemed rather more enthusiastic. Eddie Reindeer immediately saw the potential in the young singer and included her in the show business banter of the company, out of which, he told Eamonn Andrews, came Shirley's enduring nickname. 'Yeah, we used to have a little game switching names – she called me Ready Heindeer and I called her Burly Chassis.'[5]

And Shirley's fondness for Eddie's humour led to a memorable accident:

Even when the costumes did turn up there was trouble. I had a strapless dress with a long skirt. As I stood in the wings, watching Eddie Reindeer do his act, he cracked an unexpected gag. I burst out laughing – and my dress split around the waist. We patched up the damage with a broad belt and the audience noticed nothing till I started on my closing number, 'Stormy Weather'. That's a song I love and I tend to throw myself around a little while I'm singing it. On the last bar I flung my arms triumphantly above my head – and down came my skirt, leaving me standing there in my underwear! Believe me, I got the biggest hand of my career, but I wasn't pleased![6]

That's what she told a Cardiff newspaper a couple of years later, for an article coyly headlined 'Striptease! But it wasn't my act!' Since then it has become the one story Shirley trots out in an interview every time her early career is mentioned. It's perfectly unthreatening seaside postcard stuff that serves to take the conversation away from the grubby realities of life on the road in the early 1950s.

And there is, of course, something disingenuous in Shirley's telling of the story. In these first years of her career she must have been well aware that titillation was a large part of her appeal. Indeed, it was a large part of the appeal of revues like *Memories of Jolson*. The audience was as much there to see scantily clad coloured girls strutting their stuff in the chorus line as they were to listen to Eddie Reindeer's patter.

And before taking Shirley's protestations of modesty too seriously, we should look at her first ever publicity photo shoot, which took place during the tour. Three of the photos survive in the archives of the *Daily Mirror*, and it's pretty obvious that the photographer had a very clear idea of what the young Shirley's appeal was.

It's worth considering the photos in a little detail. All three are taken on an empty stage in a deserted theatre. In all three she has her natural afro hair worn short with an attempt at a side parting. The first picture shows Shirley sitting on the floor, wearing a white halter-neck dress which fans out beneath her. There's a fair amount of cleavage on view and Shirley is smiling up at the photographer. The second shows Shirley leaning against a scenery fence. The dress no longer loops around her neck. Instead the straps are hanging down and it's only Shirley's folded arms that are holding it up and keeping her breasts more or less covered. She's still smiling, but it's hard to ignore the titillation of the pose. In the third photo there's no ambiguity at all. She's sitting down again and the top half of her dress is folded down so it seems to be only her nipples that are keeping it in place, and, again, only just. Once again, Shirley is smiling broadly at the photographer.

As photos of a sixteen-year-old trying to make her way in show business go, they are blatantly exploitative. Their market would have been one of the mildly salacious weeklies of the time, like *Reveille* or *Tit-Bits*, not one of the daily papers. But while it's impossible to justify this exploitation of such a young girl, it is worth noting that nothing in Shirley's expression suggests any discomfort with the photos.

The other thing to note is that the teenage Shirley is not beautiful by any conventional standard. Indeed, by the standards of her fellow chorus girls, she was barely a contender. Louise Benjamin offers a blunt assessment of the young Shirley's charms: 'She wasn't a beauty like Pam, who had lovely fine features, lovely hair. Shirley was a bit plain, very bad skin and bad hair. She did have lovely hands.'

Well, perhaps, but what the young Shirley had, and evidently knew she had, was flat-out sex appeal, a hard-to-pin-down quality that is nevertheless more powerful than simple good looks. You can see it in these cheesecake photos, of course, but you can also see it in the photos of the ensemble, which show Shirley surrounded by rakish men, looking absolutely in her element. She clearly knew what she had, and was more than ready to use it to attract the blokes, who treated her well, and to get away from the bitching girls, always complaining just because Shirley happened to borrow one of their blouses or eat some of their food. Louise Benjamin again: 'Oh yes, she did like a bloke, Shirl! I remember her staying out after the show and getting in terrible trouble with Ben – although his morals weren't that brilliant! He was very strict with her: do as I say not as I do.'

During the tour Shirley had an affair with one of the young male dancers in the show. Meanwhile, after a couple of months on the road, the novelty started to wear thin: 'I played all over Britain with *Memories of Jolson* but I was still not sure whether I liked show business, and I was desperately homesick. Only Mother's letters, full of encouragement and love, made me stick it out.'[7]

The final dates for the show were in North London. Rather than go home immediately, Shirley decided to stay on in London. Along with Louise she took up an offer from Ben and Pam Johnson to stay with them in their house in Harold Hill, east London, in return for helping look after the Johnsons' little daughter, Maria.

The first thing Shirley did was to try and capitalise on the start she'd made by appearing in *Memories of Jolson*. Eddie Reindeer was keen to help out, happy to play the show business mentor to this impressionable young girl, no doubt hoping that a little of her lustre might rub off on him:

Well, the show was coming off at Wood Green and I thought if I make a test record with her I might get her on the discs, you know. So we went to the little place off Shaftesbury Avenue and we made this little record. Matter of fact we made two – one for Shirley to take to her mum, and one for me to take round the record companies. Well, I didn't have any luck with mine. I couldn't whip up any enthusiasm at the time, but that's show business.[8]

Listening to the recording, a duet on the decidedly corny 'By the Light of the Silvery Moon' (then enjoying a revival of popularity thanks to a Doris Day film), it's easy to see the problem, which is that Eddie Reindeer dominates proceedings, not allowing the young Shirley any space to show what she could do.

Undeterred, Shirley looked around for some solo gigs. She found an agent, William Henshall,* with an office on the Charing Cross Road. He got her at least one gig, appearing at the NCOs club on the US air force base in Burtonwood, Cheshire. Two shows for ten pounds.

Back in London she moved between Ben and Pam's and her sister Ella's place – Ella having recently moved up from Cardiff to the Seven Sisters Road in north London. Some of the time Shirley worked in a laundrette. Some time early in the new year, 1954, she realised that she was pregnant. This is how, a few years later, she explained what happened:

> It happened when I was seventeen and touring with a show called *Memories of Jolson*. I met a boy and I thought we were in love. A few months later I realised I was going to have a baby. The boy wanted me to get rid of it and when I refused he vanished and I have never seen or heard from him since.[9]

---

* Presumably the same theatrical agent of that name who, thirty-five years earlier, during his divorce action, had his character summed up thus by a judge: 'I ought to say I seldom have to try a case where a man shows himself such an utterly worthless disreputable scoundrel as he.'

Much, much later, in 1998, she would change this story. In her only other recorded reference to her first child's father, and following a court case in which she was obliged to prove that she was not an anti-Semite,* she told reporters that her daughter Sharon's father was Jewish: 'I have never told him – it would have hurt too many people. He was married and had children.'[10]

It might be worth noting that the only Jewish performer involved in *Memories of Jolson* was Eddie Reindeer, a married man who then took her down to London.

Whoever the father was, he certainly didn't stick around. One can only imagine how hard this must have been for the just barely seventeen-year-old. Characteristically, she told as few people as possible, but never wavered in her desire to have the baby: 'I was prepared to face the music. I'd loved and nobody could take that away from me.'[11]

It's from around this time, when the two girls were sharing a room in the Johnsons' house, that Louise Benjamin offers her most revealing memory of Shirley: 'At night, she'd wait till the lights were out and then I'd hear her rummaging about and from under the mattress she'd bring out a packet of biscuits – Lincoln biscuits, you remember? – and she'd eat them while she thought I was asleep.' It's a telling image of a young woman, part child, part adult, keeping things close, her comforts and her troubles.

*   *   *

But before Shirley had time to dwell on the ramifications of this unexpected pregnancy, another serious gig, her best yet, came along.

* A former personal assistant, Hilary Levy, had sued Shirley for breach of contract after being sacked, and alleged that Shirley had struck her and called her a Jewish bitch. Shirley was acquitted of all charges.

It was to be another revue, but where *Memories of Jolson* was an ad hoc affair, masterminded by the dodgy Cliff Gordon, this one had some very experienced showbiz pros behind it. One of the two producers – the other was the future sexploitation supremo, Paul Raymond – was a man named Joe Collins. From a showbiz family, Joe had been in the business for decades, running a successful theatrical agency. These days he's better known for his two daughters – the actress Joan and the writer Jackie – but back then Joe Collins was a serious name in his own right. In his autobiography he remembers how Shirley's involvement in the show came about:

One of these new shows, called *Hot From Harlem*, featured music of black American origin – shades of the famous Cotton Club – but the cast were all British black people. In the fifties there were far fewer black performers in Britain than there are today, and when I came to casting the soubrette I was stuck. I just could not find the right girl.

An agent friend of mine, Sidney Burns, stepped in. 'I've got someone you could try. Heard her singing in some dump in Tiger Bay.* That's where she lives. She's only singing part-time . . . works as a waitress too. She's still very raw, but I think with the right presentation she would be fine. Her name is Shirley Bassey.'

I interviewed Shirley Bassey in my office. She was just a skinny little thing in her mid teens, yet I sensed she had stage presence and could be made to look stylish. I did not bother to hear her sing. I reckoned that even if she wasn't much of a vocalist, she would fit in my show if she were dressed the way I had in mind.[12]

---

* Probably slightly misremembered by Joe Collins. According to Michael Sullivan, Shirley's first manager, Burns was an investor in *Memories of Jolson*, so that's where he would have heard her sing.

One can only speculate as to what kind of audition for a pretty young singer didn't involve actually hearing her sing – although a solid recommendation and her sultry looks may have been all that he required – but then Shirley was already getting used to men being more interested in her looks than her singing. And Collins was evidently happy with what he saw, as he agreed to provide the funds for a new wardrobe for Shirley.

> I telephoned the fashion designer Eric Darnell. I want this girl, Shirley Bassey, to look feline and seductive. She's only a scrap of a kid. You haven't got much to work on. But do what you can. I'm willing to spend forty-two pounds on her clothes. That sort of money was no fortune, even in 1954, but it was not too bad either, considering I was spending it on an unknown artiste in a touring revue.[13]

It wasn't too bad at all, not after the second-hand tat of *Memories of Jolson*. And nor were Shirley's wages too bad. From five pounds a week for *Memories*, she was now on the giddy heights of eighteen pounds a week. The only people who earned more than her in the show were the clutch of experienced comedians. No wonder she didn't mention to Mr Collins that she was pregnant. Most likely, with the insouciance of youth, she simply didn't consider that this might, in due course, become a problem.

Meanwhile the rehearsals for *Hot From Harlem* started. As Collins suggests, this was another 'all-coloured' show – not even a token white Reindeer on display this time. Musically, the show was something of a step forward: the minstrel stylings of *Memories* were replaced by a vague approximation of Harlem in the 1920s, the jazz age rather than the plantation age. And while the minstrel songs were already irredeemably corny, strictly for the old folk, 1920s jazz was actually undergoing a revival at the time amongst the nation's youth.

That said, *Hot From Harlem* was still a pretty cheesy affair. It didn't even feature any actual black Americans, like Ike Hatch and Chris Gill in *Memories*, to lend the show musical credibility. Its stars were the comedians Charlie Woods and Bertie Jarrett, a very popular variety attraction of the time, as Roy Hudd recalls in his guide to the great variety acts:

> A first-class teaming of two black guys. Bertie Jarrett would sing songs at the piano, *à la* Fats Waller. They had good patter and a sensational dancing finale where Charlie would dance onto a staircase built up to, and on, the piano. They played all the UK's number one theatres.[14]

Charlie Woods was a veteran of the black British music scene. He was born in Canning Town, east London, another of the original sailortowns, And along with his sister, fellow dancer Josie Woods, he'd had a wonderfully varied career in show business.* Charlie was a canny operator who, as well as being the headline act, secured himself a second wage as the show's manager. Bertram 'Nightlife' Jarrett was another veteran, a Jamaican who'd been in the UK since pre-war days.

The show's other star was an old associate of the Woods siblings, Cyril Lagey. Lagey had quite a name at the time, as a member of Sid Milward's Nitwits, a comedy mini-orchestra, specialising in notionally amusing manglings of popular classics. Maggie Regan, who worked with Cyril in a subsequent combo, Nuts And Bolts, gives the flavour of the man:

---

* The Woods siblings started out by training with the clog-dancing music hall troupe the Eight Lancashire Lads (the ensemble that, bizarrely enough, once featured a young Londoner called Charlie Chaplin). After that they joined the Eight Black Streaks, billing themselves as 'The World's Fastest Dancers', and appearing in the film version of *Kentucky Minstrels* (all this from Val Wilmer).

Cyril had an eventful life. He worked as a cigarette boy in the Nest in Carnaby Street, London, a famous club in the 1930s frequented by film stars and royalty. He played a jungle king in the movie *Tarzan* and can still be seen in old documentaries jumping from the back of a flatbed truck in the desert during the war. He was there to entertain our troops . . . Some people called (his humour) 'Uncle Tomming' or 'mugging', but whatever it was, Cyril was the master of it. His eyes rolled in fear, and his big lips gibbered with fright when asked the simplest question by Professor Nuts! His squeaky high voice and American drawl was superb. Many times I have seen audiences of every nationality bent over and gasping for breath with hysterical laughter when Cyril had only just walked on stage, before he even opened his mouth to speak. You tell me . . . when did you ever see that?[15]

The remainder of the cast comprised a clutch of male dancers, mostly of West Indian origin; the Guyanese singer and trumpet player Simmie Russ; a couple of supporting singers, Val Richmond and Naida Lane; a couple more comics, Eddie Williams and Dusty Daniels; and, as ever, a chorus line mostly made up of Bay girls who'd been recruited, once again, by Charlie Woods. Shirley's friend Iris Freeman was there; so too was Victor Parker's daughter Beryl and half a dozen others.

In charge of the dancers was another Cardiffian with a Nigerian father: a woman called Terry Link, a little older than the others, who'd been living in London's Camden Town, for some years. Her flat was a regular meeting place for the Bay girls.

*   *   *

The week of 15 March 1954, the show opened in London at the Chiswick Empire – not what Roy Hudd would call a number one theatre, but not a number three fleapit either. The show started with the whole troupe doing a dance called the Cakewalk, showing off Shirley's singing and the Jamaican dancer Harold Holness's moves.

Thereafter the first half of the show rolled out a mishmash of mostly comic vignettes – 'The Convict Escapes' and something, doubtless hilarious, called 'Jungle Antics' – and solo spots. Eddie Williams performed a comic routine and Shirley Bassey, billed with considerable chutzpah as 'Broadway's new singing sensation', sang 'Ebb Tide', one of the hot songs of the moment, if hardly one that evoked Harlem in the 1920s.*

Shirley herself was happier this time around. She wasn't just another chorus girl arguing over putting ten bob in the kitty. She was the soubrette, getting paid more than twice as much as her contemporaries, with her own wardrobe and make-up and dressing room.

This time I was happy from the start. I guess I was more confident. I was no longer the scrawny little kid from Tiger Bay. My figure was filling out, and my dressing-room mirror told me that, with my new hairstyling and good make-up, I had outgrown the 'ugly duckling' stage. If I'd wanted any further reassurance the boys waiting at the stage door, trying vainly to date me, and their notes and flowers, provided it.[16]

---

* Initially an instrumental hit written by composer Robert Maxwell. Lyricist Carl Sigman was commissioned to write words, for which he found inspiration from the beach scene in *From Here to Eternity*, inspiring him to explain that, 'If listened to in the right frame of mind the melody rises and falls in a way which uncannily resembles an orgasm, with one of the most stirring climaxes I've ever heard followed by a beautifully relaxed, restful and contented ending.' Just as Shirley was singing it, in 1954, it was a pop hit for Vic Damone and an R & B hit for Roy Hamilton.

Joe Collins was certainly happy with his investment.

> You could say I got a bargain. Shirley Bassey put the heat into *Hot From Harlem* . . . fingers snapping, hips working overtime. She was a right little tease, with a seductive, growling voice. Sometimes the wolf whistles from the audience drowned her singing. Both the audience *and* the rest of the cast went wild over her.[17]

The italicised 'and' suggests Joe Collins was keeping back a story or two here. The Trinidadian trumpeter Pankey Alleyne told Val Wilmer that a friend of his in the band had tried his luck with Shirley only to discover she was pregnant. For the first couple of months of the show, though, Shirley was mostly able to ignore her condition and enjoy the ride.

Before long the show came to Cardiff's New Theatre, a very respectable venue. This was a wonderful opportunity for Shirley to show off to old friends and family. And Shirley duly made the most of it. After all, given her condition, there was every chance that this might be her first and last appearance there.

Curiously, for all her mother's support, it seems to have been Bobo Mendi who came to see the show first. At least, that's what she told *Woman's Hour* a few years later, when asked what her father thought of her success (interestingly, she refers to Mendi as her father throughout):

> He saw me the first time he'd ever been into a theatre in his life. It was when I was playing at Cardiff New Theatre, and he came to the opening night and he was as pleased as Punch, so much so that he picked up a programme on his way out, thinking that I was in it. He went home and said, 'Missus'– that's my mother, he called my mother 'Missus' – 'I've got a programme of your daughter,' and

my mother opened the programme and it was the following week's programme . . . He said, 'I'm so proud of her, I'm going back to see her again,' and I think then he went back and got the right programme.[18]

Another visitor to the show was Ifor Harry, the barber who lived two doors down from the Basseys. He was rather less impressed, as he told Muriel Burgess: 'It wasn't a very nice kind of show. A bit on the rough side, if you know what I mean . . . Shirley sang very well on that box, [but] what in God's name was Iris Freeman doing, floating around holding a candle and wearing something that looked like her nightie?'[19] This was the 'Ebb Tide' scene. Iris Freeman told Muriel Burgess that she'd wondered much the same thing. Shirley had done her best to explain. The box she was standing on was meant to be a rock from which she was looking out to sea, singing to her lover:

'OK,' said Iris, 'you're singing "Ebb Tide", so what am I doing buggering about with a candle?'

'Jesus,' exclaimed an exasperated seventeen-year-old Shirley, 'I give up. You're the bloody lighthouse.'[20]

It's a story that offers one of the first recorded examples of Shirley Bassey's most overlooked quality: her sense of humour. Many years later she would appear on the *Morecambe & Wise Show* sending herself up as she attempts to sing 'Smoke Gets in Your Eyes' while her foot goes through the cardboard scenery and Eric and Ernie make matters worse as they pretend to help out. Not many so-called divas would allow such *lèse majesté*, but Shirley had long had a keen awareness of the absurdity of show business conventions and, indeed, her own grandiosity. These touring revues did a good job of preventing their stars from acquiring too many airs and graces.

After Cardiff, the *Hot From Harlem* tour headed north. More digs, more dressing rooms, more boys at the stage door. And a steadily dawning awareness that all this could not last. She was three months pregnant, four months pregnant, five months. Her new gowns could scarcely take the strain. And yet she wanted to keep on, both for the joy of performing and for the money.

It can't have made things any easier to know that one of her supporting singers, Naida Lane, a mixed-race Londoner with a West African father, was preparing to get married to Chris Barber, the trad jazz trombonist who was currently riding high in the pop charts with his tune 'La Fleur'.

Barber and Lane were married three months later, just as Shirley was having her baby. The story, as reported in *Jet* magazine, ran as follows:

> Pretty British-born Negro dancer, Naida Lane, 23, and white band-leader, Chris Barber, were married in London. At the wedding reception in the swank home of Barber's parents, Naida, the daughter of a West African, broke into tears, said: 'We coloured people sometimes carry a chip about prejudice when there's no cause . . . You've all taken me to your hearts as easily as though I'd come back sunburnt from a vacation.'[21]

It's hard to imagine Shirley ever sounding so grateful to be accepted by white people, and a reminder of just how rare and how powerful her lack of race consciousness was, however much she might be berated for it later. She wasn't an Uncle Tom, she was just herself, a girl from Splott. She acted as if it never occurred to her that there might be prejudice against her and as a result it seems to have rarely occurred to people to be prejudiced.

Around this time the show came back to London for a brief run. A talent spotter saw Shirley and brought her to the attention of the booking agent Bert Wilcox, but, as he remembers, she seemed to be at a very low ebb:

A feller called me up, said 'Do you book coloured singers?' I said yeah why not, he said 'D'you think you could book a girl into a West End nightclub?' I said 'I don't see why not – there's no prejudice there if she can sing.' He said 'I want to bring this girl along, she don't look much but she's a very good jazz singer,' so he brought her up, this girl. She was skinny, a bit spotty, unattractive, didn't say a word, miserable, and he said I'd like you to meet Shirley Bassey. He'd heard her because she was singing at the old Collins Music Hall in Islington in a thing called *Hot From Harlem*, and he thought somebody could develop her, but I never heard her sing, I just had a look at her and thought she's not the kind of girl that I could really push into the West End clubs, and that was it.[22]

She must have known by then that, in her condition, all talk of appearing in a West End club was just pie in the sky. Come the summer, though, there was no choice left for her to make, as she recalled a few years later, when the existence of her daughter was first discovered by the tabloids: 'I carried on in the show as long as I could. I wasn't earning much money, but I managed to save a few pounds each week for my baby. Then I had to give up and I went away to have my baby.'[23]

And that, really, should have been that.

NINE

Stormy Weather

Shirley left the show in the summer after a run in Liverpool. She took the train back home, changing at Crewe, where she ran into Louise Benjamin who was horrified to discover Shirley was pregnant. She came back to the house on Portmanmoor Road, moved back in with her mother and Bobo Mendi and her brother Henry and her sister Iris and her husband Bill. And before long, she went out and found herself a job, waitressing at a Greek café in town, the Olympia on Frederick Street, just by the side of Boots the Chemist. It's a part of her life she often refers back to, a simple time living with her mother and her baby, doing a simple job where you could laugh and talk and flirt, and where there were no troublesome dreams for you to follow. 'I didn't like the grind, the one-night stands and hot, stuffy buses rattling over bad roads, so I retired. I was 17 and I went to work as a waitress. What else could a black girl do in those days, maybe become a prostitute?'[1]

At least, that's the way it looked in hindsight.* In fact, she never

* In this instance from 1970, when she seems to have gone through a brief flirtation with black consciousness (or at least plain speaking). In the same interview she describes *Hot From Harlem* as 'the old clichés about oversexed blacks doing it in the streets' and reveals that once you leave Cardiff 'the rest of Wales is a bastion of conservatism, and the back country people used to stare at me like I was a freak because they had never seen anyone black before.'

really let go of her dreams. *Hot From Harlem* had been at least a qualified success and, if the touring life was hard, then the shows themselves, with the gowns and the make-up and the cheering audiences and the men at the stage door, were some compensation, So when she came back to Cardiff, she still made the effort to keep her fledgling career going, even though she was heavily pregnant.

She found herself an agent, a woman called Betty Kellond with an office in Churchill Way, a stone's throw from the Olympia café. Betty Kellond was in her forties and, according to another client, the actor Victor Spinetti,* looked like Olive Oyl. She didn't have much luck finding work for her new client, as Shirley remembered a little while later: 'I thought with two successful shows behind me, getting another job would be easy. For almost six months I haunted my agent's office, always to get the same heart-breaking reply: "Nothing today I'm afraid dear. Keep in touch."'[2]

One day in town she ran into Wyn Calvin and wondered whether it was worth her while having another crack at the BBC. Calvin recalls: 'I saw her and said "Oh hello, darling, you got a week out?" She said "No, I've come out of that." Then I took a good look at her and I saw why she'd come out, I saw the shape of her.'

There was no way the BBC were going be interested in featuring a pregnant unmarried teenager, so Wyn wished her all the best and carried on his way, assuming that this was another fledgling show business career cut off before it really got going. A familiar enough story.

Shirley Bassey's first daughter, Sharon Eileen, was born on 9 October 1954. Shirley gave birth in a London maternity hospital in secret. Officially she'd gone to stay with her sister Ella in London

---

* His description, in his memoirs, of Kellond's attempt to seduce him is a fine slice of tragicomedy.

'for a holiday'. It was what girls did then; they went away. They had their babies and gave them up for adoption or passed them to their own mother who would declare her delight at having such an un-expected late child and the neighbours would nod and wink and gossip behind their hands but, officially at least, accept the fiction. 'The baby was a secret. Not many people knew about it because I can be very private, just as I can be very public. But I could look after myself. I'm a rat.'[3]

The place she chose to have her baby was called the Towers Maternity Annexe, in Bishop's Avenue, Hampstead. A grand house, it was the former home of Britain's biggest star of the pre-war years, Gracie Fields, another woman who'd made her way in show business from hard beginnings. When Gracie's marriage to comedian Archie Pitt broke up, she donated the marital home to be used as a hospital for unmarried mothers. Most of the girls who found their way to the Towers gave their babies up. But not Shirley.

After she had her baby she came back to Cardiff and she wait-ressed and she haunted Betty Kellond's office and then, so she says, she resigned herself to a life of ordinary pleasures and ordinary struggles.

1954 turned into 1955. Shirley turned eighteen, not quite such a landmark back then, when twenty-one was still voting age, but still. And then, in early February, a telegram arrived. It was sent at the behest of a man called Mike Sullivan, a London theatrical agent. Let him fill in the background from his memoir of his time with Shirley:

> One morning towards the end of January, I took a call from John Marriner, controller of the Little Theatre in Jersey, in the Channel Islands. John asked if I could book him a small ballet company and

I suggested the Ben Johnson Dancers, a skilful all-Negro group. He agreed and asked me to book them for him.

When I was going to see the group rehearse it occurred to me that, as he was going to do a complete show in Jersey, Ben would need an act to keep the show together in front of the stage curtain while he changed the sets. A singer might be the answer, I told Ben. Did he know anybody?

'How about Shirley Bassey?' chipped in one of his girls while Johnson was thinking of names.

'Who's Shirley Bassey?' I said. You can ask a simple question like that without knowing what you are getting into. After all, somebody must have said one day, 'I wonder how you split an atom?'

Shirley Bassey, I learned, had been a singer in two shows in which the Johnson dancers had toured.

'Any good?' I asked.

'Not bad,' said one of the dancers, 'but I'm not sure if she's still in the business.'

Ben Johnson said the girl lived in Cardiff and offered to get in touch with her. In the event of her wanting to audition, he gave me her address: Splott! So this is what our glittering business has come to, I thought, and went for a drink.[4]

Ben Johnson sent the telegram. Shirley, however, with her baby and her steady job, was not immediately taken with the idea.

I had been working as a waitress for about a month when I got a telegram from Ben Johnson, who had been choreographer for the *Memories of Jolson* show. He wanted to know if I'd like to go to Jersey with a small ballet party.

The suggestion didn't thrill me. Working as a waitress was not my idea of heaven, but at least it meant a regular pay-packet. If I went off to Jersey there was no telling what would happen at the end of the fortnight. I would have wired back to Ben, turning down the offer, but Mother wouldn't let me.

'You take it,' she kept telling me. 'It gets you back on the stage, and you never know. Maybe some agent will be watching the show and like your singing . . . ' I sent Ben a telegram accepting and packed my bag for London.[5]

Back to Mike Sullivan:

The girl replied and I sent her the train fare. A few minutes before 6 p.m. on February 14 I climbed two flights of bare wooden stairs to Max Rivers' rehearsal rooms in Great Newport Street.

She was sitting on the dusty floor. Old crumpled jeans were rolled to her knees and a pale tan face with a short-cropped fuzz of black hair topped a dirty yellow sweater. Just looking at the girl made me half decide to send her away and find someone else. But everybody deserves a chance and I had paid her train fare from Wales to London.

'Well, I guess we had better hear this young lady sing.'[6]

Sullivan had booked a pianist called Stanley Myers* for the session. Shirley told him she'd like to sing 'Stormy Weather', by now pretty much her signature song. He asked her what key she wanted. Shirley didn't know, sang a couple of bars and Myers figured it out. Then she started singing full out and Sullivan was immediately captivated:

* Later a well known TV and film composer – he wrote incidental music for *Doctor Who*, the score to *Prick Up Your Ears* and, most famously, 'Cavatina', the theme to *The Deer Hunter*.

As she did it I shivered, an uncanny spine-tingling sensation. This had never happened to me before and I was hardened to singers and their auditions.

I told Ben the girl would be suitable and left him to fix the terms with her. Later Johnson, his wife, one of the dancers named Louise and the scruffy girl singer joined me for a drink. Shirley drank lemonade and I asked her if she had ever auditioned for a recording company.

'People have said they would fix it up, but they never did,' she replied. I told her that I expected to be going to Jersey during the summer season. 'We'll have a cup of tea and talk about it.' 'That will be nice.' She sounded as if she didn't believe a word of it.[7]

For her part, Shirley doesn't seem to have initially realised Sullivan's significance; as far as she was concerned she was working for Ben Johnson.

During a break in rehearsals I was sitting on the floor playing with the baby daughter of one of the girls in the show. I didn't look very elegant in an old sweater and a pair of drainpipe slacks.

When a tall, slender man walked in I didn't take much notice. One of the girls told me he was Mike Sullivan, who was booking the acts for the show. Ben Johnson introduced me and asked me to sing.

'Why not?' I said. I went over to the piano and did a couple of numbers. Mr Sullivan listened, thanked me politely and walked out. I didn't give the incident another thought.[8]

Shirley's thoughts, understandably, were rather more with the daughter she'd left for the first time, than with this latest promise of a big break in showbiz.

I wasn't sorry when I had to leave *Hot From Harlem* and I wasn't sorry when I went to work in the Greek restaurant, but I was very sorry when I had to leave little Sharon and go to London for that audition. She was only six months old. I hated leaving her. When I got to London I spent all my money on phone calls to my sister to see if the baby was all right.[9]

And so to Jersey, where she joined up once more with the Ben Johnson ensemble, four dancers and four musicians. They were all staying in a decent hotel in St Helier and Shirley shared a room with Louise Benjamin. Rehearsals for the show, which was now called *Caribbean Heatwave*, continued. Ben Johnson agreed to let Shirley have a dancing spot as well as singing a few songs. She would dance a duet with Ben himself to 'By the Light of the Silvery Moon', still clearly a favourite of hers despite Eddie Reindeer's lack of success with their demo.

The show opened on 28 February 1955 at the Little Theatre and seemed to go well enough. Louise Benjamin remembers it as a happy if rather cold time.

We lived in this nice hotel in Jersey, and after the show we would make sure we were fast out of the theatre. We'd make sure we got two Wagon Wheels and run back to the hotel. Then we'd get our cocoa or whatever, and get the two big armchairs by the fire, because it was winter so when the others came we were always there in the chairs with our Wagon Wheels – they had only just come out then! We would talk about what was going on with the show . . . who hated her on that particular day, whose back she'd put up!

The stage director, Peter Loftus, wrote to the *Daily Telegraph* with his memories of the show a decade or so later:

The stars were Ben Johnson and Pamela Winters with Shirley Bassey appearing, needless to say with great success, in two solo spots. I was stage director for this colourful all-Negro revue and I can well remember the hours Shirley Bassey used to spend listening to the records of Eartha Kitt on whom she modelled her act. She was a great admirer of Miss Kitt.[10]

This is interesting as Shirley has always tended to underplay the influence of Eartha Kitt on her, preferring to give credit to Judy Garland or even Josephine Baker. However the influence of Eartha Kitt is obvious and extends way beyond their superficial similarity of skin tone. No other popular singers of the time traded so heavily on a larger-than-life sexual persona as Kitt already did, and Shirley soon would. And it's telling that Shirley was listening to her now, just as she was making her first moves towards being a solo entertainer.

A few days into the run Michael Sullivan arrived: 'I caught a plane to Jersey and sat through the matinee performance listening to Shirley Bassey sing "Stormy Weather", "Ebb Tide", "Smile", and "The Sunny Side of the Street". She looked terrible in a pale-green calf-length dress she had bought for her sister's wedding and with no sense of make-up.'[11]

Again, that should have been that. A couple of weeks in Jersey and Shirley would have been back home to her baby and another job. But Michael Sullivan wasn't just another talent scout waiting to find a ready-made, fully fledged star; he was rather more ambitious than that. He was looking for someone with the raw material of stardom, someone he could mould and shape. He wanted to be a Svengali, wanted to have the satisfaction of not just finding a star, but creating one.

Sullivan himself had a suitably colourful past for a theatrical agent. One of the very few non-Jews in the business, he was the illegitimate son of a shipping executive, brought up by his aunt under the impression she was his mother. His first venture into show business was aged fifteen as a fairground barker at the Southend Kursaal, luring passers-by into a freak show, whose sole pitiful attraction was a very poorly faked 'five-legged sheep'. He started his own agency for variety artistes and by the time he met Shirley he had seventy-two acts on his books and was responsible for booking twenty-three variety theatres.

But he was a canny enough man to see that variety was on its last legs and finding bookings for jugglers and trapeze artists and ventriloquists was not going to keep him in the style to which he had become accustomed. And that was some style: in his early thirties at the time he met Shirley, he was a sharply dressed ladies' man and looked a little like Danny Kaye. He'd been married three times and counted Errol Flynn amongst his boon drinking buddies. A wolf in wolf's clothing, then.

So Mike Sullivan was not a man to be put off by details like the wrong outfit and bad make-up. 'None of this made any difference. It could all be changed. What mattered was that I still got that shiver when she sang. All of the Svengali that lives in every real agent was getting to work within me. I would mould her, teach her stagecraft, lighting, build her into a star.'[12]

To his credit, Sullivan saw Shirley's racial mix as an asset rather than a problem:

'Because she was coloured it would be easy to persuade people to think of her, properly presented, like Lena Horne or Eartha Kitt.'[13]

That's to say that, in practice, Shirley's skin colour would make it easier for the British public to treat her as a 'proper' – read 'American'

– artiste and not another feeble home-grown imitation.

Sullivan decided to get some of his local show business associates over to the Little Theatre to see if they agreed with his hunch. So a man called Sydney James, a booker from Guernsey, came to watch Shirley in action.

The audience applauded loudly, but Sydney was unimpressed. 'I think you're out of your mind, Sullivan,' he said. 'Sydney, you are so wrong. Look at the audience. This kid's got them eating out of her hand. Wait till I dress her up, teach her to move, get her made-up properly, get her some special numbers. Use your imagination.'[14]

But Sydney James evidently hadn't eked out a living in the variety game by using his imagination.

'My knowledge and experience are what I use,' he said. 'She sings out of tune and you can forget the audience. Audiences are like sheep. One claps, they all follow. You have to get her past the bookers before the public will see her and no booker is going to go for her.'[15]

All of which has the authentic tang of hard-won knowledge, but Sullivan was not to be dissuaded. That evening he came over to the hotel lounge with Sydney to meet Shirley. Ben, Pam and Louise were there too. Sullivan had had his eye on Louise for a while: 'Physically I had been attracted to Louise from the time I first saw her in that rehearsal room and if she had been able to sing – just a little – I would never have asked Ben to send that telegram to Cardiff.'[16]

This came as something of a shock to Louise years later: 'I would have been absolutely terrified if I'd known. I thought he was sleazy.

I was very, very green. If he'd ever made an overture to me I would have had a fit. He was not a bad looking man, but he was too London for me, very flash . . . gave me the creeps.'

Shirley, however, was made of sterner stuff. She let Sullivan take her off to another part of the lounge and ask her about her life. With characteristic reluctance, she gave him the basic details, culminating in her experiences of singing in the revues.

'I wasn't sure I liked it,' she said. 'I enjoyed the singing, but not the travelling, nor living in digs. And I didn't get on too well with some of the people in the show.'

Sullivan took all this on, then asked how she would feel about going out on the variety circuit as a solo act.

'On my own. Oh, I don't think I would like that.'

'Well, not exactly on your own. You would have a pianist and I would be with you. You see,' I said, 'I believe that if you will work with me I can make you into a star.'

Her response was to break into soft, silent tears. She had been told things like this before and nothing had happened. She was eighteen and disillusioned.[17]

At least, that's the way he tells it in his autobiography. What he leaves out is the more likely reason for her tears. Shirley also told Sullivan that she had a baby girl back home in Cardiff, and he had told her that there was no way Sharon could be part of Shirley's new life. If she wanted to be a star then Sharon would have to be adopted, and her existence denied. As stark a choice as you could wish for.

Let Michael Sullivan describe what happened next.

I got up and held my hand out to her. 'It's time you were in bed,' I said. 'I'm going back to London tomorrow. Come to see me as soon as this job is over and we'll see what we can work out.'

She nodded and smiled through the tears.

Moments like that I cannot resist. I kept hold of her hand and led her upstairs to bed with me.

That was the first and only time I made love to Shirley Bassey. Had I done it more often everything might have been different . . . But that night showed me a side to her that was surprising.

That doubting insecure girl from Tiger Bay was a tigress in her own right. My back was so badly mauled and scratched by her that the following day I telephoned my office and my wife saying that I had to stay on in the Channel Islands. Then I went to Guernsey for five days to let the scars heal.[18]

'Moments like this I cannot resist.' Shirley Bassey was scarcely the first or the last young woman with show-business aspirations to be seduced by Mike Sullivan. As Louise Benjamin indicates, he was that kind of man, you could see it a mile off. Clearly he was taking advantage of a very young woman in a vulnerable situation. But it would be too simple to paint Sullivan as nothing but a predator and Shirley as nothing but a victim. At eighteen she knew men pretty well, certainly well enough to see a man like Sullivan for what he was. So it may be that Sullivan's telling of the story makes his seduction of Shirley sound more exploitative than it actually was. After all, this is how Louise Benjamin remembers what happened:

Shirley had a little fling with him. I actually remember when it happened. We were in Jersey. I must have been a little bit dopey because I couldn't believe it. She came back and told me and she was full of it: 'You'll never guess what happened!' And I was 'God!' And then she told me he said he would spend a hundred pounds on frocks for her. A hundred pounds in gowns, in lovely dresses!

Next day, with Sullivan gone to Guernsey and thence to London, Shirley had her decision to make. Did she take up the charming Mr Sullivan's offer or not? She asked Louise for advice.

She told me that Mike Sullivan had said she'd have to have the baby adopted . 'If we're going to make a star of you we can't have that.' She said to me, 'Oh, I don't know what to do,' but, well, I knew nothing of babies, and I certainly didn't want to have one, and I was very dismissive of the whole thing. I look back now and think what a hard decision that must have been to make, but back then I just thought, 'Oh, if you have a chance of becoming a star . . .'

Mostly when people talk about turning points in a life it's just a conceit; lives generally turn slowly, but in the case of Shirley Bassey it's clear that this really was a pivotal moment. She absolutely had to choose which way her life would go. Up till then, reckons Louise – and this chimes with pretty much everyone else's memories of the young Shirley – she was really not so driven to succeed, didn't have that self-belief. It was Mike Sullivan in those few days in Jersey who made her believe in the possibilities. It was Shirley herself, though, who decided not just to give it a go, but to throw her whole self, her whole life into it. Louise Benjamin:

The thing is with Shirley she didn't have big dreams, not really. I don't ever remember her talking about how I'm going to be a big star in the future. She never realised how good she was until she met Mike Sullivan. It was only then that she actually thought, I have got something. She was never one to be star-struck. It was only after Mike Sullivan started to tell her. I mean, Ben used to tell her how good she was, but not as much as Mike. Mike Sullivan knew he had gold dust there.

TEN

Talk of the Town

Her new life started awkwardly. Having decided to forgo the simple life of motherhood and waitressing and chase the dream instead, Shirley called Mr Sullivan: Mickey, her Svengali seducer. He didn't reply. Seemed like an old, old story: 'I called not once but half a dozen times. And every time his secretary told me, "Mr Sullivan is not in the office." Bitterly disappointed, I decided he was pulling my leg. I thought it was a pretty dirty trick to pull on an out-of-work singer.'[1]

At least, that's how Shirley told it a year later. Sullivan's own version cast this the opposite way round.

> After my return to London I waited for Ben Johnson's group to finish in Jersey, then every day when I walked into the office I asked my secretary: 'Did a coloured girl call today? Someone called Bassey?'
>
> She had not called and she did not call. After more than a week I started chasing her. Nobody knew where she was . . . most of the people I telephoned had never heard of her anyway . . .[2]

Who has it right? Most likely a bit of both. Shirley calls up, gets no answer, gives up rather than humiliate herself with repeat calls. Sullivan calls the number she gave him, her sister's or her friend's or her sister's friend's, gets no reply. Either way, it was an early indication this was never going to be a relationship in which both parties saw things the same way.

Finally, as Sullivan tells it, he called Ben Johnson at the rehearsal rooms and Ben arranged for Shirley to come round at 5 p.m. the following Saturday. Even then things failed to run smoothly. Sullivan came down with the flu and Shirley ended up coming to see him lying on his sickbed in the Mapleton Hotel on Coventry Street, just round the corner from the Soho rehearsal rooms. Sullivan's wife and business partner, Juhni, was there too. Juhni was old-showbiz through and through, the niece of one of the Crazy Gang, no less. She was to be charged with giving Shirley a makeover.

Shirley arrived wearing a transparent raincoat over a salmon-pink dress and Juhni was not impressed. She was even less impressed when Sullivan proceeded to offer this gauche teenager a contract that gave her twenty pounds a week for the next year, payable whether she worked or not. Given that Sullivan was virtually bankrupt, this seemed a foolish and unnecessary risk. On the other hand, it was certainly enough to persuade Shirley to sign up. As Sullivan recalls: "'It's a gamble,' I said, 'and you can't lose.' 'Oh, all right then,' Shirley said. I blew my nose and a star was born.'[3]

After the business came the pep talk. One that Shirley took to heart:

'I believe you have the making of a great star,' he told me. 'You could be another Lena Horne. But you've got a lot to learn, and you need a deal of experience. Put yourself in my hands and I'll get you to the top of the tree. But remember, it won't be easy. You'll have to work harder than you've ever worked in your life before, and you'll have to obey me implicitly. Now, is it a deal?'

My heart was beating like a hammer. I could only stare at him, unable to believe he was really serious. Me – a star? It didn't seem possible. But just for the chance I'd work till I dropped.[4]

Sullivan told Shirley to come back in a few days to collect her contract. She left and Juhni had a word with Mickey: "'I just hope you know what you're doing,' she said. "She's not bad looking but she's no raving beauty. She'll need a lot of working on to give her presence."'[5]

Sullivan went off to discuss his new discovery with another couple of old showbiz hands, both of whom he knew had already worked with Shirley: Joe Collins and Sydney Burns.

Collins was dismissive. In his autobiography he may claim to have spotted Shirley's talent right away, but back then he was less than enthusiastic, still annoyed that she had quit *Hot From Harlem*. 'She walked out of the show before the end,' was all he had to say about his former soubrette. Sydney Burns was more forthcoming, but little more encouraging: 'She is still a beginner. A baby. She sang out of tune and she shouted more than she sang. She's not much.'[6]

Stubborn as ever, Sullivan still wouldn't be swayed. He gave Shirley the contract he could scarcely afford to pay and she took it back to Cardiff where her mother gave it her blessing (as she had to, Shirley still being only eighteen, and twenty-one being the legal age of maturity at that time). When Shirley came back to London with the signed contract, Sullivan went into full Professor Higgins mode:

Late at night we would sit in my office in Shaftesbury Avenue discussing the timing and phrasing of songs. I made her speak the words until she was able to break up a lyric and make every syllable count.

Shirley and a pianist called Bob Wardlaw worked together for four hours a day until she developed a style of her own.[7]

Juhni meanwhile went to work on the visuals. Shirley's repertoire was heavy on the torch songs, sophisticated rather than teenage fare, so her look had to match. Together the Sullivans devised an appropriate stage outfit: 'Black velvet with elbow-length gloves and a false hairpiece to give her height.' Juhni's mother then did the actual dressmaking. The result was not exactly the way Shirley saw herself and she initially tried to object before being reminded of her promise to absorb and obey her master's diktats. As Sullivan summed up the situation: 'She hated the dress and swore she would never wear it. She did.'

Next came lessons in stage deportment, especially the tricky business of exiting the stage while looking in control. Also the crucial matter of making contact with the audience.

'After the first sixteen bars of a song their attention wanders,' I said. 'Until then they are busy taking you in. That's when you have to get them and hold them. Take them one side at a time and let your eyes go from the front to the middle to the back. You don't have to move much and when you get a high note throw your head back and give it to the people upstairs. That way you get all of them and keep them.'[8]

The impact this kind of old-school showbiz know-how had on the young Shirley is obvious, and it would serve her over all the years to come.

After a month or so of this intensive – and expensive – preparation, the hard work broken up for Shirley only by regular afternoon visits to the cinema (she was a very keen cinemagoer, with a particular predilection for science fiction), Sullivan decided his protégée was ready for a road test. His major gig at the time was booking actors into the Hippodrome circuit – not the top-of-the-range Moss Empires, but not the shabbiest either. Well, mostly not the shabbiest. The particular variety bill Sullivan decided to launch Shirley out on was at the Hippodrome, Keighley – not exactly the jewel in the Hippodrome crown.

The Yorkshire variety theatres were a particularly hard training ground. Harry Secombe's improbably excellent novel, *Twice Brightly*, gives a wonderful flavour of their down-at-heel magic. And Secombe's fictional account matches almost precisely with that of Don Auty, who stage-managed a show in Keighley just a few weeks before Shirley arrived there.

We opened at the Hippodrome, Keighley, which is now a car park. The show was called *Don't Be Shy, Girls* . . . Keighley was one of the first theatres to dispense with a pit orchestra and we were accompanied by a Hammond organ, piano and drums that sounded a bit thin. We had no scenery; I had to borrow what I could from the theatre which did not have much in the way of stock drapes and scenery, so the show looked to say the least a bit scrappy . . .

The show was headed by an Irish comic who . . . was very funny but had such a broad Irish accent that he could only be fully understood at the Met in Edgware Road, London, and the Pavilion Theatre in Liverpool where there were large Irish audiences . . . We also had a miniature circus and one of the girls in the troupe used to do a trapeze act. I used to help her tie off the trapeze apparatus in the grid and pray that the knots that we had tied would hold for the week. A few months later, when with another show, she fell from the trapeze at the Theatre Royal St Helens and was killed.

We also had two ladies who, although a little long in the tooth, did a dance act in tights and a conjuring act. During their dance routines they produced bunches of flowers from nowhere whilst they tapped away to the band playing 'Happy Feet'. They also made up the numbers of the chorus because we had only four other girl dancers, one of whom was aged around forty. She also acted as wardrobe mistress. We had our own musical director who played the piano in the pit at Keighley and conducted the resident bands at the other dates. He was a mean little man and he lived with one of the dancers. His wife and two sons did not know this and we all put on acts of great subterfuge when they visited the show. He was the only member of the company that I never got on with. A juvenile lead and feed was also in the cast, his hair slightly greying around the temples![9]

So, given that the Hippodrome Keighley's other claim to fame was that Peter Sellers caught pneumonia in its dressing rooms as a child, this was going to be a definite test of character.

Sullivan put his protégée on the bill in the second-to-top slot, closing the first half of the show. She was understandably nervous but Bob Wardlaw came with her to accompany her on the piano, and so did Mike Sullivan, for the first night at least. There was a Monday morning band call, then two afternoon dress rehearsals. By the end of all that Shirley was utterly petrified.

As well she might have been. Monday night audiences on the variety circuit were notorious: precious few paying punters would show up for anything but the biggest attractions, so the crowd, such as it was, would be largely made up of people who'd been given complimentary tickets. These were mostly pensioners, plus a sprinkling of fearsome theatrical landladies. Michael Sullivan takes up the story:

By the time it came for Shirley to go on stage and close the first half of the show she was near to panic. At the back of the stage I stood with her, rubbing her numb, cold hands, trying to stop her shivering. 'Don't worry. Just go out and sing. It doesn't matter if you make mistakes. Just try to do everything we have worked at all these weeks,' I said.

As the pit orchestra played 'I Can't Give You Anything but Love' I gently pushed her forward and then ran through the door from the stage area into the auditorium. She had already finished her first song when I got round there and the applause sounded good. After her second song it was much louder. It was the old people I watched. They were applauding as keenly as anybody else in that theatre. For me that was all the confirmation I needed of my faith in Shirley Bassey. These are the very last people her act is aimed at and yet she has got them, I thought. The girl really has something.[10]

His faith was further vindicated at the end of the week when the manager, the traditional 'taciturn Yorkshireman', vouchsafed that 'I've heard better, you know, but I must say she goes over bloody well.'

After that minor triumph Sullivan decided to take Shirley off the road for a couple of weeks to fine-tune the act, then sent her off on an eleven-week tour of provincial theatres, from Guernsey to Glasgow via Birmingham and Workington. Things mostly went well: Northampton was a blip, and so too was Guernsey, where Sydney James seemed only to have booked Shirley in order to complain about her some more. He called Sullivan after the first night to say he was thinking of pulling her off the bill, and then cut her slot from twenty minutes to eight. However, the real testing ground of the tour was meeting the most feared audience on the circuit at the Glasgow Empire. The memory was still vivid in Shirley's mind fifty years later: 'It was like a bear pit. I stood in the wings and heard them boo the acrobats when they all but lost their balance, and boo the comedians when their jokes weren't funny enough. When I walked on, they began hooting and hollering and telling me to get my clothes off.'[11]

Rather than do the obvious trouper's thing and simply launch into her first song, trying to ignore the crowd, Shirley instinctively behaved like the star she was hoping to become. She stood there in silence and simply waited, and after a little while the crowd hushed, staring at the teenager shaking in front of them. 'At first I just stared at the audience. Then I spoke into the microphone. "Now, look here," I said, "I've come here tonight to entertain you lot and, if you don't want to listen, then I'll go home. But you could at least give me a chance."'[12]

And so they did and once again, just like the Keighley pensioners, they went for it. A standing ovation at the end of 'Stormy Weather'. It's a show Shirley comes back to again and again in interviews. And that's because it was an absolutely key moment in her career. After this standing ovation all the others would be easier. Whether she was singing in front of London high society at the Astor Club, European jet-setters in Monte Carlo, or the Queen herself at the Royal Variety Performance, the Glasgow Empire became her benchmark. No other audience would ever be so intimidating. From this moment on she knew that she had what it takes.

And then the tour was over. A year later Shirley was smart enough to call it 'the most worthwhile schooling I ever had'. She had done her bit. The next move was up to Mike Sullivan.

Sullivan had a problem to solve. He had an act, he was sure of that now, but how was he going to make her a star? He knew as well as anyone that the variety circuit was in terminal decline.

Theatres were closing down or going over to all-nude shows with monotonous regularity (the Hippodrome Keighley, for instance, would be closed for good within the year).

On the other hand the record industry was starting to take off in Britain. The *New Musical Express* had started publishing a singles chart the year before and there was a new breed of singing star emerging in Britain, whose fame was not based on slogging their way round the variety circuit honing their act and eventually making it to the top, but on a handful of 78s and some nice publicity snaps, all aimed at the new teenage audience.

Sullivan considered this route, but he figured that Shirley was essentially a live phenomenon, that an audience needed to see her to appreciate her. The question then was where should she perform? If variety tours were not the answer, what was? 'Piece by piece I put my mental jigsaw together: A coloured girl, sexy looking, singing sophisticated moody songs. Like Lena Horne, like Eartha Kitt, like Josephine Baker. In the bottom of my glass I saw images of them performing. Around them were audiences sitting at tables. I had found the answer. Cabaret.'[13]

It made sense. If Shirley on stage was powerful enough to win over audiences of Yorkshire pensioners in cold and dank theatres, how much more powerful would she be at close quarters in a smoky nightclub? The next question was, which club to go for?

The London nightclub scene of the time divided into actual cabaret clubs where the entertainment was the thing, like the Astor or Al Burnett's Stork Club, and hostess clubs like Murray's and Churchill's, where the floor show was secondary to the serious business of pretty girls separating out-of-town businessmen from their money in exchange for endless 'champagne' cocktails. Sullivan fixed on the Astor in Berkeley Square, run by a classic cigar-chomping entrepreneur in the shape of Bertie Green. The Astor was old established, upmarket and known for the quality of its house band: George Shearing had been the resident pianist a while before.

Booking the unknown Shirley into such a prestigious joint was no formality. Sullivan finessed the deal by persuading a fellow agent, Sonny Zahl, of Shirley's talents and then getting him to recommend her to Bertie Green. The plan worked. Green agreed to pay Shirley the handsome sum of £65 a week for a two-week engagement. Now it was up to Sullivan to prove that he did indeed have a British Eartha Kitt on his books.

Sullivan schemed some more and realised that the one thing his protégée lacked was any of her own exclusive material. If she confined herself to songs like 'Stormy Weather', which was known as a Lena Horne vehicle, she was bound to be seen as derivative at best. He decided to get a pro songwriter to compose something tailor-made for Shirley to sing.

To that end he headed up to London's Tin Pan Alley, Denmark Street, to meet his friend Benny Lee, a singer and comedian, at Lee's regular lunch spot, the Universal Chinese. Lee mentioned that another regular at the Universal was a songwriter called Ross Parker. Sullivan jumped on the name. He remembered Parker's two big wartime hits, 'We'll Meet Again' and 'There'll Always Be an England', both performed by Vera Lynn. He presumably didn't dwell on the fact that they were both written the best part of two decades before and that since then Parker's success rate had been pretty minimal: his last hit of any kind was a couple of years in the past, a co-write on an Alma Cogan song.

Sullivan badgered Lee for an introduction. Lee demurred. Sullivan persuaded him to come and see Shirley sing on a variety bill in Chatham, fill-in work before the Astor. Lee came down and was impressed enough to recommend Parker take a look. He was also impressed and agreed to a meeting with Sullivan. At the meeting Parker, with considerable élan, set about negotiating his terms:

> 'Yes,' said Ross, 'I'm prepared to write a couple of songs for the girl, but I suppose you know how much I get?'
> 'I've no idea. You'll have to tell me. I've never bought a song.'[14]

Parker replied, 'I usually get in the region of two hundred guineas.' As this would be four thousand pounds or so in current terms, Sullivan was a little alarmed. But never one to back down, he simply persuaded Parker that he'd pay on the instalment plan. Parker must have thought it was Christmas.

Parker proceeded to play Sullivan a selection of songs he'd already written. Sullivan liked them well enough, but couldn't see any of them working for Shirley, as he later recalled:

> Politely I explained this and he said, 'What the hell do you want?'
> 'I want some bite in the lines, something saucy. I want her to sell sex.'
> We talked around this and talked of the people we wanted to interest, the international nightclub set . . . the people who burn the candle at both ends. At last we had the idea and Ross said 'I'll go away and work on it.'[15]

The song he came up with suggests that Parker saw the whole gig as a joke, a ridiculous song for a ridiculous fee. From the man responsible for the pieties of 'There'll Always Be an England' came an extraordinary piece of work called 'Burn My Candle (At Both Ends)'. It's a song that bears the same relation to the sophisticated American cabaret material of an Eartha Kitt as the British pulp novels of the time did to the American crime novels they tried to imitate: that's to say it's tacky, gaudy, obviously fake, and features some surprisingly explicit sex. Sullivan, of course, loved it from the start.

He renewed his charm offensive on Ross Parker. Would Parker consider playing piano for Shirley on her final warm-up week in the none-more-glamorous surroundings of the Tivoli, Hull? Well, yes, for just twenty-five pounds a week Parker agreed to it. Presumably he'd heard Shirley sing his song and render its cartoon sexiness into something real. The two of them went to Hull and, after a few days, a thoroughly enthused Parker gave Mike Sullivan a ring to say that he was enjoying himself so much he'd play for Shirley at the Astor as well.

And so the duo returned to London. Mike Sullivan put Shirley up at Olivelli's,* a theatrical restaurant and hotel just off Tottenham Court Road, and she embarked on her two-week stint at the Astor. Showtime was at one in the morning, which suited Shirley fine. The former factory girl had grown fond of sleeping late and left strict instructions that she should never be woken before noon.

The Astor was another triumph. The hard weeks on the variety circuit had toughened Shirley up, and the cabaret rooms held no terrors for her. 'Burn My Candle' was developing into a show-stopper, its uptempo raunch contrasting perfectly with all the torch balladry that surrounded it.

Both on stage and off, Shirley was showing the first signs of turning into a star. On stage that was all to the good. Off stage, however, her new-found success seemed to be going to her head.

---

* A place with a fine history: everyone from Duke Ellington to Groucho Marx and Tex Ritter had stayed there before Shirley, while the downstairs restaurant was the first place in Britain to serve pizza. Remarkably enough it's still in business, though in considerably reduced circumstances.

Towards the end of her variety theatre tour she'd already had her first bust-up with Sullivan. She had stopped sending him his share of her earnings. When she returned to London he called her into the office to ask for his money. 'This is my money,' she told him. 'I pay you.'

Sullivan read her the riot act and threatened to cancel their arrangement if she really thought she was the boss and he was the employee. Shirley responded by breaking out the tears. Sullivan made her sweat till the next day when she apologised profusely and explained that she'd kept the money back because she'd had to pay off her former agent, Betty Kellond. Sullivan OK'd that but realised that Shirley was not going to be the most pliant of protégées.

Ten days into the run at the Astor, on 25 August, Ross Parker called Sullivan up with a piece of news. Jack Hylton was going to be coming to the club that night. This was exciting: Jack Hylton was one of the major players in the showbiz industry of the time. A hugely popular pre-war bandleader, he was now the most successful impresario in Britain. He'd discovered talents as diverse as Audrey Hepburn and Arthur Askey. He promoted major American musicals and British variety shows. He was responsible for booking the Royal Command Performances. In this year of 1955 his productions included a Royal Command Performance, five shows running in London, and a Royal Variety Performance in Blackpool (featuring amongst others Alma Cogan, Morecambe and Wise, and George Formby). If there was one man in Britain who could make an unknown into a star, it was Jack Hylton.*

---

* As long as the would-be star had some ability, that is. Hylton made a considerable fool of himself later in the 1950s when, blinded by infatuation, he decided to make a pneumatic Italian called Rosalina Neri into a star and gave her her own TV show which all too clearly revealed her lack of any discernible talent.

Sullivan assumed Parker must have been responsible for this coup, as the songwriter had done a lot of work for Hylton over the years. In fact it was pure happenstance. Hylton was taking a new discovery, a French actor/comedian called Robert Dhery, out on the town, and Dhery fancied the Astor Club. And so Hylton and Dhery arrived and, just around midnight, Ross Parker introduced Mike Sullivan to them. They talked about the variety business for a while and then Shirley came on stage and Hylton stopped talking and started paying attention. When she'd finished, having brought the house down one more time, he turned to Sullivan and said, 'She's very good, you know. Do you think she could open at the Adelphi tomorrow night?'

Sullivan looked bewildered and Hylton elaborated: 'I'll tell you. This girl I've got, Pavlou, she's been taken off with peritonitis and I've got to find somebody to fill a small spot. You know lad, it's only a little time, not important to the show, but we need some girl and this one's not bad.'[16]

The show in question was a Jack Hylton revue called *The Talk of the Town*, a vehicle for two popular new comedians, Tony Hancock and Jimmy Edwards, with comedy sequences from the new writing team of Frank Muir and Denis Norden. It had been a big hit, but not without its problems. Tony Hancock had become increasingly erratic and was absent from the show at the time due to 'nervous strain'. Add in Maria Pavlou's illness and Hylton definitely needed a new added attraction.

Sullivan jumped at the offer, and assured Hylton that Shirley would be more than happy to appear the following night. She would still be able to make it over to the Astor after the Adelphi show finished. They sorted out the details the next morning at Hylton's office. Shirley would sing four numbers, including 'Burn My Candle'. Did Sullivan have an arrangement for the song? No, he didn't, she'd always sung it to Ross Parker's piano alone. A series of emergency phone calls and Sullivan tracked Parker down, and Parker in turn called Billy Ternant, Hylton's veteran Geordie musical director. Parker sang the melody line down the phone and Ternant promptly arranged it for the full band.

Then Hylton sprang another surprise. He told Sullivan that he had just signed a deal to become Advisor of Light Entertainment for Associated-Rediffusion, one of the companies providing programmes for the new commercial television channel, ITV. Would Sullivan like a job, running his new television department? Sullivan thought about it and agreed in principle, while insisting that his contract with Hylton should not interfere with his management of Shirley Bassey.

That settled, Sullivan called up his fledgling star to tell her the good news. Six months later she recalled what happened in breathless showbiz prose:

> I was woken by the shrilling of my bedside telephone. It was my manager, hoarse with excitement. 'Get dressed and come round here,' he said. 'You've got to take over the lead in *Talk of the Town* at the Adelphi tonight.'
>
> I like a joke – but not at that time of the morning. 'Quit your kidding,' I snapped. 'I've got to get my beauty sleep.'
>
> 'I'm not kidding,' he said. 'Jack Hylton was in the club last night and he heard you sing. Maria Pavlou has gone sick and Mr Hylton wants you to fill in for her. Snap out of it Shirley, this is your big break.'
>
> When that evening I stepped into the Adelphi's 'star' dressing room I still couldn't believe it. I kept pinching myself hard to make sure I wasn't dreaming. Me, Shirley Bassey – the kid from Tiger Bay – the star in a West End show![17]

Another challenge, another triumph. It was a close-run thing getting Shirley on stage in *The Talk of the Town*. The band were still
practising her songs when the doors were meant to open. The dress
Hylton provided for her, a gold sheath, didn't fit and had to be held
together by safety pins at the back. It would look all right from the
front but she had to make sure not to turn round. Shirley was terribly nervous and then, to make things worse just as she was about
to make her entrance, the MC, the comedian Dave King, forgot
her name. No matter: once she started singing the nerves vanished
and she was in her element. The hard work of the preceding summer
was paying off and she had the crowd transfixed.

The next morning she had her first notices in the press, all playing
up the dream-come-true angle – typical was the *Evening News* which
devoted half a front-page column to a story headlined 'Shirley –
star who arrived in a rush' and beginning, 'Two years ago 19-year-
old Shirley Bassey was a £3-a-week factory hand in Cardiff. Last
night she was a West End revue star . . . '

By the end of her run at the Adelphi it was obvious to everyone
around her that Shirley was a potential star. And if she had what
it took, it was up to those around her, Sullivan and Hylton in particular, to harness and exploit her.

*   *   *

That wasn't Mike Sullivan's only problem. He also had to make sure
he kept control of his protégée when all the signs were that Jack
Hylton was looking to take her over. To make matters worse, all
the press that followed her appearance in *The Talk Of The Town*
credited Hylton with discovering her in a West End nightclub, with
no mention of Sullivan.

The obvious next step was to put Shirley on the television, in one of Hylton's variety shows. With both Hylton and Sullivan involved in booking the ITV shows, getting her a slot was a done deal. But it would inevitably associate her name even more closely with Hylton's. Hylton himself started to court Shirley in person. The songwriter David Lee remembers meeting her at Hylton's place around that time: 'He wanted me to write a musical show which unfortunately did not get off the ground. We were in his Mayfair apartment when this sweet, demure young thing brought us in our coffees. He told me then that she had a bright future.'

Sullivan decided to move quickly and offer Shirley a new contract. He invited Eliza Jane and Shirley's sisters up to London for the last night at the Adelphi. And after the show he invited photographers along to the dressing room to take pictures of Shirley signing a new contract, witnessed by her mother. The contract was for five years. The presence of family and photographers made it hard for Shirley to do anything other than sign a contract that gave Sullivan a very sizeable chunk of her earnings, as he recalls: '(The contract) guaranteed her twenty-five pounds a week for the first year and sixty pounds a week for the second. From then on we had a partnership. I got forty-five per cent of all income and paid for gowns, publicity, music, pianists and travel. She got the rest.'[18]

Happy that he now had his discovery firmly under his control, Sullivan went ahead and arranged her first TV spot, on a show called *Jack Hylton Presents*. This was good news inasmuch as this new ITV channel was attracting huge audiences looking for something a little less worthy than the BBC's output. On the other hand, *Jack Hylton Presents* was a rough-and-ready affair which didn't always present its stars in the best light. TV in the 1950s wasn't exactly renowned for high production values, but even so, these early Jack Hylton shows had a deserved reputation for particularly amateurish shoddiness. As his biographer explains:

Hylton's contract initially required 1½ hours of broadcast time per week and this seemed to be the perfect opportunity for him to promote his shows and his artists. He thought it would build new stars for the stage whilst exploiting established stars on his roster. Unfortunately, his simplistic approach of pointing a camera at a stage show and hoping it would work as television fell far short of the expectations of the viewing public . . . Many celebrities (Elsie and Doris Waters, Eric Barker, Cyril Fletcher, Alfred Marks) had jeopardised their careers, appearing in shows which were poorly scripted and cheaply produced. These shows were not only received very badly by both the critics and the management of A-R, but also by the artists appearing in them, some of whom apologised on air for the quality of programming.[19]

However, the risks were less severe for singers than for comedians, who were dependent on script and set-up, and anyway the shows were very popular. So really there was little for Shirley to lose. She sang 'Burn My Candle' and, unlike so much TV of the time, a copy of it still survives in the National Film and Television Archive.

It's the first and best recording of the young Shirley. As soon as you see it, it's blindingly obvious why everyone around her talked of her star quality. Backed by a middle-of-the-road orchestra, dressed in a simple black gown with her natural hair cut short and in no particular style, and shot in Hylton's signature fashion – one camera, medium close-up – she is nevertheless mesmerising.

The song, taken in isolation, is blatantly sexual but hardly convincing, as the double entendres of the title give way to single entendres in the bridge – *'There's "S" for Scotch, that's so direct / And for straight and simple sex / "I" for invitation to / A close relationship with you / "N" for nothing bad nor less / "S-I-N", that's sin, I guess.'* But no matter, Shirley turns this base metal into gold. She is flagrantly sexy but in such an exuberant kind of way that it would have taken a very committed prude to object.*

And that, right there, is the key to Shirley Bassey's early success: she was blatantly sexy and yet somehow, if not innocent, at least not too knowing. And how does she manage that? It's her lack of self-consciousness. So much of what passes for sexy is excruciatingly self-conscious – pretty girls offering a presentation of 'sexy' that has one eye firmly on the money. Where most sex sirens, then and now, tend to look as if they see their sexuality as something to be exploited as ruthlessly as possible, Shirley looked as if she saw it as something simply to be enjoyed.

---

* It's instructive to compare and contrast Shirley's TV debut with that of another entertainer born on the same day two years and a continent apart: Elvis Presley. When Elvis appeared on the *Milton Berle Show* in the summer of 1956, the US press expressed near-unanimous horror. Where Shirley received raves, Elvis was all but run out of town. The New York *Journal-American* referred to 'primitive physical movement difficult to describe in terms suitable to a family newspaper'. And the New York *Daily News* suggested that the Tupelo Flash was guilty of giving 'an exhibition that was suggestive and vulgar, tinged with the kind of animalism that should be confined to dives and bordellos'.

ELEVEN

Burn My Candle

Autumn turned to winter 1955 and things were moving fast. Mickey Sullivan's plans were working out as well as he could possibly have hoped. Less than six months after her Keighley debut, Shirley was taking a West End theatre by storm and appearing on the telly. Sullivan's job was no longer to beg favours for his unknown protégée, but to sift through the offers that were coming in, and strategise the way forward.

The most interesting of these offers was for Shirley to make a record. A man called Johnny Franz, from Philips Records, had seen Shirley's second TV appearance on *Jack Hylton Presents*, performing her favourite ballad, 'Stormy Weather'. He was so impressed that he immediately approached Sullivan and offered Shirley a recording contract, based simply on seeing her on TV.

Sullivan was only too happy to accept. Franz was one of the most successful men in the record business at the time, with a string of hits from one of the more unlikely stars of the 1950s, a Trinidadian honky-tonk pianist called Winifred Atwell. A year earlier Winnie had become the first black artiste to reach number one in the British pop charts. Like Sullivan and Jack Hylton, Johnny Franz was to be the latest in a line of older men to take a significant role in creating the Shirley Bassey phenomenon.

At that time Johnny Franz was in his mid thirties. He'd started out as a piano player in the clubs by night and a Denmark Street office boy by day. He'd been employed by the BBC for a while as an orchestrator. He'd worked with Vera Lynn, and played piano for the big 1940s star Anne Shelton. Then the newly formed Philips Records made him their head of A & R. Apart from Winifred Atwell, his roster of the time also included Shirley's compatriot Harry Secombe.

Franz wasn't just an A & R man. With his background as a pianist and arranger he was establishing himself as a record producer (or a 'recording manager', as they were known at the time). Philips had their own studio in Stanhope Place, near Marble Arch. This was Johnny Franz's fiefdom, a rival operation to EMI's Abbey Road studio a mile or two to the north.

In his biography of the Walker Brothers – later Franz protégés – Anthony Reynolds offers a vivid portrait of the man: 'He was addicted to (sugarless) cups of tea, dapper in a deep-grey fifties style pinstripe suit, dark brown hair slicked back, his groomed moustache pencil thin. He always seemed to have one hand in his pocket, while in the elegant piano-player fingers of the other, a cigarette perpetually burned, swathing him in smoke.'[1]

While the details of the record contract were being sorted out, Sullivan went back to planning Shirley's next live appearance. Again, the solution was obvious: ask Jack Hylton for a decent spot for Shirley in his next big London show. Hylton was amenable enough. He was about to launch a new West End production, featuring the radio comedian Al Read, and there was a second-on-the-bill spot going for a singer. Shirley was an obvious fit. And a relatively cheap one too: Hylton secured her services for sixty-five pounds a week, and everyone was happy enough with the deal.

Al Read was a very big name of the period, a Lancashire comic with a fine line in dry observational humour. His weekly radio show, with its deceptively well-crafted tales of dodgy builders and gossiping housewives, was listened to by anything up to half the British population. He also – and this sounds unlikely but is actually true – had a sideline in running a sausage-making business. Radio was Read's ideal medium, but his enormous popularity made him a big live draw as well.

The year before he'd had a big West End hit show called *You'll Be Lucky* under Hylton's aegis (and co-starring a singer/actress called Shani Wallis whose path would cross Shirley's again). He'd spent the summer of 1955 at the Opera House in Blackpool, with a new revue called *Such Is Life*, and it was this show that Hylton was planning on bringing to the Adelphi.

Al Read's autobiography offers this, not necessarily entirely reliable, account of his introduction to his new supporting attraction:

During the run-up to the show I was approached by an agent, Michael Sullivan. He told me he had a singer under contract, still very young . . . Jack Hylton had already been introduced to her at the Albany Club and wanted her in the show. Shirley oozed star quality but she was still very raw. In the middle of our first rehearsal the assistant stage manager Johnny Russell came up to Jack and myself looking as if he was about to press the panic button . . . 'She can't walk – she's got no idea of stagecraft.'

'OK then, we'll stop her from walking, won't we Al? Ask wardrobe to make up a gown so tight that it'll lace her knees together. And put a big flare on the bottom.'

'Well, that still leaves her hands,' said Russell. 'She's equally hopeless with them.'

'Easy,' said Jack, 'get her to stroke her tits and wave her arms about. That should just about do it.'

Thus, in a few minutes in the stalls of the Adelphi, the Shirley Bassey style – right down to the slinking walk and the outstretched hands – was dreamed up.[2]

Or at least, that's the way he tells it. It's an account that obviously ignores the hard work Mike Sullivan had put in with Shirley, but it does give an unvarnished glimpse of the sexism of the times.

Such Is Life opened at the New Theatre Oxford on 5 December. Al Read, of course, topped the bill. Shirley had second billing, and the extensive supporting cast included the comic Jack Tripp, a French acrobatic dance troupe, the American/Hungarian comedy dance team Bob and Marion Konyot, a French actress/singer called Odette Crystal, and the Tiller Girls.

Marion Konyot, like Shirley, was one of the new additions to the show that had run in Blackpool. A former child dance star and *Hellzapoppin'* veteran, she moved from the US to Britain in the 1930s, as the variety circuit fizzled out earlier on the far side of the Atlantic. She now lives in South London, where I interviewed her, and recalls the show well: 'Oh yes, it was basically a George Black show and they added us, a wonderful French adagio dance act, and Shirley, but all the scenes were the same as Blackpool. It was basically a variety show except we had a grand finale with all of us in it.'

The Shirley Bassey Marion Konyot encountered was a girl caught up in a whirlwind. Marion and her Hungarian husband Bob found her charming: 'I thought she was lovely: very vivacious and a good artist. We used to live in Brixton and she used to come up to the house and my mother-in-law used to cook goulash for her. And she was really quite down to earth.'

On 14 December *Such Is Life* opened at the Adelphi in London. And, household name though Al Read might have been, it was immediately clear to both audiences and critics who the real star of the show was. Elizabeth Frank in the *News Chronicle* may have confused Shirley's geographical origins but offered a pretty decent appraisal of her appeal:

> She is a willow-slender, coffee-coloured eighteen-year-old girl from Jamaica with a voice as powerful as Lena Horne's. Her face which, in smiling repose is that of cheerful urchin, can assume a kind of wild ecstasy and despair as she sings of sex and sin . . . her technique is already that of a seasoned artist and her natural assurance is tempered by something childish and strangely touching. Without hesitation I nominate Shirley Bassey as one of the big stars of the future.

However, the sheer impact the young Shirley had on the London audience was best summed up by Thomas Wiseman,* writing in the *Evening Standard*. 'She sang her songs in a way that amounted to vocal arson. She was all electric and uninsulated. She is an eighteen-year-old coloured girl from the docks in Cardiff who hit rain-soaked London like a freak heatwave.' Wiseman went on to put down the rest of the show by comparison: 'On the whole this is a revue for the charabanc trade. Except that Miss Bassey, as she is in the limousine class. But go and see her, even if your normal means of transport is by rickshaw, roller skates or drosky . . . '[3]

All electric and uninsulated. Uninsulated may not even be a word but it sums up the young Shirley perfectly. The rest of the press followed suit. Al Read was less than chuffed. The very polite Marion Konyot, who was fond of Read, simply says that 'I don't think they got on. He liked to be top dog.' One look at the photos of the two of them together, doing publicity for the show, confirms that all

* Later a successful novelist. While at *The Standard* he was responsible for naming a generation when he referred to 'That angry young man John Osborne'.

right. Read looks spectacularly unimpressed at being comprehensively outshone by the glamourpuss next to him.

Those early reviews in the papers confirmed what everyone around her had come to believe: Shirley was a star. All at once her status within the company changed, as Marion Konyot remembers:

> She did become temperamental. Once she had some row with the stage manager and she was refusing to go on stage – so he hit her! And she went on. In those days stage managers were the boss. And Mike Sullivan and Jack Hylton, they sort of kept a wall around her. They didn't mind her coming up to us though, as they figured we couldn't do much harm. The stage manager looked after her. But she managed to find some men anyway!

Oh yes, the men. One of the many remarkable things about Shirley Bassey, at least in these early years, is that she appealed almost equally, though in rather different ways, to men and women. The ballads, the dramas, the frocks, the glamour, all appealed to a female audience. But for the male audiences of the time, used to the decorous likes of Anne Shelton, the honest direct sexiness of Shirley Bassey was not something they were minded to resist.

A vivid account of how Shirley was, the week stardom came looking for her, is offered by the Irish journalist Paddy McGarvey, writing in the *Sunday Dispatch*, under the headline 'Coloured Girl is Sensation of the Week'. It's worth reproducing here in full (plus a few annotations), and not only to wonder at a time when journalists on the Sunday papers were allowed to write up their interviews in a mock-Kerouac stream of consciousness:

> The show sensation of the week was an 18-year-old coloured girl from a back street in Cardiff who stopped the new Al Read show

Such Is Life at the Adelphi Theatre, London. Her torch singing sent the critics back to their desks looking for superlatives to describe her. Her rendition of her hit song 'Burn My Candle' makes the other blues singers look green. I could not find the proper superlatives. So I just got down my jazz train of thought:

Walking along the Strand, London. Thinking. Wet night. Wonder if she's the red-hot momma type, Shirley Bassey. Adelphi Theatre. Al Read show. Excuse me. Where's the stage door? Maiden Lane. Ta. Miss Bassey. Yes sir. Why hello. It's her manager. How are you? Yes. Shirley's a big hit. Have noticed.

Dressing room. Camel-hair-coat-coloured girl curled up in chair. Miss Bassey. Mr McGarvey. How do you do? How do you do? Place full. Me Manager. Manager's wife (pretty). Theatre press officer. All talk talk. Shush Shirley is saying:

I was born in Cardiff, 132 Portmanmoor Road. My mum is English, my father is a West African seaman. No, we're not from the Tiger Bay district. Not that it matters. Tiger Bay is not as dirty as they say. Yes, I'm a blues singer.

It's a sign of a more innocent time that a starlet would happily give out her home address. Interesting too to see which stereotypes the young Shirley was prepared to sign up to. The Girl from Tiger Bay? Well, no, but . . . 'not that it matters'. And a blues singer? That's not a label she was happy to have stuck on her for long.

Feline look. Has African's gift of expressive eyes. Talks with hands. Not pretty. Lovely mouth. Pink lips. Skinny? Perhaps. See when she stands up. She doesn't stand up. No Welsh accent. She lost it. Where? Ha ha. All join in. Ha ha. She laughs. Nice. Nice talker. Poise and only eighteen. She's talking again.

Sullivan must have done a hell of a job with the elocution lessons, then. A Splott accent is not easily removed from the vocal chords.

> I started singing in school and working-men's clubs. Then I went into a touring show called *Memories of Jolson*, the one after that was *Hot From Harlem*. My mother takes a great interest in my career. My dad doesn't know a lot about it. He just knows I'm making a lot of money, that's all.

This was the first faint hint of the importance that Shirley's money would have to her family.

> Rum title 'Hot From Harlem'. Still, experience for her. Then Michael Sullivan, manager now, saw her. Then Jack Hylton. Adelphi lights success success. Celebrate. She ate two steaks. Money now. She wants to buy a Jaguar. Drive? No. Another Diana Dors case. Ha ha again. All join in. Ha ha.
>
> Shirley's on stage now, Sullivan says. Like to watch? OK. Long walk. Long corridors. Bar half way. Two scotch and ginger. Cheers. Shirley's a nice kid. Cheers. Up to the circle now. She's singing her hit 'Burn My Candle – at both ends'. Strewth. Girl's transformed.
>
> Like Eartha Kitt? No, more friendly. Lena Horne? No, warmer. She's herself. Velvet mouth. Wide open with yelling note. Melodious. Crikey. Could put an ashtray in it. Words a bit blue. 'Burn My Candle' again. Someone threw matches on stage. Ha ha. Everybody. Ha ha. It's a riot. They're stomping the floor.
>
> Dressing room again. Full again. Door opens. A woman with another woman. And another woman. And two kids. Her mother. Sisters, nieces. Mrs Bassey Mr McGarvey. How do you do? How do you do? Proud. Yes. Seven children. Shirley the baby.
>
> Out in the Strand again. Thinking. Still wet. Taxi. Some baby.[4]

One thing that comes out of this article is that Shirley was still closely involved with her family at this stage. How difficult it must have been for her to see her infant daughter Sharon being passed off as her sister's is hard to imagine. She managed it, though. Marion Konyot, who saw a lot of her, says she never talked about her family at all, never gave any inkling that she had a baby daughter. 'No, she never talked about her background at all; she was very close about that. And we didn't pry.'

It's hardly surprising, though, that Shirley didn't want to talk about her family, given what happened back in Splott, just a few days after her family had come up to London to see her at the Adelphi. Eliza Jane and Bobo Mendi had not been getting on well for some while. It may have been that Eliza Jane's daughter's success was breeding dissatisfaction with her own lot in life. But whatever the reason, the week before the Adelphi show matters had come to a head. She hadn't cooked Bobo his preferred rice and foo-foo for his tea, but gave him the meal she'd prepared for the rest of the family. To general amazement the normally quiet Bobo lost his temper and told her that, 'A fucking dog would not eat that. If I had a gun I would shoot your brains out and finish myself as well.'[5]

Things stopped short of outright violence that time, but the big blow-up came two weeks later, on 23 December. This time things ended up in court. Let the court reporter pick up the story:

On the day of the alleged offence Mendi had a dispute with Mrs Iris Denning, a married daughter. Mrs Bassey asked what was wrong and Mendi left the room saying, 'Wait a minute, I got something for you.' When he returned he was holding the gun, pointing it at Mrs Bassey and trying to cock it.

Mrs Denning, with great presence of mind, pushed him out into the passage. As she pushed him he stumbled and fired the gun . . . Mrs Bassey thought Mr Mendi intended to point the gun at her and shoot at her.

Mr Mendi left the house and when he returned in the afternoon told police officers that he had thrown the gun away.[6]

In fact, when the police came to arrest Bobo, he was sitting in the front room reading the paper, apparently unconcerned, certainly not acting as if he felt anything serious had occurred. Eliza Jane didn't see it like that, though. She had him arrested, charged with attempted murder, and taken to the police cells.

In his defence Bobo said he had only intended to frighten Iris and Eliza Jane: 'I bought the gun on my last voyage with three bullets,' he told the police. 'I bought it to protect myself in foreign countries.'

Eliza Jane was having none of that: 'He intended to shoot me. There is no doubt of that,' she told the court. 'Iris was holding the baby and she pushed him off with her shoulder and the gun went off.'[7]

In cross-examination, however, Eliza Jane did concede that Bobo's actions hadn't come out of the blue. And that prior to his fetching the gun she had repeatedly hit him over the head with her shoe. However, she said that this was in response to Bobo calling her names.

The court seemed minded to accept Eliza Jane's version of events and Joseph Mendi, 'a 64-year-old African', was committed for trial at the next Glamorgan Assizes. He died of cancer the following March, before the trial could take place.

It's clear that Portmanmoor Road was not exactly the oasis of domestic harmony that an up-and-coming starlet would want to boast about. The day after the shooting Shirley came down to Cardiff for Christmas. She must have been mightily relieved that the local press didn't make the connection between Shirley Bassey, the local girl who was making good up in London, and the misadventures of a Mrs Eliza Bassey of Splott.

Indeed a local journalist, Gareth Bowen, came to visit the rising star over the Christmas period, and the Bassey family, well versed in the keeping of secrets, gave no indication that anything untoward had been going on: 'I remember spending Christmas Day with Shirley,' he wrote in the local paper a few years later, 'at the humble terraced house in Portmanmoor Road where she grew up. She was starring in Al Read's show at the Adelphi Theatre, and the toast that day was in home-made rice wine.'[8]

Cardiffians often give Shirley Bassey a hard time over her lack of enthusiasm for her roots. But after this latest family scandal, it's hardly surprising that the young Shirley decided her past was something to be left behind as fast and as completely as possible. She came up with her own version of her family history, a heavily edited one in which all her siblings shared the same father, who then proceeded to vanish for no particular reason. Her oldest sisters, the Middlesbrough girls Doris and Florence, she never acknowledged at all. And gradually Bobo, too, would be airbrushed out of the picture. Her mother was a nice quiet Yorkshirewoman and Shirley was a citizen of the world, thank you very much. Remarkably enough, no journalist has ever bothered to check into her background, and so Shirley's version has persisted. Nice and simple, but only half true.

TWELVE

My Body's More Important
Than My Mind

Eliza Jane was not the only Bassey to have trouble with men. As Marion Konyot noted, despite the best efforts of Mike Sullivan and Jack Hylton, a constant stream of suitors found their way to Shirley's stage door – some after her body, some looking for a piece of her success, and some hoping for both. As Marion remembers:

> Oh yes, there were always people trying to take her over. Most of them were the men she was seeing. She was awfully bad at picking men, I'm afraid. That boy Pepe Davis was backstage all the time, he was . . . oh, not my type! The other guy was nice, the actor she was going round with, quite a well-known British actor.

Trying to disentangle the young Shirley's love life is tricky, but she seems to have had two major relationships during the year-long run of *Such Is Life*, which was now booked into the Adelphi all the way up to Xmas 1956. The men concerned were a study in contrasts. On the one hand there was the aforementioned Terence Pepe Davis: a callow seventeen-year-old just out of public school: he'd fallen hard for Shirley and wanted to marry her. On the other, there was Robert Hartford-Davis, a friend of Mike Sullivan's: a working-class boy made good, older and much slicker than Pepe, starting to make his way as a television director. Later his distinctly chequered CV would include directing early British sexploitation and American blaxploitation movies, as well as discovering the teenage Gary Glitter.

Hartford-Davis was the one Shirley really fell for. 'I was looking for a father figure,' she told the *Sunday Mirror*'s Trudi Pacter a decade and a half later, 'and Robert fascinated me because he was nearly thirty and he knew his way around. He was the first man to take me to a real restaurant. He bought me my first bottle of perfume.' The relationship carried on for eight months, but ended badly:

> During that time Robert had another girlfriend and even though he was romancing me he never dropped the other girl. It didn't alter the way I felt. Then one night he took me in his arms and told me it was all over between us. He was going to Africa. I was devastated, I cried my heart out . . . The experience with Hartford-Davis hardened me towards men. It affected my future relationships. I always have to be the one who ends it. The minute I feel there's something wrong between me and a man, I'm out of the door fast.[1]

The lesson may have been a harsh one, but it did at least have a positive impact on her art, as Shirley pointed out in the same interview:

> I remember going on stage when I was eighteen and putting across as much emotion as a plank of wood. Sullivan said to me, 'You're singing this song and it's beautiful. But you're singing from your head not your heart.'

'What's the difference?' I'd say. And he told me, 'When you've loved a man and he doesn't love you – then you'll know.'[2]

You might have thought that being abandoned by the father of her child would have taught her that lesson already, but perhaps that lacked the glamour of being dumped by a film director.

There's a sense that this first year of stardom was a kind of year zero for Shirley. It was as if everything that happened before then had happened to a different person, an ordinary girl from Splott, and should be forgotten. In her new life she was Shirley Bassey the star. And stars have dramatic, tempestuous lives. If a star is dumped by her film-director boyfriend then she reacts dramatically. She reacts on stage. So Hartford-Davis was hardly the first man to hurt her, but he was the first man to hurt Shirley the star, and really he was doing Shirley the star a favour, allowing her to suffer spectacularly. From now on the counterpoint of the Shirley Bassey act was in place. For every song like 'Burn My Candle' that celebrated her sexuality, there would be another one, at least, that wallowed in the grief and bitterness of lost love.

And yet the transformation into Shirley the star was not complete. Pepe Davis was not the kind of boyfriend a star had; he was the kind of boyfriend an ordinary teenage girl had. He was a regular kid with a job as a salesman. He hung around the theatre and when Shirley didn't have a better offer she went out with him. After a while of being treated like this, Pepe became both jealous and possessive. Mike Sullivan soon saw the evidence of this:

I was stopped in a backstage corridor of the Delphi by Shirley's dresser Helen Cooper.

'Mike,' she said, 'I must have a word with you. You have got to talk to Shirley. Her mouth is bruised and it's all because of some boy.

She won't tell me about it, maybe you can get it out of her.'

I crashed into Shirley's dressing room and found her dabbing make-up over a swollen lip and jaw. There was also a small cut on her arm. The start of the show was still an hour away and for most of the hour I shot questions at her. She simply turned away and refused to answer me.[3]

The silent treatment might have worked against most people but Mike Sullivan was always a match for Shirley and eventually she gave in and answered.

She told me that she had, indeed, been burning her candle both ends with casual boyfriends . . . and in the middle with a boy who, for months, had considered himself her steady date. She had stood him up so many times that he had flared up and threatened to beat her up if she went out with anybody else. The previous night she had gone out with another casual pickup and when she got home to Olivelli's her angry steady was waiting for her. He pushed her into her room and – amid a lot of shouting – punched her in the face. 'Do something, please do something. I never thought it would get like this,' she begged.[4]

Sullivan duly swung into action. He called Pepe's mother – the family lived in Queensway, near Hyde Park – and threatened to call the police unless loverboy cooled it. Pepe's mother was happy to do her bit to try to put an end to the relationship, suggesting that her boy was far too good for the likes of Shirley. Just to make sure Pepe got the message, Sullivan persuaded a policeman to have a word in his ear.

And that should have been the end of it, but Shirley wasn't one to be given instructions in matters of the heart and within a month or two she was seeing Pepe again. She assured Sullivan that 'Everything's all right now. He's never spiteful the way he used to be and I'm quite happy.'

The explanation for the to-ing and fro-ing was simple enough. Shirley the star had still not quite taken over from Shirley the overawed young girl from Cardiff. One side of her was swayed by the sophistication of the Hartford-Davises of this world. But at the same time she liked having a regular boyfriend her own age, and one who did really love her. Pepe's own account of their courtship is touching:

> Shirley and I met in a Finchley, London, club. I was seventeen, educated at Blundell's public school in Tiverton, Devon. She was nineteen and from the drink and music clubs of Cardiff's notorious Tiger Bay. She sat alone on a high stool, sipping an orangeade. She looked like a lithe and sinuous kitten. But she seemed rather frightened. It was before her meteoric rise to the crest of world fame. Our eyes met. We talked all evening. I spoke of how I was just starting work in my father's textile business. She spoke about the audiences who were already applauding her every night and the loneliness of the big city. I took her back to her hotel in Bloomsbury. Next evening we had a meal together.[5]

It's clear that Shirley did feel close to Pepe, as she immediately let him in on secrets that she had kept well away from all her show-business friends.

> Then Shirley told me she had to go back to Cardiff because her father had just died.* I took her to the hotel and helped her pack. It was as I entered the room that I noticed something which suddenly drew

* Referring to Mr Mendi, of course.

me violently to her. On her dressing table was a photograph of a baby – the cutest I ever saw. Written on it was 'To mammy with love'. Shirley said simply, 'The child is mine. Everyone at home knows. Her name is Sharon. I couldn't look after her myself in show business. But I still pay for her upkeep.' At that instant I took Shirley in my arms. I felt a surge of love for this lonely little girl who spoke without hate or anger of what had happened. During the next few months our friendship became closer. We were both very much in love. When she came back from Cardiff I began helping her with her fan mail. How we used to joke about her bad spelling. I introduced her to smart West End restaurants. I was very proud to be helping her.[6]

One consequence of going out with a middle-class boy with no real connection to the showbiz world, a boy who just wanted to take her home to his family and get engaged and do the whole straight thing, was that Shirley's colour soon became an issue:

Four months after we first met I took her to meet my parents. It was difficult. I called Shirley my little chocolate drop. I loved her so I had no thought of the Colour Bar. All I wanted was to marry Shirley and bring up her little girl as ours and in my name. But some of my best friends shunned me. My mother realised I was very much in love and she accepted Shirley as one of the family. Soon Shirley spent nearly every weekend at the family's Bayswater flat. By then her records were beginning to sell well and she was appearing often in cabaret and on TV. Once we were televised together arriving for a film prem-iere. She invited me to Cardiff to meet her family. She was so very happy when she saw that I was more than attracted to her baby.[7]

So the relationship carried on – Pepe devoted and Shirley keeping him hooked, while continuing to play the field. Mike Sullivan accepted the situation and got on with the serious business of making as much money as he could out of Shirley while he still had her under contract. From Sullivan's point of view, Pepe had at least one thing to recommend him: unlike a lot of Shirley's suitors he had no designs on becoming her manager.

Shirley's basic employment for the year of 1956 was already secured with the extension of her run at the Adelphi. Even so, Sullivan was happy to take as many other gigs for his new star as he could. She might be doing two shows a day at the Adelphi, but they were over before eleven and the cabaret clubs didn't get going till then, so he booked Shirley in for a run at the Embassy Club in Bond Street. Two hours after her curtain calls at the Adelphi she'd be back on stage. It was a punishing schedule but she was young and excited and managed to pull it off.

At least, she did until Sullivan pushed his luck even further and booked her in for a slot on one of Jack Hylton's TV shows to be broadcast live on a Friday night. She would have to fit it in between the Adelphi and the Embassy. Ill and exhausted, when the time came to take a taxi over to the TV date, Shirley threw a tantrum and refused to go. Sullivan acted in the approved manner of the time:

> She started throwing clothes and pots of make-up at me and screaming. Here was the Bassey I was to come to know and shudder over. Screaming and temperamental. The more I tried to calm her the more hysterical she became. I slapped her in the face.[8]

This did indeed calm Shirley down temporarily and Sullivan was able to get her into the cab and over to the Albany where the TV show was to be filmed. On arrival, though, Shirley broke down again. This time one of the supporting attractions, a comedian called Eddie Arnold, administered the slap to the face. This didn't help matters at all and only the intervention of the avuncular Jack Hylton, tranquilliser in hand, succeeded in calming Shirley down. Sullivan quickly realised that he was in grave danger of alienating his meal ticket.

> I couldn't get near Shirley for the rest of the night. Jack Hylton made sure of that. 'Get away from her,' he said. 'You've done enough.' As I quietly left the place I saw Shirley take her seat at Hylton's table. She looked at me and smiled . . . a superior, arrogant smile. The star was starting to take over the singer.[9]

Or perhaps the singer was starting to appreciate men who looked after her, rather than ones who exploited her relentlessly, however much they'd done for her in return.

While the live performance side of things was moving forward at pace, Shirley's recording career was advancing rather more sedately. During her year in *Such Is Life* Johnny Franz had released just three singles by Shirley. The first of these featured the two songs she'd first performed on the television: 'Burn My Candle', the uptempo A-side, and 'Stormy Weather', the ballad B-side.

The songs were recorded in February 1956 at the label's Stanhope Place studio. By now, Johnny Franz had a crack team of musicians, arrangers and recording engineers around him. Among the people who worked on these first Shirley Bassey sides were two remarkable characters. In the role of recording engineer was a man called Joe Meek, while the arrangements were the work of one Wally Stott.

Joe Meek would later find fame as the pre-eminent British pop producer of the pre-Beatles era. His trademark 'Phil Spector in a bathroom above a shop on the Holloway Road' sound produced hits for Heinz and the Honeycombs and a worldwide number one with the Tornados' 'Telstar'. Troubled by – and persecuted for – his homosexuality, and eccentric at the very least, he later went mad and killed his landlady then himself, making him the stuff of music business legend, and the subject of a recent biopic.

Back then he was in his mid twenties and just making his start in the music business. Fascinated by electronics since childhood, he had worked as a radar operator for the RAF, and as a technician for the Midlands Electricity Board. He was obsessed with the possibilities of recorded sound and had started to make a name for himself as a man who could give pianos and drums a distinctive compressed sound. His work on Chris Barber's 'Petite Fleur' had been noticed, and Shirley's debut single was one of his first jobs for Johnny Franz.

The arranger on the session, Wally Stott, was in his late twenties, a dance band veteran whose considerable musical skills had seen him rise through the ranks from the brass section till, in 1953, he was appointed as the musical director for Philips, when the label launched in the UK. He was effectively Johnny Franz's right-hand man, with responsibility for writing the arrangements and conducting the orchestra during a recording session, while Franz concentrated on production. Over the next couple of decades, Wally Stott would become one of the most respected arrangers in the business, working with singers from Harry Secombe to Dusty Springfield to Scott Walker, and writing music for film and TV from *The Goon Show* to Michael Powell's paranoid masterpiece *Peeping Tom*.

In 1972 he caused something of a sensation in the tight-knit world of the British recording industry by going off on holiday to Scandinavia and coming back, having had a sex change, under the new name of Angela Morley. His career didn't suffer, however, and within a couple of years Angela was in Hollywood winning a string of Emmys and working closely with the film composer John Williams, before dying of a heart attack in 2008.

The record they all made together, 'Burn My Candle', is an odd concoction. Wally Stott's arrangement goes all out for sophistication and works pretty well, but rather shows up the song's dashed-off quality. Shirley sounds lively, but not half as lively as in her live performances. Overall it was a confident debut for a new artiste, if a rather conventional one. On it, Shirley already sounds a lot older than she actually was at the time. Which was what both her manager, Mike Sullivan, and her record company boss, Johnny Franz, wanted. Together they'd made the decision that Shirley should not be marketed to teenagers, but to an older audience. It was a brave call at a time when rock and roll was just starting to make an impression on the charts. There must have been a temptation to turn Shirley into a distaff Tommy Steele, a Welsh sparrer. Of course Shirley's subsequent fifty-year career shows that theirs was a shrewd decision.

'Burn My Candle' wasn't a hit but it made a mark. The BBC banned it, presumably on grounds of general salaciousness, and while that didn't help sales of that particular record, it did no harm to Sullivan's plan to build Shirley up as a sex siren. A second single, a rather staid reading of 'Born To Sing The Blues', backed with a livelier rendition of the pop country song 'The Wayward Wind', a big US hit for Gogi Grant, came out that summer, and again failed to chart but received some nice reviews. A review in the august *Gramophone* magazine noted that 'She is very young, but with a good producer might develop interestingly. She has started right by going on the stage, the hardest, cruellest training ground.'

There would be one more single later in the year, but as far as

Sullivan was concerned Shirley's recording career was no more than a sideline. It was the live work that mattered. And as the run at the Adelphi came towards its end, he managed his finest coup yet, booking Shirley into the Café de Paris, the absolute acme of the London cabaret scene at the time.

The Café de Paris, set in a grand basement just off Piccadilly, was the regular London venue for the likes of Cole Porter, Noel Coward and Marlene Dietrich. It stayed open during the war and paid the penalty when two large bombs crashed through the cinema above and exploded on the Café's dance floor. Eighty people died in the ensuing carnage, including the black British bandleader Ken 'Snakehips' Johnson and many of his band.

After the war, the Café de Paris was refurbished and resumed its position as London's smartest nightspot under the direction of its impresario, Major Donald Neville-Willing. Neville-Willing, a fantastical individual who had worked for ENSA during the war, was vividly described by Tommy Steele in his autobiography:

> He stood five foot two with a full head of blue-rinsed hair, a waxed moustache, a red velvet smoking jacket and a monocle. 'You will follow in the footsteps of Noel Coward and Marlene,' he cooed. 'My patrons will take you in their arms and cry "Hosanna". With that he snatched the flowers from the vase on the table and threw them into my lap, all wet and sticky.[10]

Sullivan had courted Neville-Willing for a while and was delighted when, late that summer while on holiday in Monte Carlo, he got word that the Major had finally agreed to give Shirley a try. The Café de Paris was about as far from teenage as you could get. Sullivan decided that Shirley needed to make herself as grown-up as possible.

The role model he decided on was Eartha Kitt. For that to work he needed to get Shirley some more original material that would play on the sex-kitten angle. His business relationship with Jack Hylton was on the decline, so there was no way he'd be able to get Ross Parker to write any more songs. Instead, he sought out another songwriter whose biggest hit was some way in the past. His name was Ian Grant and he had co-written the cabaret standard 'Let There Be Love', back in 1939. Grant agreed to write Shirley a couple of songs. A pianist called Les Paul (no relation to the guitarist), who'd served time with Gracie Fields, was brought in to be the accompanist.

Once again Grant's songs teetered on the edge of parody. One was called 'My Body's More Important Than My Mind', the other simply 'Sex'. Neither was exactly a classic but they did the job. The team went to work grooming Shirley for her latest challenge:

> Ian, Les and I worked night and day to teach Shirley every trick we knew. I had a tight black gown with a band of mink around the bust made for her . . . The Major was impressed by all this work and enthusiasm and decided to make Shirley's first performance an invitation-only night and insist upon evening dress. The invitations went out to the aristocracy, the well-heeled, the socially acceptable and show business personalities.[11]

The mind boggles as to just who 'the socially acceptable' might be. Shirley was alarmed too, especially when Sullivan told her she might be invited to join the nobility at table after the show. 'I can't. I just can't,' she told him. 'All those knives and forks. I won't know what to do.' So Sullivan had to demonstrate what a full service management operation he was running by taking Shirley out to a smart restaurant, and teaching her to distinguish her soup spoon from her fish fork, and to do what the quality do with their napkins when they finish eating (leave them in a crumpled heap).

On 30 September there was a final dress rehearsal at the venue. It was tense and difficult and ended with Shirley bursting into tears. On balance Sullivan reckoned this was a good thing. Better to release the tension before the big night than during. When they finished, Shirley headed off to the cinema with a young singer called Barry Hamilton, who was also staying at Olivelli's, and Sullivan headed back to his hotel suite, confident that he had everything well prepared.

A late-night phone call from Papa Olivelli dispelled that illusion. Shirley was distraught, could he come over? So Sullivan headed over to the hotel to discover his star lying in bed looking puffy-eyed and exhausted. What was the matter? The matter was Pepe Davis once again. He had recently been called up for his national service, as he later recalled:

In September '56 I was called up for the RAF. I still cherish the wonderful love letters which Shirley wrote to me when I was in the RAF: 'I'm longing for you to come home, I'm dying to see you.' 'When I said goodbye at the station last night part of me seemed to go with you and I felt terribly lonely.' In those letters Shirley used to sign herself 'Chutch', as she was known at home, or 'your baby'. And often after each few sentences there were rows of crosses for kisses . . . My success in RAF boxing helped me to get regular 36 hour passes. Those weekends were always so happy. I saw very little of my family, for Shirley and I both felt we couldn't waste one precious second of our time together.[12]

Or at least the weekends were happy until Pepe read in the papers that Shirley had a new boyfriend called Barry Hamilton, from the

Three Deuces vocal group. So when she'd got back to Olivelli's, Pepe had been waiting for her. They rowed and then, Shirley told Sullivan, she said she'd had enough and they were finished. What happened next? Sullivan asked. Shirley told him:

He said, 'Well, you won't be seeing me any more,' and I said, 'Good.'

He went out, I hear his car start up and roar down the road. Then there's silence. He must be turning. I hear it roaring back. Then a crash. I put my coat on and run downstairs. Two boys are in the doorway. One says, 'Over there.' And points across the road. There's that big petrol station over there and the car is rammed right into the gates.

I was first there. I found him lying on the ground near the back of the car. I think he must have got out after the crash and collapsed. I lifted his head a bit and started crying. His face was covered in blood. The ambulance came and he got hold of my hand and kept saying, 'Will you go with me?' I said I would but Barry gets hold of our hands and unclasps them and says, 'You can't, you've got the show to do tomorrow.'[13]

Shirley said she still wanted to go to the hospital, but Sullivan put his foot down: 'I had to put a stop to this affair,' he wrote. 'I had never even seen this boy, but he had struck twice at my livelihood.'

Pepe's life was saved but he suffered severe head injuries which would affect him very badly over the years to come. Later on Shirley would visit him regularly and even promise to marry him in an attempt to help him recuperate – a promise that would have unfortunate ramifications. In the short term Sullivan's wife Juhni came over to be with Shirley, and by the next day the livelihood was back to her usual self and managed to do two shows at the Adelphi before heading over to the Café de Paris for her big debut.

As ever, she rose to the occasion effortlessly. He mother was in the audience, and so too were Liberace and his mother. Liberace's mother – clearly every bit as camp as her son – held a lace handkerchief in front of her son's face during the racier numbers, apparently to prevent him from getting overexcited.

Sullivan himself wasn't really able to enjoy his protégée's triumph as his own love life was going through one of its regular crises. His wife Juhni, who had played such a big role in grooming the young Shirley, was there at the Café, but so too was Sullivan's new lover, a Greek dancer called Lily Berde. Sullivan went home with Juhni that night, but two days later their relationship was over for good. Lily Berde in due course became the third Mrs Sullivan.

It wasn't just Sullivan's love life that was in turmoil either. His professional life was also in perilous straits. The Shirley Bassey project was going well; the Café de Paris was a great success. Neville-Willing extended her booking from the original fortnight to an impressive nine weeks. However, Sullivan's outgoings were still outpacing his income. He had to explain this to Neville-Willing when they came to extend Shirley's contract.

Shirley was clearly being advised that she was being exploited by Sullivan. She said as much to the impresario, who'd become very fond of her, and he took the matter up with Sullivan, who pointed out that he was paying for Shirley's gowns and publicity, her pianist and her dresser, her hairdressers and songwriters. Once all these overheads were factored in, he argued, the run at the Café de Paris was actually losing him money.

Losing money it may have been, but it was certainly gaining friends. An upmarket crowd started to take notice of the new singer in town. Shirley was featured in the *Sketch* and *Tatler*, and in the entertainments columns of the Sunday broadsheets. Offers for more work came in, and not just in Britain but abroad. A season at the

Café de Paris offered an entrée to Paris, New York and beyond.

Sullivan jumped at the offers: here was the chance to take the project to the next level, to make Shirley a star of the international cabaret scene. He agreed to take Shirley to do a show at the Olympia, Paris, in December, as soon as the run at the Adelphi finished, and started to plan a trip to the US in the new year.

Money was not the only area of conflict between Sullivan and his star. He was convinced that her future was as a cabaret singer and took little interest in developing her as a recording artiste. Shirley, now boundlessly ambitious, was sure she could be both. Johnny Franz, of course, tended to agree with her. So, for the next record, he decided to take Shirley away from the cabaret material and towards something more obviously commercial and fashionable.

Britain was having a mini calypso boom at the end of 1956. This wasn't so much a product of the current wave of West Indian immigration into Britain as a manufactured affair based on the popularity of a new American star called Harry Belafonte, a New Yorker of West Indian parentage who had developed an enormously popular line in West Indian accented pop. His signature tune was a Jamaican folk song, adapted by Belafonte's fellow New Yorker, Lord Burgess, as the 'Banana Boat Song'. This was already a major hit in the US and so Franz lined it up as Shirley's next single release.

Whether Shirley's racial origins had anything to do with the choice of song remains moot. Certainly in his sleeve notes to Shirley's first album, released the following year, Franz refers to her as 'The daughter of a West Indian seaman'. Shirley's enthusiasm for the song can probably be judged by the speed at which it disappeared from her repertoire. She had doubtless heard calypsos ever since she was a child – they were a part of the Bay's musical landscape – but she was certainly no West Indian.

Before the record could come out it was time for her next great adventure to begin. The seaman's daughter was to leave Britain for the first time. That December she travelled with Mike Sullivan to Paris.

> Shirley had never been out of Britain before and she was like a little girl, full of wonder and excitement. The Christmas spirit must have grabbed me because when we were arrived at her hotel in Paris I told her: 'Shirley, you are getting one hundred pounds for this broadcast. For once I suggest you take the whole damn lot and go shopping.'[14]

The show was a success. Shirley was invited back for a season the following spring. And on their return to London Sullivan was able to finalise the American trip. He worked a deal with the William Morris Agency to co-promote her in the States. They would go to New York, then the El Rancho in Las Vegas and finally Ciro's in Hollywood.

Shirley was thrilled, naturally, but was also starting to see herself as a fully fledged star. She began issuing Sullivan with list of demands: Could he please buy her a mink coat and a Jaguar?

Sullivan, meanwhile, was utterly broke, dodging the alimony demands from his ex-wives. Getting Shirley and himself on the plane to the States was an obstacle course. He had to borrow money from his accountant and from Bob Konyot, and, at the airport, he had to dodge the detectives sent to arrest him for non-payment of maintenance. But Mickey Sullivan being Mickey Sullivan, he dodged and ducked and one way or another he and his protégée made it to New York, ready for their biggest challenge yet.

THIRTEEN

Viva Las Vegas

Shirley Bassey, accompanied by Mike Sullivan and Mike's new girl-friend, the Greek dancer Lily Berde, arrived in New York in the depths of winter. Things started to go wrong before they'd even left the airport.

Mike and Lily were waved through immigration without any problems. Shirley was made to wait till all the other passengers had passed through. Sullivan was relieved to see that Shirley didn't appear to notice the racial significance of this.

For the first couple of days Shirley mostly stayed in her room, entranced by the vast choice of TV channels available and watching film after film. Mike Sullivan, meanwhile, was out hustling. His first port of call was Columbia Records, the company who represented Philips in the US. And once again Sullivan acquitted himself very well indeed. He got Columbia to agree to set up a recording session for later in the week, the session to be produced by Mitch Miller, no less.

A dapper middle-aged man with a distinctive goatee, Mitch Miller was the most powerful figure in American popular music during the 1950s. Columbia was the era's most successful record label and he was their main man. He was directly responsible for many of the label's key acts, including the phenomenally popular Johnny

Mathis.* Miller was also a star in his own right, thanks to his dia-' bolically popular series of *Sing Along With Mitch* albums (these featured an all-male chorus bellowing out simple versions of famous songs, from 'You Are My Sunshine' to 'She Wore A Yellow Ribbon' – pretty much the Black and White Minstrels repertoire – while the American public was urged to sing along, helped out by the inclusion of lyric sheets).

The session was booked for Shirley's last day in New York. In the meantime Sullivan engaged a publicist, Ed Gollin, to take her out on the town, to see and be seen. First stop was the Broadway Theatre where they caught the Sammy Davis, Jr. vehicle *Mr Wonderful*, a show that had been running for nearly a year and featured a song, 'The Birth of the Blues', that Shirley had already recorded herself.

After the show, Gollin engineered a meeting between Shirley and the star. Sammy was clearly taken with the British starlet, and invited her along for dinner at a local celebrity haunt, a steakhouse called Danny's Hideaway. And then, to cap it all, he whisked his new friend off to see his Rat Pack confrère Frank Sinatra at the Copacabana. By the end of the night Shirley was sitting round a table in New York with Mr Sinatra himself.

Two years earlier she'd been waitressing in the Olympia Café, Cardiff and now she was at Frank Sinatra's table at the Copacabana, New York. No wonder she was starting to acquire airs and graces, and had blown out her first rehearsal for the Mitch Miller recording date. This was the life.

The idyll was interrupted when Mr Sinatra's lovable mob of

* That one of the biggest recording stars in 1950s American music – as far as albums sales went Mathis's only rival was Frank Sinatra – should have been a flamboyantly camp African American is one of the era's enduring oddities.

gangster and would-be-gangster associates started to take notice of little Sammy's friend. As Shirley told Sullivan the next day:

> The owner of the Copacabana, Joe Padella, sat next to me. He looked big and tough too. He gave me a dig in the side and said 'Wadda you do?' I said 'Sing.' He said 'Where?' I said 'I open in Las Vegas next week.' Then he said 'Sing for me.' I told him I couldn't because I had a contract and he didn't like that. He told me 'You can sing for Joe Padella' and he started getting mad and walking up and down. He said 'Hey Frank, wadda you think? She won't sing for me.' Sinatra was busy talking about Sinatra and he just waved his hand and said 'Never mind Joe, never mind.' But I was getting scared and I whispered to Ed Gollin, 'Let's get out of here. These people frighten me.' I walked to the door with Ed and Sammy Davis sent us home in his car. All the time I was expecting something awful to happen to me.[1]

It would have been a lot worse if she'd turned up ten years earlier. The Copa's manager, whose name was actually Jules Podell, was a staunch racist who was put in place by the celebrated mobster Frank Costello. And until the mid 1950s the place operated a strict colour bar. Even Harry Belafonte had been turned away. The colour bar was only broken when Davis showed up as a guest of Sinatra's one night. The club's bouncers initially tried to stop Davis entering but Sinatra threw a fit and Podell backed down. Shortly afterwards Davis, accustomed as he was to these situations, agreed to headline and Podell started to make an exception for black entertainers who could attract well-heeled white audiences into his club.

A day or two later it was time for the Columbia recording session. This did not go well. Shirley, busy enjoying New York and imagining herself already a fully fledged star, had blown out both the scheduled rehearsals and failed to learn any of the material properly. Mitch Miller, a lot less tolerant than Johnny Franz, was not impressed. New York was full of great singers and they were expected to turn up ready to go. Sullivan was once again called on to smooth over troubled waters and succeeded well enough. Three songs were recorded, among them a lively novelty called 'I Wish I Had a Needle and Thread' that would be Shirley's next single back in Britain, and 'The Wall', an excursion into straight country pop that would be a hit for Patti Page later in the year (and one of the few songs to be recorded by both Shirley Bassey and Johnny Cash).

The New York professionals were less than convinced by Bassey. It was a sign of Shirley's new self-confidence that, as far as she was concerned, it was all Miller's fault, as she told Mike Sullivan: 'I thought they would have been a little more professional in America. In England Johnny Franz takes me over a number several times.'

And so to Las Vegas. Shirley had originally been booked into the New Frontier hotel, the place where Elvis Presley had made his Vegas debut six months earlier, but that had fallen through at the last moment as the New Frontier was having financial difficulties. Thankfully, the William Morris Agency had managed to switch the booking to the neighbouring El Rancho.

The El Rancho was the first of all the Las Vegas resort hotels, and the first to open on what is now known as the Las Vegas Strip. Before the El Rancho opened in 1942 Las Vegas's casinos and entertainment were all concentrated in the downtown area and hardly constituted a major tourism destination. The El Rancho – and by extension the whole Las Vegas strip – was the brainchild of a man called Tom Hull. Legend has it that Hull's car broke down on the primitive road leading through the desert to Las Vegas and that, while waiting for the repair truck to show up, he noticed how busy the road was. There and then he decided that what the place needed was an upmarket motel with a casino and a theatre. It turned out he was right. Within a few years the mobster Bugsy Siegel had also spotted the potential of the Las Vegas Strip and soon the El Rancho was just one of a line of lavish hotel/casino/entertainment hubs strung along the road.

Compared to the places that came after it, the El Rancho was a relatively down-home kind of joint, just a more elaborate spin on the classic American roadside motel, albeit one sufficiently lavish that its lawns required ten million gallons of water a month to be pumped in. However, it did have a good reputation as an entertainment venue. The principal auditorium, the so-called Opera House (previously the rather more Okie-sounding 'Round-Up Room'), had attracted a stellar line-up over the past decade. As Las Vegas venues went it was also more open than most to black entertainers.

Dorothy Dandridge and Nat King Cole had performed there. So had the Katharine Dunham dancers. Eartha Kitt was a regular, and had been there just a couple of months before. Even Shirley's teenage favourite Billy Eckstine had graced its stage, further evidence of just how far she'd come, how quickly. The biggest attractions, though, or at least the most regularly featured, were the comedian Joe E. Lewis and the stripper Lili St Cyr,* who had been headlining the week before Shirley arrived.

Manager and protégée alike were thrilled to be there:

* 'A stripper de luxe who appears on stage in such radiant undress that audiences are rendered not only speechless but gaspless. Her appeal is particularly demonstrated by the finale of an act called "Bird in a Gilded Cage", in which she soars out over the audience in a gilded cage dropping beaded panties, frilly garters, and sequined bras on the hands-outstretched spectators below. It is not what anyone conceivably could call a domestic-type act, and nobody could have been more startled than Miss St Cyr herself when she began getting letters from women asking for instructions on how to make "those darling panties and bras". As a matter of fact, there have been so many requests of this type that she has established a lingerie-manufacturing company in California called Lili St Cyr Unmentionables, Inc. "Now there are not many women," she says, "faced with the problem, as I am, of getting out of underthings in one second flat, but business is good, and I am not going to allow it to mystify me."' (*From Playtown, USA, Katherine Best and Katherine Hillyer, 1955*)

We drove by taxi to El Rancho, goggling at the huge, ever-open hotels with their neon signs. In our tinsel world this was close to the centre of the universe. Here glamour reigned as it never would at the Hippodrome, Keighley. Enormous billboards announced the appearance of stars like Peggy Lee and Tony Martin. Looking at names like that I was almost relieved when we arrived at El Rancho to see that Shirley's name was not in lights. As she stepped from the taxi she looked crumpled and tired . . . hardly the sort of thing to set the desert on fire[2].

The El Rancho's current owner was a man called Beldon Katleman, and he'd arranged for Shirley and her manager to be put up in adjoining cabins in the grounds. On discovering that the cost was fourteen dollars a day Sullivan made new arrangements for himself and Lily. Until Shirley got paid money was going to be very tight.

Still, when the money did come in, there was going to be plenty of it: Shirley was due to be paid $1,800 a week by the resort. And, even though she was unknown, the local press came down to see Shirley on her first night at the grandly titled Opera House (in fact a pretty standard hotel ballroom with the stage set up in front of a dance floor surrounded by seating for three hundred diners). It was a lot less intimidating than the Café de Paris. On the other hand, at El Rancho Shirley had to put up with the punters eating during the show, something she would refuse to accept in later years.

Still, she didn't let that put her off, and the local press were duly wowed, none more so than the *Las Vegas Sun*, which reported that:

'The El Rancho has discovered another Eartha Kitt, an ex-factory worker from Wales. And it's like finding uranium. Savage, sultry and sleek, Shirley Bassey whams home songs of sin and sex.'[3]

So the New York music business folk might not have warmed

to Shirley, but they hadn't seen her in her element, on stage. In Las Vegas they knew a natural performer when they saw one. Mike Sullivan made smart use of this exposure. Not only did he circulate the reviews to magazines across the States, but, more importantly, he was able to tell the press back home in Britain that his protégée was a hit in the US. Then, as now, the British papers were only too keen to believe any such stories, and the week after Shirley opened at the El Rancho, the *New Musical Express* ran a story headlined 'Shirley Bassey is a big hit in Las Vegas' in which 'the Welsh thrush' phoned in an interview to vouchsafe the remarkable revelation that 'The audience was marvellous and if it's like this every night I'm going to love it.'[4]

It didn't take long, though, for Las Vegas's less appealing side to emerge. After they'd been there for a couple of days Mike Sullivan received an urgent summons to come and see the resort's owner. Katleman told Sullivan that he'd heard he'd been out on the town with Miss Bassey. Sullivan concurred; he'd taken Shirley and Lily out to see the sights the night before. Katleman then explained the way things were in Las Vegas. White men and black women should not be seen together in public. Sullivan was horrified:

> First the wait at immigration and then this. If you move in the big money and big hotel circles you can travel a long way before it hits you, I thought, but now we had come up against it. I had no intention of making a martyr out of Shirley. I never told her about my meeting with Katleman.[5]

Sullivan instead did his best to protect her from the unpleasant realities of Las Vegas, making sure that she basically confined herself to the El Rancho – singing at night, sleeping, watching TV and playing the slot machines by day. The only thing that might have alerted Shirley to the race relations situation was the fact that none of El Rancho's all-white punters tried to ask her out: 'Mickey,' she said, 'I've always had dates before. What's the matter with me?'

In truth it's hard to believe she wasn't aware of what was going on. The one time on the trip that Sullivan discussed the matter of her skin colour with his protégée she had this to say: 'Now if I go into a place and people stare at me I never think it's because I'm coloured. It's because I look attractive and striking when I'm wearing a wonderful gown. Otherwise it would drive me mad.'[6]

But as it turned out, Shirley had a remarkably easy time of it in Las Vegas compared with most black entertainers. Las Vegas in the 1950s was a Jim Crow town through and through. The Las Vegas hotels were prepared to book leading black entertainers, but not to treat them like human beings. The likes of Sammy Davis, Jr. and Pearl Bailey and Duke Ellington were barred from eating, drinking, gambling or even sleeping at the hotels that hosted them. If a black star wanted a drink in Vegas he had to head over to the city's Westside ghetto. Indeed, they had little option, as after their shows all the Lena Hornes and Nat King Coles – huge stars at the time – were bussed back across the tracks to rooms in boarding houses. For a brief while, during 1955, an integrated casino, the Moulin Rouge, had been opened in the Westside itself, but it closed within six months amid rumours of Mafia involvement.

One anecdote sums up the racial climate of 1950s Las Vegas: Sammy Davis, Jr., always forced into the role of trailblazer, was performing at a hotel on the Strip. One day he decided to jump into the swimming pool. Next morning the pool was drained and scrubbed by a cleaning crew.

And if it was bad for the stars, it was worse for the black porters and maids and cooks who kept the town going. The downtown stores wouldn't let a black man try on clothes before buying them, lest their white customers consider the item of clothing defiled.

So the fact that Shirley actually got to stay on the premises and gamble on the slots and so forth was pretty remarkable. Presumably it had a lot to do with her being a foreigner and not an all-American Negro. The colour bar had a range of rather random exceptions for dusky-skinned folk from across the water. It's likely the management of the El Rancho played up to them, which may explain why Shirley told *Picturegoer* magazine on her return that: 'In Las Vegas they all thought I was French. They'd send notes to my table. I'd just read them, smile and tear them up. Everyone thought I was snooty and playing hard to get. I didn't dare admit I didn't understand French.'[7]

Or American racism, either. Or perhaps she was just keeping the tone of the interview nice and light – as, a few years later, she was rather more candid about her Las Vegas experience:

> When I received my invitation to sing in Las Vegas I was terrified. I had heard about Jim Crow. But I thought to myself, this must be faced if I'm going to become an international star. In fact no hotel turned me away. The Americans said, 'Well, let's face it, you don't look coloured, you look Mexican or Puerto Rican.' In America apparently only (American) Negroes are considered coloured. It made me ill.[8]

Either way, Shirley survived her three weeks at El Rancho. All concerned were happy and the resort invited her back the following year at a salary of $5,000. Next stop LA.

In Los Angeles Shirley was due to appear at Ciro's, on Sunset Strip. This was another classic post-war American entertainment hot spot. Everyone from Frank Sinatra to Billie Holiday, Mae West to Marlene Dietrich, had played there. The owner, Herman Hover, was a big cigar-chomping man, a New Yorker who'd served time in the Mob joints back east. It was still a prestigious place to play but what Mike Sullivan didn't know was that it was on shaky financial ground. The Las Vegas strip was steadily putting the rest of the nation's cabaret hot spots out of business.

The Sullivan crew settled in LA for a few weeks. Sullivan eventually managed to find a place with a pool that didn't mind housing a coloured singer. Shirley took some driving lessons around Hollywood, and dated playboy Arthur Loew, Jr. Loew was born into a movie business dynasty, and his Connecticut-style farmhouse just above the Sunset Strip was pretty much the coolest place to hang out in LA at the time. By all accounts he was an extremely funny man as well as a very good-looking one. His previous girlfriends included two women who would later become good friends of Shirley's: the British starlet Joan Collins, with whom he had a celebrated public row,* and Eartha Kitt, whom he might have married had it not been for his family's objections.†

Meanwhile the run at Ciro's went as well as ever. The *éminence grise* of Hollywood reporters, Walter Winchell, came to see Shirley and reported that 'She has an appealing song style and holds the eye and ear from the moment she belts out the first note. Her figure is another major entertainment.' The only thing to go wrong was the matter of actually getting paid. This was a serious problem as Sullivan was depending on the money to pay for the flights home to Britain. As a holding operation he got the William Morris Agency

---

*A much-told Hollywood story involves the pair having an argument at the La Scala restaurant in Beverly Hills. This culminated in Collins storming out with the words, 'Arthur, you are a fucking bore.' Loew then got to his feet and retaliated with the precisely calibrated 'Well, that's OK, because you've always been a boring fuck.'
†'The man I wanted to be the father of my daughter was Arthur Loew, Jr.,' Kitt told the *Daily Telegraph*, 'but his mother said, "I'll shoot him in the foot before he marries a brown-skinned woman."'

to book Shirley into the Riverside Room in Reno, Nevada. Shirley had a good time there. She played to a convention of midgets, two of whom proposed marriage to her. Then a taller fellow chatted her up and also proposed marriage, so she told Sullivan:

> I thought it was marvellous, being proposed to and I also thought that, being in Reno, I could get a quickie divorce before I left, so I accepted. We went in his car and drove around all over the place, talking about the wedding, for hours. He even got a friend of his with a radio station to congratulate us over the air. Then it got light and I thought, 'Bit weird. He's got no intention of marrying me.' All he wanted to do was take me home and get me into bed. What he did do was waste the whole night talking. Why couldn't he just come out with it instead?[9]

Meanwhile Mike Sullivan still didn't have the money from Ciro's. It turned out the club was in severe financial difficulties and within a year it would close down for good, while Herman Hover would be arrested for nearly killing his brother who was having an affair with his wife.

Salvation came in the shape of a letter from Johnny Franz, back in London. The 'Banana Boat Song' was in the charts. Sullivan parlayed this news into a headlining slot at the London Hippodrome, booked with Leslie Grade. The deal was for £500 a week plus £50 per cent of the profits. And two flights from Reno to London.

> Then I called Johnny Franz and asked him to meet Shirley at the airport with a big model boat with cellophane sails and a huge bow on the mast with Shirley's initials on it. And full of bananas. That, I thought, should make pictures for the papers and let people know Bassey was back.[10]

FOURTEEN

Sophisticated Lady

Shirley arrived back in London on Good Friday, 19 April 1957, sporting an elegant new short haircut. Mike Sullivan hit the ground running. Within a week there were stories in the press about Shirley's first dates for Leslie Grade, a hometown run at the New Theatre, Cardiff, in May.

There was obviously going to be local interest in the show – Splott girl makes good and all that – but to get the national press interested Sullivan needed to find a new angle on the story. He recalled Shirley telling him about the youth club where she used to sing and dance. What was its name? The Rainbow Club, she told him. In no time a friendly London Welsh journalist, Jack Thomas, was running a story proclaiming Shirley's intention to give regular donations of £250 to the Rainbow Club out of her earnings. The organiser, Mrs Capener, was quoted as saying, 'We will never be able to thank Shirley enough. I am sure it will please her to know that we've already decided that the first of the money will be used to build a stage at the club.' Shirley, herself, simply adds 'I'm just glad to help my own people.'[1]

It didn't take long for Sullivan to find a way in which the Rainbow Club could repay the favour. He suggested they might like to put on a welcome party for Shirley at the station when her train arrived. They agreed and Sullivan managed to turn the Bassey homecoming into a full-scale jamboree. He even persuaded British Rail to put a banner on the front of the train announcing the star's arrival.

While this was all being set up, Sullivan parked Shirley at the Mayfair Hotel, in a deluxe suite costing £60 a week. Shirley was happy enough with this till she realised that it was she, ultimately, who was paying for it. Meanwhile her friend Gloria, Pepe Davis's sister, invited her to come and stay with the family in Bayswater. Shirley decided to take her up on the offer. Given that Pepe was suffering the after-effects of the head injuries suffered in the car crash, and was still madly in love with her, this seems a curious decision. But £60 a week was, after all, £60 a week, and she was going to be on tour for most of the next few months, so . . .

Before she went on tour there was also the matter of her recording career to attend to. The 'Banana Boat Song' had done well for her, staying in the charts for almost the whole time she'd been away in the States, but now the Harry Belafonte version, which had been all over the American radio stations, was a hit in Britain too, a bigger hit than Shirley's had been. Should she try another calypso-style record or try for something more sophisticated? One thing was for sure: she was no longer happy to let anyone else tell her what to do, as the journalist John Ennis observed on seeing Shirley at work in the Philips studios in Stanhope Place:

Two men chain-smoked cigarettes from open packets on the desk of a large brightly lit, green-carpeted office near Marble Arch. A grand piano strewn with sheet music filled the corner opposite the door. A radiogram against one wall boomed an American recording of a new popular song. A slim light-skinned coloured girl with candid brown eyes stood at one corner of the desk. She wore a mauve cardigan, a grey skirt and a green and mauve headscarf. She flipped the pages of a showbiz periodical snapping her fingers and writhing slightly to the rhythm of the record. The song ended, one of the men, Johnny Franz, asked the girl 'Like it, Shirley?'

'Oh yes,' the girl said, 'but it isn't me.'

'You're a bad one for liking a song the first time you hear it,' Franz said. He put on another record. It compared a lover's emotions to a see-saw. Miss Bassey sang the lyric. When she finished Sullivan said 'It'll be a hit.'

'Who wants to sing a hit?' Miss Bassey demanded. 'If I sing something I can be sincere about, people will like it.'[2]

As these last words make apparent, even at the age of twenty Shirley was starting to outgrow her mentors. She knew, even if they didn't, that the key to her long-term appeal would be her identification with her material. It didn't matter how gaudy or clichéd the emotion; if Shirley felt it then she could sell it to her audience. What she couldn't do was fake it.

The dilemma remained: was Shirley Bassey a transient pop singer or a long-term cabaret artiste? For the moment, both Sullivan and Franz hedged their bets. They decided to release two of the pop songs recorded with Mitch Miller in New York – 'I Wish I Had a Needle and Thread' and 'Tonight My Heart She Is Crying' – as a single. After all, they could hardly do otherwise without offending the most powerful man in the record industry. They also decided to release an EP of songs recorded live at the Café de Paris, and cut a selection of cabaret takes on the blues with a view to putting out a long-playing record.*

---

* An emblematic move – back in the 1950s pop artists were generally confined to releasing 45 rpm singles. Long-playing 33 rpm albums were considerably more expen-

And so to Cardiff. Shirley's return home had caught the imagination of the media. The BBC, just a few years after snubbing her, celebrated the event with a special radio show, and the *Daily Sketch* sent a reporter, Michele Dearing, to accompany Shirley on the train. The star showed up just about in time to catch the 8.55 from Paddington, a mink cape slung under one arm and a torn paper bag under the other. Dearing began by asking what was in the bag, and got a reply that reminded her just how young Shirley still was:

> 'I'm taking some sweaters home for mum to wash and the mink to show my sisters . . . No, I never eat breakfast,' she said tossing back the long ends of an amber-coloured scarf tied around her cropped black hair.
>
> Over bacon and eggs, toast and marmalade, two glasses of milk, coffee and two chunks of fruit cake, Shirley (ten minutes later) was blithely telling me all about the sheer fun of being Shirley.
>
> 'I'm sophisticated all the time now,' she says contentedly, taking a mighty mouthful of bacon. 'I want to have a mews cottage with the biggest bed in the world and a mink carpet. It would be practical in the long run because mink never wears out. I want to marry Frank Sinatra: I probably will, because I always get what I want. Trouble is I'm always in love, but only for a few weeks at a time.'

After a pause for more breakfast, she carried on telling Dearing about Mr Sinatra:

> 'Frankie's the unhappiest man alive with the most exciting personality in the world. But boy, he's bitter. I want to cuddle him, he's

---

sive and aimed at an older audience, so generally confined to crooners, musical soundtracks, jazz and classical.

such a skinny little fellow. I want to marry him and find out why he's so sad all the time.'

And after the big reception at the station from the Rainbow Club, the Girl Guides, Boy Scouts and Boys' Brigade, and anyone else Sullivan could drum up, Dearing accompanied Shirley back to Splott:

No mink carpet, just linoleum to cover the floor of this shabby terraced house. To Shirley this was HOME. She bounced into the kitchen with a 'Hi Mum.' Mrs Bassey was fumbling through her handbag on the lino-topped table looking for money to pay the milkman. Three of Shirley's sisters and three of her eight nieces were in that tiny room. The unglamorous, warm-hearted, matter-of-fact women in worn cardigans watched the steam rising from a nappy on the fireguard. Shirley produced a £5 note for the milk. 'That ring's a bit flashy,' said sister Eileen.

'How do you like my mink? See, the collar turns up to make a hood. Wait till you see my new handbag, I paid 17 guineas for it. And my new shoes, they cost £10. They're beautiful but they cripple me. Look, I've learned how to Charleston . . .'

And the sisters watched and listened, patient and a little exasperated in the way of older sisters.[3]

From the house, the Shirley Bassey show moved out onto the streets. She bought sweets for the neighbouring kids, then headed over the road into the working-men's club where she used to dance on the table and sing for coppers. This time she announced the drinks were on her. Lawrence the barman hoisted her onto the piano and one of the locals accompanied her as she sang, or at least clowned around pretending to sing, for the newspaper photographs.

Shirley and her class at Moorland primary school, Splott. Spot the odd one out. (1947)

Shirley's father. The only known photo of Henry Bassey, taken from his merchant navy registration card. Has his daughter's eyes. (1919)

Shirley and her mother, Eliza. Eliza modelling Shirley's new mink stole at home in Cardiff. (8 May 1957)

At home with the family. Back row – Pat (Marina's husband), Mary (Henry Bassey's wife), Henry Bassey, Eliza Bassey, Iris Bassey plus baby Sharon, Shirley. Front row – Elaine Bassey, Marina Bassey with Russell, Susan, aged 6. (9 December 1955)

Shirley on the street where she grew up, Portmanmoor Road, Splott. (9 December 1955)

Shirley in costume from her first West End show, *Such Is Life*. (16 December 1955)

Shirley's first photoshoot, aged sixteen. Never again would she be so shamelessly exploited. (September 1953)

Shirley comes home to the New Theatre, Cardiff. Griffe Lewis is the pianist), and the other gent is the theatre manager, Mr Reg Phillips. (15 September 1958)

Backstage at the Astoria, Brixton, the young Shirley realises that her manager, Mike Sullivan, needs her more than she needs him. (1957)

Shirley the pop star, flanked by a young John Barry and David Jacobs. They're at the Empire Pool, Wembley, where Bassey and Barry have been performing at a benefit for SOS – The Stars Organisation for Spastics! (27 March 1960)

Shirley in the kitchen of her first home of her own near Hyde Park, London. (16 December 1959)

Shirley backstage at The Chiswick Empire Theatre, her first UK show following the tabloid revelations about her daughter Sharon. (6 March 1959)

Shirley goes on holiday. With Samantha aged 3 and Sharon aged 11. (9 August 1966)

Shirley reclining. (16 March 1967)

A defiant Shirley enters the sixties with a home of her own and without the management of Mike Sullivan. (18 January 1960)

A shaken Shirley following her escape from a gun-toting Pepe Davis. She's accompanied by her friend, the stage cartoonist Peter Quinton Honey. (11 November 1957)

Shirley's turbulent professional relationship with Mike Sullivan comes to a temporary truce as they settle their differences out of court. (January 1961)

Shirley in rehearsal before a season at the *Talk Of The Town*. (26 September 1962)

Shirley smoking at the Mayfair Hotel, following the unfortunate incident of Kenneth and the chauffeur. (23 November 1962)

A reunited Shirley and Kenneth en route to Beirut, Kenneth bearing reassuring reading matter. (6 May 1964)

Shirley gets married. With Kenneth Hume immediately after their wedding at Paddington Register Office. (8 June 1961)

Shirley and friends at a London nightclub. Next to her is Reggie Kray. Next to Reggie is Ed Pucci, a former American football star and bodyguard to Frank Sinatra. (circa 1965)

Shirley in Milan, living *la dolce vita*.

Over the next week there were more photos, many more photos. Six months earlier *Picture Post* had taken photos of Shirley at her mother's house and she'd looked like a contestant in a talent show, an ordinary girl distinguishable from her sisters only by the fierceness of the glint in her eyes. This time, as she posed with the kids of the Rainbow Club, or was snapped sitting on the dock of the bay, she looked like she'd dropped in from another world, a star come down momentarily to earth. No wonder she complained that her old friends didn't know what to make of her. 'It's hateful,' she told a local journalist, responding to accusations from former friends that she no longer had the time of day for them. 'Just because I can afford some things now that I couldn't before doesn't mean I'm big-headed.'

Shirley rarely looked happier than in the photos from this week, whether out on the streets, or on stage at the New Theatre, or, most of all perhaps, with her brother Henry and his new wife Mary, toasting their wedding. She was still a young woman with her roots in the place she came from, but her life was fast taking her away from those roots. Gradually her sense, both real and imagined, that people back home were jealous of her success and her money would alienate her from the town of her birth. Already she was starting to plan out her future. As soon as she had enough money she would buy a new house for her mother and sisters. Then she would sign the adoption papers that would formally hand Sharon over to her sister Iris. And after that she would be free of obligations and responsibilities, free to live the life of a star. And stars most certainly didn't live in Splott. So it was a celebration, then, this return home, but also an ending.

Back in London, after the tour of the provincial theatres, there was a gap before Shirley's run could start at the London

Hippodrome. Sullivan, keen as ever to have his protégée out there earning, booked her some dates on the Continent. She was to play Stockholm and Belgium, then a week in Monte Carlo which would double as a holiday. Shirley decided to take her roommate, Gloria, along to Monte Carlo, leaving poor Pepe behind in Bayswater.

Shirley loved Monte Carlo immediately. The contrast with 1950s Cardiff could hardly have been more pronounced (and must have struck her very hard indeed, as it's the place in which she seems set to live out her later years). The French Riviera in the late 1950s was as glamorous and sophisticated as glamorous and sophisticated could be. Regulars around the casinos and plages included the magnates Warner and Zanuck, Beaverbrook and Agnelli, as well as a slew of writers and artists from Picasso and Matisse to Chagall and Graham Greene, not to mention those great exemplars of nouveau riche post-war Britain, Lord and Lady Docker.

The real powers behind the scene in Monte Carlo were not the Ruritanian royal family, but the Greek shipping magnates Aristotle Onassis and Stavros Niarchos, both of whom lived there in fabulous chateaux and kept yet more fabulous yachts in the harbour. Onassis was also responsible for building the principality's leading night spot, the Sea Club, where Shirley was due to perform for a week.

First, though, she had to go through the notorious showbiz ordeal of performing at a Friday gala night at the Sporting Club in the Casino. This attracted one of the snootiest audiences on earth and, sure enough, Shirley Bassey, like Marlene Dietrich and countless others before her, failed to rouse them out of their moneyed stupor. Shirley didn't mind, though: she had already met a boy called Nicky, the son of another Greek ship-owner, and was happily letting him show her the sights. And while the Sporting Club may have been a drag, the Sea Club jet-setters loved her.

Then it was back to London to open at the Hippodrome, head-lining a variety bill. This was the first time she'd headlined a major London theatre in her own right, but by now such milestones were becoming routine. The loyal Jack Thomas was there to report on her first night. And he didn't let his mate Mike Sullivan down.

'I've just been through one of the most exciting theatrical experiences of my life – the West End variety debut of a great international star – and she's Welsh,' he trumpeted, before going on to hymn 'the magic of those fabulous hands, that vibrant sex-throbbing voice.'[4]

Backstage Shirley, settling into her role as an international cabaret star, told the smitten Mr Thomas about her Monte Carlo experience: 'My first night audience included Mr Onassis and Greta Garbo. Garbo was wearing slacks so she had to sit in the gallery. On the last night Prince Rainier and Princess Grace took in the show. Afterwards I saw the Prince tap Grace's arm and point at me like I was a celebrity or something.'

Also backstage were assorted greetings and flowers from well-wishers, including twenty-one telegrams – 'my lucky number because I'm not twenty-one for five months' – one of them signed, enigmatically, 'Pound of Sugar'. Shirley wouldn't tell Jack Thomas who this was but Mike Sullivan later revealed it was the shipping heir, and 'Pound of Sugar' was 'a phrase Shirley used as a child as the answer to How much do you love me?'

As it happened that was the last Shirley heard from her Greek boyfriend, but she was hardly starved for male companionship in London. She was still living with Pepe's family, and her behaviour, going out on dates with one man after another, was torturing the devoted Pepe.

Her increasingly imperious demeanour wasn't endearing her to Mike Sullivan either. As far as he was concerned there was still plenty of work to do. The Hippodrome show was a success, but something less than a triumph, and had attracted the first bad reviews of her career, suggesting that the ingénue was not quite a West End headlining act just yet. Her last single, 'I Wish I Had a Needle and Thread', had flopped and her new single, another calypso-style affair called 'Fire Down Below', was only just crawling into the lower regions of the charts. Shirley seemed to take every new step up the showbusiness ladder as nothing more than her due, while the stress of continually trying to maintain this forward momentum was starting to tell on Sullivan:

> As the show neared its end I managed to catch pleural pneumonia, but talked my doctor out of sending me into hospital and carried on working from my bed at the Mapleton Hotel. Being sick was not helped by the fact that Shirley had started behaving in a very demanding manner. She was twenty years old, she was reading the posters I had written which said she was a fabulous star and she was living the part in the way she saw it. Getting her to rehearse a new song was like leading a reluctant schoolgirl to her lessons. She was temperamental with the theatre musical directors and one day she cost Philips Records a lot of money by going to her hairdressers instead of keeping a recording date and leaving forty musicians cooling their heels in the studio.[5]

Shirley's fondness for the nightlife was also starting to get her into the gossip columns. For example, after a night out at the 21 Room in Soho, she was involved in an altercation with the owner,

Bertie Meadows, over the bill, culminating in Shirley giving Meadows a slap. As she explained to Sullivan afterwards:

> I went to the club with my friend Verne O'Hara and Mr Keith Hamilton. Nobody was high. I only drank red wine. My girlfriend (O'Hara) was drinking ginger beer and Mr Hamilton had three gin and tonics. The bill came to eight guineas, including three pounds ten for eggs and bacon. I come from a family who live on eight pounds a week. I had a little argument with Mr Meadows. He yelled all over the room like a baby whose mother has taken his toys away. His head just happened to be where my hand went.[6]

Sullivan booked Shirley some more provincial variety dates after the London run finished in August, but his health didn't recover and he was diagnosed with tuberculosis. Shortly after this piece of bad news he received an offer of work for Shirley in Australia. Attracted both by the prospect of recuperating in the southern hemisphere summer, rather than facing the British winter, and by the chance to get Shirley away from the Soho nightclub habitués who, to a man, seemed to be scheming to take her away from her manager, Sullivan accepted. They would fly out in November. Meanwhile Sullivan would recuperate in bed and Shirley would perform at the Bagatelle Club in Mayfair.

Shirley was still living with the Davis family, still apparently oblivious to the effect this was having on young Pepe. By his own account, the months since she'd been back from the US had been very difficult for him:

> I had been invalided out of the RAF as result of the car accident, and I was working again for my father. I was overjoyed to hold Shirley in my arms again. But I had yet to learn that though she

still purred, she had learned to bare her claws. She became more nervy still, living in hotels. So, with my parents' consent, Shirley came to stay at our luxury flat. She shared a bedroom with my 21-year-old sister Gloria and life was very happy. Mother always got in the specials, as she called them, for Shirley. Special butter, best olives, smoked salmon. And I used to cook her omelettes and spaghetti dishes. My mother even looked after her shoe repairs and clothes cleaning. Shirley always came to kiss me goodnight.[7]

Things had deteriorated that summer when Shirley went off to Monte Carlo and Pepe's condition got worse:

Then in July I became very ill from the effects of the car accident. I started to get blackouts and had to go to hospital. Only my mother can reveal the full story of Shirley's deathbed promises to me of love and marriage. All I know is that when I got better Shirley seemed to grow distant. Shirley and my sister went to the South of France for a holiday. My mother has since told me that what she had heard about that holiday made her worried.

Pepe, an increasingly sorry figure, a damaged and undignified loser in love, resorted to taking an overdose of sleeping tablets. He survived, but still Shirley stayed on in the flat. Even Pepe was starting to doubt her motives now:

Perhaps it was out of kindness to me that she stayed on in our flat. But it is a very luxurious flat. And she had our Bentley car at her disposal. A maid to attend to her every want. And I still adored and worshipped her. When Shirley was afflicted with spots on her face I used to kiss the spots every night and rub cream on to make them better.

Things came to a head when Shirley brought round her latest boyfriend, a South African 'stage cartoonist' called Peter Quinton (or sometimes Peter Quinton Honey), a slick piece of work in his mid thirties, with a cad's moustache. Pepe could no longer delude himself as to what was going on:

> She told me he was a photographer. That night when she came to my room to kiss me goodnight I asked her if she still loved me. She said 'Yes, but as a brother.' My fears turned to suspicion that Peter Quinton Honey, a married man living apart from his wife, was becoming her new boyfriend.

His suspicions were soon confirmed when, a few days later:

> Honey phoned her at 11.45 p.m. Shirley spoke a few words and hurried out. She did not return till 3.30 a.m. I was waiting in the lounge. She went into her bedroom and a few minutes later came out wearing a flimsy green negligee. She said 'Pour me a drink of Drambuie.' Then she swung round: 'You're jealous, aren't you, Pepe. I like him better than you. But I'll never forget the wonderful times we had together.' I flung a heavy ashtray at the wall. She smashed her glass on the floor. Next day, my mother asked her to leave.

Shirley wasn't too bothered. She was off to Australia in less than a week. She packed her clothes, helped by Peter Quinton, and took a room not far away in the Cumberland Hotel, close to Marble Arch. Pepe was at the end of his tether:

> The three days that followed were a nightmare. I realised how desperately in love I was. I phoned Shirley at the Cumberland and said I wanted to bring her some flowers. But she told me to give them away and she put the phone down.

The day before Shirley was due to fly out to Australia was a Sunday, 10 November 1957. She had a last-minute dress fitting scheduled for that evening at her hotel. While she waited, she went to the cinema with Peter Quinton. Meanwhile Pepe decided this was his last chance to win Shirley back:

> Then began the hours when my love turned to frenzy. I went to a drawer in my bedroom. From it I got an old revolver. It had been given to me by a man I met as security for a £1 loan. Then I took a taxi to the Cumberland Hotel.

Let Shirley pick up the story of what happened next from an interview she gave to the *Daily Sketch* the following morning:

> They call me the Tigress of Tiger Bay – why, I don't really know because just now I feel like a small, very frightened girl. I am trembling from head to foot after the two most terrifying hours of my life.
>
> From 12.45 a.m. till 2.45 a.m. today I was locked in my hotel bedroom at the mercy of a love-crazed man with a gun. What girl would not feel scared after that – even somebody like myself from the tough sort of place that Tiger Bay is supposed to be? Over and over again, the man threatened to kill me.
>
> It began when my friend Peter Quinton, South African stage cartoonist, brought me back after seeing *The Bridge on the River Kwai*. I was in the bathroom when a shot rang out. I ran into the bedroom and found Peter struggling with a young man. I recognised the visitor at once. He was a man with whom I became friendly last Easter when we were both feeling lonely. I have since stayed at his parents' flat in Bayswater. He wanted me to marry him but there was no romance as far as I was concerned.

174

He was gripping a revolver in one hand and Peter was bleeding from a nasty knock on the head. The young man pressed the revolver against my stomach and warned Peter that he would shoot me . . . Peter dashed out of the room for help. The man locked the door and piled chairs and other pieces of furniture against it to form a barricade. At gunpoint, he forced me to play two records for him on my radiogram. One was Frank Sinatra's 'Swing Easy'. He made me play them over and over again. He also forced me to keep lighting cigarettes for him. Every few minutes he helped himself to a drink from a bottle of Drambuie. I was too frightened to cry. I thought that in his state he would really murder me if I broke down. All the time I kept pleading with him to be sensible and go. Suddenly he forced me on the sofa. I think he wanted to kiss me. He kept saying he loved me. When I tried to shout to the police he said he would kill me. He said he knew that I had been with Peter that night and if he couldn't have me, neither would Peter.

He made me telephone his mother. He snatched the receiver from my hand and told his mother that he had shot and wounded Peter. He said he was going to shoot me and himself. His mother apparently said something which infuriated him. He put the gun against the receiver and fired a shot into it. It was blown to pieces. It seemed an eternity before the police forced their way in and overpowered him.

The man was in a car accident. He was seriously ill with a brain injury and doctors thought he was going to die. I spent night after night at his bedside. Once I told him I was going to marry him, and that might have something to do with what happened. Before the accident he was a sweet and charming person. But he changed afterwards.[8]

The story made headlines across the next day's press. Gradually more details emerged. It turned out Peter Quinton had not been shot, but hit over the head with the revolver. The only person who had actually taken a bullet was Pepe himself. He'd managed to shoot himself in the leg just as he was being arrested. This explained why he was limping as the police bundled him out of the hotel. In true 1950s fashion, however, the newspaper photos show Pepe managing to light up yet another cigarette as he was taken to hospital under armed escort.

While Pepe was having the bullet removed from his leg, Shirley was at the airport, giving interviews to the press and being photographed having a last kiss with Peter Quinton before embarking on the 36-hour journey to Sydney.

While she was in the air reporters talked to her mother back in Cardiff. Eliza Jane, unsurprisingly, failed to mention the remarkable coincidence that she herself had been involved in a shooting incident just a couple of years earlier. Instead she simply reported that Pepe 'was a very nice boy and I visited his people at their home in London. She doesn't love him enough to marry him and, anyway, I don't think she wants to marry at all yet, because a career in show business and marriage don't mix.'[9]

At the same time, in what has become a time-honoured tradition, the *Daily Mail* let loose its star female columnist, Eve Perrick, to run a piece disparaging Shirley as a silly little girl from Splott, out of her depth in the big city. In these pre-Twitter days the general public were unable to run to Shirley's rescue, but, in a sign of just what an impression Shirley had made on Fleet Street's male columnists, there were answering pieces written by the likes of Alan Bestic in the *People* ('This Girl Has Guts!') and Gareth Bowen in the *South Wales Echo* ('Be sorry for Shirley: She's really not so sophisticated').

By this time Shirley was in Australia. She was exhausted when she arrived and gave Sullivan, who had come out in advance, hell for putting her through the whole journey in economy class. She calmed down a little when Mike introduced her to the man who'd booked her to appear in Sydney, Bruce Gordon, the general manager of the Tivoli Theatres. ('He was tall, he was handsome and he soon impressed Shirley.') Then she told Sullivan what had happened back in London, a rather more lurid version than that she had told the newspapers, involving Pepe forcing her to strip naked, and looking as if he intended to rape her, before finally coming to his senses and letting her go.

*   *   *

Australia was the perfect environment for both star and manager to recuperate. Shirley began a romance with Bruce Gordon: there was even, for a while, some talk of marriage (which might have worked out well for Shirley as Gordon, these days, is a reclusive billionaire Australian TV magnate based in Bermuda).They spent Christmas and new year in Sydney. This was Shirley's first Christmas away from her family and Sullivan went the extra mile by getting his girlfriend Lily Berde* to dress up as Santa Claus and put a stocking full of presents at the end of a homesick Shirley's hotel bed.

A week into the new year Shirley turned twenty-one. This was the legal age of majority and was to have serious consequences

---

* Lily Berde was also appearing as a supporting attraction to Shirley. The Tivoli programme described her as 'the girl who has danced her way around the world' and announced that she would be performing 'her sensational marijuana dance: a study in rhythm and movement of a drug addict's emotions and sufferings. This dance has been banned from television in America, Britain and even France and has won her the title of The Sexiest Girl In The World.'

for the business relationship between Shirley and her manager. The two of them had, however, been planning for it. For instance, as soon as Shirley returned to Britain, she would sign the papers to buy a new house for Eliza Jane and her sisters.

A fortnight after her birthday, on Friday, 24 January 1958, the Australian idyll was rudely interrupted. Just as she was about to go on stage for a matinee, performance Shirley received a call from the *Daily Sketch*. They wanted to let her know that they had found out about her daughter, Sharon. They had Sharon's birth certificate and they were going to run the story on Monday morning. Did Shirley have anything to say?

No, she did not. She was devastated. Mike Sullivan had always told her that Sharon's existence had to be kept secret. Now the secret was out. She was concerned that her career would never survive this. Not in 1958. Not in an era when 'unmarried mothers' were pariahs expected to live in punitive 'mother and baby homes' until they gave their babies over to be adopted. She knew what the newspaper readers would say. How keen they would be to be given the chance to say what they really thought of people who looked and acted like her. Coloured girls, girls from Tiger Bay, working-class girls who didn't know their place, girls from families who had never lived by the rules, girls who didn't live by the rules themselves, girls who acted like they were happy in their skin and their sexuality. She was sure she was about to be hated, hated simply for what and who she was, and she couldn't bear it.

Before she had time to formulate any kind of plan, Shirley had to go on stage. For once she was unable to leave her troubles behind as she started to perform. Instead she broke down in tears and had to leave the stage midway through her act. Mike Sullivan was called and arrived at the Tivoli to find his star in hysterics. Shirley explained what had happened and Sullivan immediately realised the gravity of the situation. He had two days to head off a potential disaster.

FIFTEEN

Cruel To Be Kind

Mike Sullivan was always good in a crisis. He called his newspaper contacts in the UK and found out the background to the call from the *Daily Sketch*. It was all to do with the Pepe Davis shooting case, which was about to come to trial. Pepe's mother had been telling every reporter she could get hold of that her Pepe had been driven to violence by Shirley's terrible behaviour. In particular she claimed that Shirley 'had got rid of four different babies by four different men'. There was no evidence to support this outlandish claim, but once the reporters started to dig they soon discovered the kernel of truth in the allegation: Shirley had had a baby and she had 'got rid of it' inasmuch as she'd passed Sharon to her sister Iris to be cared for.

Sullivan took all this in and came up with a damage limitation strategy. The *Daily Sketch* were due to run the piece on Monday and would most likely present it with a hostile slant. There was no denying the truth of the story, so the only option was for Shirley to appear to come clean of her own accord before the *Daily Sketch* story could run. He selected a friendly journalist, the *People's* Arthur Heliwell, and arranged for Shirley to call him straight away so he could run an exclusive in his Sunday column and take the wind out of the *Daily Sketch's* sails.

In fact the story made the front page of the *People*. The head-line ran 'Shirley Cries "I Did Have a Baby"'. Underneath it Shirley was allowed to make her case.

'I want the world to know the truth about my baby. Yes I did have a child three years ago and I vowed then that I would never reveal my secret. But now I must tell the facts. I want you to print them. People have been saying dreadful things about me,' she sobbed. 'They have said that I got rid of four babies. They are suggesting that I was wild and irresponsible and went with all sorts of fellows. It's all untrue. I had one unfortunate romance in my life and I've been paying the penalty ever since. It happened when I was seventeen and touring with a show called *Memories of Jolson*. I met a boy and we thought we were in love. A few months later I realised I was going to have a baby. The boy wanted me to get rid of it and, when I refused, he vanished and I have never seen or heard from him since. I carried on in the show as long as I could. I wasn't earning much money, but I managed to save a few pounds every week for my baby. Then I had to give up. I couldn't carry on any longer and I went away to have my baby. She is a lovely little girl I named Sharon. I thought then that my career was finished, that all my dreams of becoming a big star were over. And so they would have been if I hadn't met my manager Michael Sullivan.

I gave little Sharon to my married sister to look after and I went back to work. It broke my heart having to leave her but, whenever I could, I went back to Cardiff to see her. Sharon is three years old and she calls me Auntie Shirley. She must never know the real truth that I am her mother. I made up my mind about this just before I left on tour last November. Before I went I arranged to have little Sharon legally adopted. After all, as a star earning big money, I can do so much more for my little girl than if I had stayed in Cardiff and worked in a factory or as a waitress. I have already bought a £3,500 house and it is in her name. Every week I set aside a certain sum from my earnings for her.'

Sobbing even more bitterly Shirley went on: 'Why do they call me a bad girl? Why do they want me to suffer for one little mistake I made when I was so young?'[1]

The strategy worked, and not just in Britain, where Shirley had plenty of friendly journalists willing to fight her corner, but also in Australia, a very conservative place at the time. An exclusive in the local press ran with the headline 'Give the Girl a Break' and the audiences for her live shows that week were overwhelmingly on her side.

Meanwhile, in London, Pepe went to trial. His father repeated the allegations against Shirley and echoed his son's obsession with the desirability of their apartment ('for a few months she seemed at home among my £8,000 collection of Queen Anne furniture' is a particularly winning line of his). Pepe himself just wanted to take his medicine, as he told the police on his arrest: 'I could have shot Shirley if I'd wanted to. But why should I? I love her. I just went mad at the time and now I want to suffer.'

The judge decided to let him suffer to the tune of three years in prison for 'unlawfully and maliciously shooting at a police officer with intent to resist arrest' and 'having in his possession a pistol with intent to endanger life.'

Following this news from London, Shirley was emboldened to write her own piece for the next Sunday's edition of the *People*. This time, rather than carry on apologising, she stands up for herself with remarkable courage for the times. The piece is headlined 'I'm Human and I'm Not Ashamed' and the central passage runs like this:

I am a coloured girl. I come from one of the world's tough corners – Tiger Bay in Cardiff. But because I have fought my way up to the top as a singer, because I sing songs about sex that shock a good many women, I am nevertheless still a human being.

Yes, I stand up in nightclubs and sing 'Who's going to help me burn my candle at both ends?' Yes, I throw all I've got into the job of singing my way to big money. But if a girl plays Lady Macbeth does it follow that she's a mass murderess? Because Peter Cheyney wrote some fine thrillers, was he a master criminal? With me it's the old, old story. When you're famous, the mud sticks. And those who hate me, and the sort of world in which I make my money, turn around and whisper: 'Of course it's all true about that Bassey girl – four babies and she got rid of them all.'

They never look into their own narrow, smug little lives. They never pause to think that having an illegitimate baby is a pain and a shame for any girl – even if she does sing sexy songs for a living. There's no halo around my head – I have known the temptations of being human and all the heartache that goes with it.[2]

She follows that up with a forthright defence of her particular art form:

Singing even songs like mine is a form of self-expression. Whatever some people may think, I am acting a part when those burning, and to me beautiful, rhythms take possession of me. When I get out there under the lights and get wrapped up in that softly, fiercely seductive beat of music, something happens to me. The words come out with a throb and a quiver. A feeling springs from deep down inside my body and makes everything glow and burn. So unless you've ever felt like that about something that expresses *you* – dancing, poetry, music, painting – don't sit back in judgement on me. Because that emotion is life to me.

As for the accusations made at the trial:

> Terence Davis, a man who genuinely loved me, has gone to gaol all because, as the judge put it, 'you don't go courting with revolvers'. Terence – Pepe to me – it was said, was crazed with jealousy because of the things his mother said about me. When I read the things that were said about me at Pepe's trial I sobbed for shame. It seemed that nobody could be as vile as the wicked, flaunting, two-timing little hussy they talked about. When I met Pepe we were both very lonely. He pleaded with me to marry him on countless occasions. I turned him down repeatedly – but gently. Finally, after an accident in which he was involved, I said 'Yes'. That seemed to help him recover. But I never really loved him. To that extent – to the extent that I said 'Yes' without really loving – I may have erred. But he pestered me and I did like Pepe. Because I turned him down I have been made to sound a vamp.
>
> Isn't it much more terrible for a girl to marry a man she can never *really* love? And isn't it better to find out in time? I have sobbed about the Pepe I knew. I know what goes on inside a man or a woman who is possessed by that demon called love. All I can say is – *I tried to be kind.*

The following week Pepe went public with his side of the story, as detailed earlier, and this thoroughly incensed Shirley, particularly the fact that the article was illustrated by photos of the love letters she'd sent Pepe. So she returned to the charge, in rather less forgiving mode, the following Sunday:*

* Just to give a sense of the world in which these events were happening, here's a selection of the artefacts on offer in the small ads that appeared below Shirley's article: a Tommy Steele-style guitar, corsets for both men and women, a telescopic sight for a Winchester rifle, a record cabinet, a 'James Dean hip jacket' and, worryingly, a two-for-one offer on 'brand new ex-Wren officers' panties'.

I have never regarded myself as an old-fashioned girl, but now I think I must be. Because, you see, I can't help feeling that love letters are private things . . . And what makes it all the more galling is that I only wrote some of them to be kind. But now I realise with Pepe I should have been cruel to be kind . . .[3]

And as for her personal morality:

Why shouldn't a girl look around a bit before she makes her final choice? What a world it would be if everyone married the first person for whom they felt an infatuation or an attraction! Many women have misunderstood me, envious bitter women who have written to me. I am convinced a lot of the gossip so-called 'good' women spread about me is sheer envy. I know that a lot of them would just love to take my place.

*　　*　　*

With all that was happening back in the UK, Mike Sullivan and Shirley were in no hurry to get home. They stayed in Australia for another month or so, attended a garden party with the Queen Mother, and then decided to break their journey home with a stopover in Honolulu. By the time they got there Shirley, too, was in poor health, suffering from a grumbling appendix. Their respective ailments may have contributed to a flaming row that took place when they were due to leave Hawaii. Shirley had overspent her allowance and Sullivan refused to pay her hotel bill, leaving her to be arrested at the airport for non-payment. Shirley eventually managed to get hold of her bank in London and placate the hotel, but, sick and angry, she left Sullivan a note saying, 'I hope you're feeling happy with what you've done. May God forgive you, because I never will.'

On return to London Sullivan did try to make amends. He organised delivery of the Jaguar Shirley craved and, when her stomach pains got worse, persuaded his accountant Leonard Beresford Clarke and his dancer wife Sylvia to look after Shirley at their house till she recovered.

Next Sullivan went to Leslie Grade to organise another variety tour. Grade was concerned that Shirley had been away too long, her recent singles hadn't done too well and the illegitimate baby story might have hurt her popularity. Sullivan promised to whip up some press interest to help sell tickets for the shows. To this end, he came up with the one really stupid idea of his career as Shirley's manager. He decided that Shirley should pretend to vanish in the week before her first variety date at the Chiswick Empire on 28 May. Shirley wasn't convinced, but agreed to go to Bath for a few days, chaperoned by an old friend of Sullivan's. Back in London, Sullivan waited for two days then went to the police to say that Shirley had gone missing. The police weren't particularly bothered, but Sullivan persuaded his friends at the *People* to run with the story, and that Sunday the front page splash was 'Shirley Bassey Vanishes' with Sullivan quoted as saying that it didn't look like she would be appearing in Chiswick and that she was frightened of singing in front of British audiences again after all the newspaper revelations.

The next day the *Daily Sketch* rubbished the story, having tracked Shirley down to Bath, and, sure enough, later on the Monday she appeared as expected at the Chiswick Empire. Still her troubles weren't over. The following day the *Daily Mail* reported that Bassey had been 'pelted with eggs and tomatoes' by three men sitting in the gallery. They were chased away by the assistant manager but then another man in the crowd started shouting abuse as Shirley sang 'My Body's More Important Than My Mind'.

It seemed that Mike Sullivan's attempts to capitalise on Shirley's misfortunes were simply making matters worse. Add in the relative failure of her latest recording, 'Puh-Leeze! Mister Brown', and for the first time in their three-year association the Bassey–Sullivan team were confronted by an undeniable dip in their fortunes.

Shirley's health hadn't really recovered either. The following week, when she was due to be performing in Birmingham, she collapsed and was diagnosed with peritonitis. She spent a week in a nursing home in Birmingham and called a friendly journalist to complain that Mike Sullivan hadn't been anywhere near her. Her only visitors had been the singer Maxine Daniels* and, oddly enough, the man she'd upstaged a year or so before, Al Read.

After that, the variety tour carried on successfully enough as far as audience numbers went, but with further regular interruptions for ill health. On 25 July, for instance, she had to abandon a show at the Finsbury Park Empire because of laryngitis. By now even the old-school Sullivan was having to accept that live work alone was not enough: Shirley needed to be on TV, and she needed another hit record.

The TV break came first. The week after the Finsbury Park booking, ITV was screening a charity gala show called *Night of a Hundred Stars*, nominally organised by Laurence Olivier. Shirley, however, had not been invited to appear. Mike Sullivan came up with a cynical strategy to change this state of affairs – a strategy inspired by a rash of recent news stories.

---

* A fine jazz singer and sister to the comedian and singer Kenny Lynch.

The summer of 1958 was the point at which Britain's initial limited enthusiasm for its new wave of post-war immigration started to turn sour. Later that summer there would be race riots in Nottingham and Notting Hill, but already the signs of unrest were there. In the same issue of the *People* that had announced Shirley's alleged disappearance, there was a full-page story headlined 'For Their Own Sakes – Stop Them Now: The coloured invasion has gone too far'. It's an unsavoury piece in which the paper, while claiming 'to fight as strongly as ever against all forms of discrimination, whether of race, creed or colour', argues that because the economy was in a downturn, all 'coloured immigration' should be stopped and any coloured immigrant who was already in the country but didn't have a job 'should gently, but firmly, be made to go'.[4]

Liberal folk, as one might hope, were outraged by this kind of talk, and were eager to show their opposition to this kind of blatant racism. Mike Sullivan decided to give them the opportunity:

> I dialled the number of the organiser and said, 'I notice that Miss Shirley Bassey has not been invited to appear on your show even though she is prepared to give her services. Am I to assume there is some colour prejudice?'
>
> 'No, of course there's not,' the organiser assured me. 'I'll phone you back.'
>
> This was pure blackmail on my part. I was gambling on my infamous reputation of rushing to the newspapers with any story that I thought would raise some dust and I knew that no reputable body would like to be tainted with the cry of 'colour bar'. Ten minutes later my telephone rang and Shirley was on the show.[5]

Indeed she was. The news that she was to be part of *Night of a Hundred Stars* helped to speed her recovery from laryngitis, and, as ever when confronted by a challenge, Shirley rose to the occasion. She performed the standard 'Birth of the Blues', from her new album of blues songs, accompanied by Eddie Calvert, 'the man with the golden trumpet'. She was a hit, the show drew a huge audience, and her career was once more on the up.

What she was desperately in need of, however, was some more new material that hadn't already been sung by Frank Sinatra, Sammy Davis, Jr., Bing Crosby et al. The first new song Johnny Franz came up with for her to record was an American ballad called 'Hands Across The Sea', a rather uninspiring rewrite of 'You'll Never Walk Alone'. Franz wanted to pair it with an uptempo number, but Shirley fought for another ballad – one her long-time pianist Les Paul, who also worked as a music publisher, had played her. It was a song called 'As I Love You'. Count Basie had recorded it four years earlier without much success, but Shirley saw something in it for her, and she was right.

It wasn't a typical American show ballad. There was a light-operatic, European tinge to the melody that turned out to suit Shirley perfectly. Up to this point her uptempo numbers had had far more character than her ballads, which still tended to sound like imitation Lena Horne or Judy Garland. With 'As I Love You' she sounded like no one but herself.

Franz was a smart enough producer to go against convention, and he agreed to put this second ballad on the B-side* of 'Hands Across The Sea'. Wrapped in a particularly effective Wally Stott string arrangement, this was an obvious step forward for Shirley. Whether it would be a hit, of course, was another matter. The *NME*

---

* In later years, putting a song on the B-side of a single would be tantamount to burying it. In the 1950s and early 1960s, though, it was commonplace for reviewers and disc jockeys to play both sides of a single, and there were plenty of occasions when both sides of a single became hits in their own right.

reported that 'it may not be hit parade material but Shirley Bassey's next disc is her best ever.'[6]

And indeed, on initial release, 'As I Love You' failed to perform any better than Shirley's last few singles. Johnny Franz immediately decided that the next release needed to be another fun uptempo number. He came up with a song called 'Kiss Me Honey, Honey, Kiss Me'. This was written by a Trinidadian sax player and singer called Al Timothy.

Timothy had been in Britain since 1948. He started out in the new country backing the great calypsonian Lord Kitchener in a Brixton pub. He moved on to writing his own calypsos. These included 'Gerrard Street', a satire on the British jazz scene and a reminder of what a melting pot the London music scene of the early 1950s was, and the risqué 'Don't Touch My Nylon' which was recorded, improbably, by Louis Farrakhan under his stage name 'The Charmer'. Timothy became friendly with the great jazz patron, Baroness Nica de Koenigswater, and was the resident bandleader at her London jazz club, Studio 51. Another regular gig was with the great West Indian trumpeter Shake Keane, at Mayfair's Celebrity restaurant. This may be where his path crossed with the Shirley Bassey crowd. One thing was for sure: the song he had for her fitted perfectly – Caribbean-inflected but distinctly British, saucy but seaside-postcard saucy, not Bessie Smith saucy.

She recorded the song along with a similarly bouncy, almost rock and roll B-side called 'There'll Never Be A Night'. Johnny Franz had clearly decided that, since her recent ballads had failed to hit, maybe the great British public would show more enthusiasm for an uptempo Shirley. But even if the record buyers were proving somewhat resistant to Shirley's charms, TV producers were definitely starting to show some enthusiasm. First she was booked to appear regularly on a new late-night sketch show called *After Hours*, helmed by *The Goon Show*'s Michael Bentine and directed by Richard Lester.* Then came a bigger break. ITV had a variety show called *Sunday Night at the London Palladium,* and with a new host, a young comedian called Bruce Forsyth, it was becoming a huge success.

On the last Sunday in November one of the performers who'd originally been booked had to drop out and, not for the first time in her career, Shirley Bassey stepped in and managed to steal the show. She sang 'As I Love You', even though it was ostensibly only the B-side of her single before last. The next week it started to move up the charts. So too, in its wake, did her new single, the perfectly contrasting 'Kiss Me Honey, Honey, Kiss Me'.

As 1958 turned into 1959 the two records took up residence at the top of the hit parade. Both spent four months in all in the charts, 'As I Love You' reaching number one, toppling Elvis from the summit, and 'Kiss Me' number three. Shirley Bassey became the first woman to have two records in the top five at the same time, the first Welshwoman to have a number one hit. Shirley was now an unquestionable star, not just on the cabaret or on the variety circuit, but in the living rooms and on the record players of Britain.

Interviewed in the first flush of this new success, Shirley was very clear what it meant to her:

> I'll never tour in variety again. All that traipsing around. All those lousy provincial orchestras. They hate me when I complain about their playing, but what else can I do? They're a horrible bunch. You

---

* All footage sadly lost. Intriguingly Shirley's co-stars on the 2 November show included Stirling Moss and a flea circus.

know what, I've collected my music at the end of a week's run and found Big-Head written all over it.

Shirley Bassey was not going to take any disrespectful treatment from anyone any more. She was a star now, and she was going to make some changes. Starting with her manager.

SIXTEEN

Shirley the Weirdie

Shirley's row with Mike Sullivan in Hawaii, and her subsequent sense that he'd abandoned her when she was seriously ill with peritonitis, clearly made a deep impression on her. Even though he'd helped her career pick up in the latter half of the year, and though she was still under contract to him, she started to manage her own day-to-day affairs, determined to establish her independence.

The first thing she did was to rent a flat of her own. This was in Dolphin Square, a massive upmarket apartment complex built in the 1930s. Its Pimlico location, close to Westminster, made it a favourite for politicians, but there were plenty of show people living there too. It had its own swimming pool, brasserie and gymnasium and was an eminently sensible, safe, if rather impersonal, location for a single young woman to live.

Her only companion in this new abode was a white poodle called Beaujolais who had been given to her by the Beresford Clarkes that summer and to whom she had become completely devoted, as is clear in an exceptionally revealing interview she gave to the *Daily Mail* in November 1958, in the wake of her series of high-profile TV performances.

The interviewer was not another showbiz hack but a man called Robert Muller, a German Jew, who'd arrived in the UK in 1938, aged thirteen. He had been entertainment editor of *Picture Post* before becoming the theatre critic of the *Daily Mail*. Later he would move into writing TV dramas himself, including a damning account of the exploitation of a starlet, *Afternoon Of A Nymph*. It's not hard to imagine that some of the inspiration for the play may have come from this encounter with a clearly troubled young Shirley.

From the beginning it's obvious that independence is something she's new to. Without a manager or assistant to look after her, she has very little idea as to how you're supposed to behave:

> 'Do you mind if I have a bath?' Miss Shirley Bassey, the girl from the slums of Cardiff who set quite a few TV screens aflame again last night, inhabits an expensively empty flat in Dolphin Square, bare of individuality except for an emotionally demanding poodle called Beaujolais and a tortuously autographed still of Liberace.
>
> From the bathroom Miss Bassey explains that she feels at home here: she really does. She has no wish to go back to Cardiff. She is waiting for a theatre to become available so that she can get in with a production called *The Shirley Bassey Show* or something.
>
> After the bath the first impression of endearing naiveté persists. On stage Miss Bassey may explode twice nightly in a shimmer of talent and sensuality, but out of the spotlight she is rather plain, uncertain and awed, see-sawing between childish boast and dismal self-apology.[1]

This seems like a pretty accurate assessment. The twenty-one-year-old Shirley starts out sounding like any recent lottery winner or talent show contestant:

> 'I'd rather be alone here than with the wrong sort of company,' she explains airily in an accent that has been neutralised out of existence.

'I'd rather sit here looking at house magazines: you know, magazines about houses. I've gone house magazine mad. I'm going to build myself an American-style ranch house. I don't know where. Outside Surrey. With all mod cons.'

And then she lurches into a revealing account of her emotional state, a girl barely out of her teens and suddenly scared that she's out of her depth:

I'll have a maid because I'd be terrified to be alone. I pretend to be brave but I'm not. I'll have the record player going like mad. I always sleep with the lights on, always have. I don't know what I'm afraid of, but I'm afraid of something.

That's why I like to get to the top of the ladder and be a star. I like to sing at nice places, nice nightclubs. I like money. I like to buy nice things. It makes me feel I've achieved something. Know what I mean? I'm going up and how high can you go? No one knows.

It's only when the conversation turns to her music that her confidence returns:

What have I different from other girls? I don't just sing a song, I've learned to *sell* a song. I sing with feeling. Like you sing about love. I know about love. I have experienced heartaches and fear and all those things help to make an entertainer.

I want to be as good as I can possibly be, you know. Everything must be right. Perfectionist. That's why you have to be ruthless when the occasion arises. But how can I be ruthless? If I were 25 I could be, but when you're only 21 you can't get away with it. People watch me rehearse and they say 'God she's tough.' They don't bother to find the real me.

Living on her own for the first time, it's clear that Shirley has had time to think about her life and the changes she's been through. She's had the time to be introspective and what she's had to confront is the loneliness of a life in the public eye. It's a subject that would become one of the central themes both of her life and her art:

> I want to get married some day, because I think marriage is good for an artist. The strain is too much. I need somebody to love. On stage they say I look unapproachable but off stage I seem to be very approachable. I attract all sorts of weirdies. I'm not big-headed and I come from nothing, but when you come from nothing and you work hard, you're entitled to have nice things and be with nice people. Only sometimes I get these terrible moods, sometimes I hate myself. I feel I've hurt somebody. Then I'd rather be alone and play Sinatra's saddest record and call myself all the silly sausages under the sun. I'm weird. I don't know what I want. Weird.

Could a man be the answer to her loneliness? At twenty-one she hopes so, but even here there's a note of uncertainty:

> I know the kind of man I want. I like older men, as old as 30 even. They're mature. My man has to be intelligent because I'm not intelligent. He has to love me madly and put me on a pedestal, because it's a wonderful thing to be loved. And he has to be tall and sort of rugged. He doesn't have to be rich. The trouble with rich people, they're such slobs. Millionaires are either fat or old, you know.

The interview ends on a note of real poignancy as Muller asks her about Sharon, the daughter she handed over to her sister.

'No, no I don't have a longing to see my little girl,' she says emphatically. 'I signed an adoption paper for my sister to have the girl. I couldn't give my daughter the love she needs.' Beaujolais has jumped on Miss Bassey's lap. 'I'm never in one place for long. I don't think it's right. I see her when I go home, but I'm not her mother any more.' Miss Bassey nurses the dog and strains its muzzle to her breast. 'I'm her aunt. I don't feel unhappy about that. I've accustomed myself to the idea. I'm her aunt. I've just got to be cruel to be kind. I'm her aunt. That's all there is to it.'

*　　*　　*

This was not the kind of interview that any star with a halfway competent manager would have been allowed to give. The fact that it took place at all was testament to the rift between Shirley and the man who'd made her a star. The full extent of the communication breakdown between Shirley and Mike Sullivan is clear from a piece in the *South Wales Echo* the following week. The *Echo*'s reporter has evidently been contacted by Bassey herself: she wants to know why she hasn't had an audition for a new British thriller called *Tiger Bay*, then being filmed in Cardiff.

'The producer and director came to the first night of my show,' she told the *Echo*. 'Afterwards there was talk of me playing the part of a nightclub singer in the film. It was understood that I would have to travel down to London for the test. I can only think they've given the part to someone else, but I wish they'd let me know.' She then goes on to add that she would love the challenge of making a film, as she's worried that her stage work is getting too easy and familiar: 'I feel myself that I am becoming too . . . mechanical,' she says.[2]

The *Echo*'s reporter duly called the director, J. Lee Thompson, who told him that Shirley's manager had already been informed that she had not got the part. He then elaborated, explaining that, 'the girl in *Tiger Bay* will stay a second-rate singer who does no more than sing in a pub. I am a personal fan of Miss Bassey. She is a wonderful artiste and it would be grossly unfair to ask her to take on this part. It would throw the film off balance.'

This would not be the last film-related disappointment for Shirley Bassey. Mike Sullivan had been talking about getting her into the movies from the time of their first trip to Hollywood, but the reality of the situation was that cinema was far more discriminatory than the music world and parts for black women were few and far between. It's revealing, in a depressing kind of way, that J. Lee Thompson tells the *Echo* that the American stars Dorothy Dandridge and Eartha Kitt had both asked after this bit part of the nightclub singer in a low-key British thriller.

Another sign of Shirley's new independence was the fact that she decided not to go back to Cardiff for Christmas. Instead she had a brief rapprochement with Mike Sullivan and went to his place for Christmas dinner. She brought along her new boyfriend, a man called Clive Sharp. Sullivan didn't think much of this at the time; Sharp was just another face about town, the co-owner of a Soho drinking club.

Two weeks later Shirley celebrated her twenty-second birthday in a joint celebration with a man called Maurice King, described in a newspaper gossip column as the part-owner of the Show Business club on Wardour Street. The other part-owner, none other than Clive Sharp, gave Shirley 'a magnificent cake'. Shirley told the gossip columnist that 'As a matter of fact Clive is my best friend at the moment.'

Two records in the Top Ten, a new boyfriend and a magnificent birthday cake. Life should have been tasting sweet to Shirley at the dawn of 1959. To cap it all, a West End theatre, the Prince of Wales, was now available, and the following month Shirley would be starring there in a new show. It was an adaptation of another Black-pool summer spectacular, *Folies Bergère*, that Mike Sullivan had seen and liked. Shirley could do a Josephine Baker routine and sing her hit songs. Her co-star would be a fellow Welsh person, the comic conjuror Tommy Cooper, and the show would be called *Blue Magic*.

Before the show, Mike Sullivan booked Shirley in to do some warm-up dates in Colchester, and she did another round of press interviews, still in a mood to bare her soul, even when talking to a frothy fan magazine like *Picturegoer*. Their interviewer Sarah Stoddart is struck by just how insecure Shirley is – 'she's one of the few stars I know who carries round her press cuttings – not to impress others, but to impress herself,' she notes, before Shirley elaborates:'Before a performance – especially if I'm feeling low – I reread those fabulous notices I had two years ago after my big suc-cess in cabaret and Al Read's show.'[3]

And, as for her appearance, talking to another woman, Shirley is franker than ever about her perceived shortcomings:

It's my face. I've got spots. They don't show under television make-up. But once on tour I went shopping barefaced – no war-paint at all. I heard a shop assistant say to another: 'Is that Shirley Bassey? Don't think much of her.' I wanted to curl into a hole. I felt a nobody. From then on I vowed I'd be loaded with glamour wherever I went.

And the rejection by the producers of *Tiger Bay* clearly still ran-kled, as she ends the interview with a defiant statement that 'I'm still determined on a film career. I just know that one day I could be a great actress.'

For the *TV Mirror*, she welcomed Godfrey Winn into her Dolphin Square flat, where he found her lying on the floor reading home-making magazines and taking notes, and she told him her three resolutions for the new year. Number one was 'I intend to choose my own friends instead of letting them choose me.' Number two was to buy a home of her own. Number three, poignantly, was 'to find myself, the real me, completely. And when I do, then I can live in my new home in peace, can't I?'[4]

Oddest of the round of interviews was a frankly bizarre piece written by the *Daily Sketch*'s star columnist, Angus Hall. Hall had been a long-time admirer of Shirley's; he'd given her Café de Paris show a rave review. This time, however, he interviewed Miss Bassey while wandering around the streets of her new stamping ground, Soho. Shirley was still finding fame difficult, but this time she was also sending herself up.

The piece rejoiced in the unlikely strapline 'Angus Hall tries hard to hate Shirley the Weirdie' and began with the observation that 'It was the combination of country-style tweed suit, vivid ginger hair and a tipple of brandy and honey – so good for the nerves – that marked Shirley Bassey as a weirdie.' Before long Shirley is warming to her preferred topic of the moment – her remarkable unlikeability:

> I'm too strange and weird to be likeable . . . I have two other great disadvantages. I'm unintelligent and I have spots on my face. These things just don't appeal to nice people. Men have been my downfall. Publicists who have smeared my name. Wolves who have treated me like dirt and a man in Australia who jilted me because I was too weird for him. When you're coloured, famous, rich and stupid, men are always taking you for sucker rides.[5]

Hall happily plays along with this and elicits Shirley's thoughts on her rivals in the world of pop music: 'Most pop singers have no polish,' she tells him. 'They either dress badly or lack sex appeal like most British singers – or they're ugly.' Bravely, Hall wonders which of these categories Shirley falls into:

> All three! I'm weird. There are days when I just hate, hate, hate the world and all the people in it. A psychiatrist I met in the States said I'd be a natural for him. But I want to stay weird.

And just to prove the point Shirley and Angus proceed to take to the streets of Soho and sing Ella Fitzgerald songs together, before heading off for more brandy and honey.

There's no mention of Clive Sharp in the piece but when, a week or so later, Shirley's by now distinctly hands-off manager, Mike Sullivan, went over to Colchester to see how the warm-up shows for the West End were going, he found that Sharp had his feet securely under the table:

> There were two men in her dressing room, two young West End faces who ran a drinking club in Soho – Clive Sharp and Maurice King. I wanted to speak to her privately but she said 'It's perfectly all right, anything you wish to say can be said in front of these gentlemen.' Clive Sharp and I had met before. To me he was just another boyfriend, but he saw himself playing a role in her business life as well as her romantic one. Clive Sharp was, softly and quietly, taking her away from me.[6]

Indeed he was. By this time Shirley had already mentioned that she was unhappy with Sullivan who was, in effect, both her manager and booking agent. Sharp had suggested contacting Peter

Charlesworth, a partner at the Jock Jacobsen Agency and one of the most successful agents in Britain at the time, with Shirley's friend Max Bygraves amongst his clients. A former record-plugger, Charlesworth had known Shirley for a while. Shirley liked the idea and, on her return to London, she had a showdown with Sullivan at her flat in Dolphin Square.

> She gave it to me absolutely straight. She thought I had been taking too much money from her and that a normal manager was entitled to only twenty per cent of her earnings. 'I'll go along with that,' I said. 'Twenty per cent will suit me fine, so long as I no longer have to pay out for agents' commissions, fares, new music, costumes, flowers, hire of jewellery, entertainment and all the other things I have been finding money for.' We agreed to tear up our old contracts and sign new ones . . .

The following day, however, it transpired that this wasn't enough.

> Shirley told me I was finished! She said that her two new advisers, Sharp and King, had told her that I had cheated her out of her share of the Colchester show, which incidentally made a loss. I said I would sue her. She said our original contract had been illegal all along. It did not matter what we said. The only important thing was: Bassey and Sullivan were washed up.[7]

So they were. Clive Sharp took over as her personal manager. He was a little older than Shirley, mid to late twenties according to Bernard Delfont's right-hand man Richard Mills, who used to host a regular poker game that often included Clive Sharp and Maurice King as well as Peter Charlesworth. 'Clive Sharp?' says Mills. 'Yes, he ran the New Showbiz Club, a tiny little room on Wardour Street, just up from the Prince of Wales Theatre. It was up some rickety stairs on the third floor, had a bar in it and a few chairs and that was about it. Clive and his partner Maurice King were looking after Shirley, they used to go off in a corner with their solicitor, Michael something, and have these private meetings.'

Maurice King had had some success booking clubs in the north of England and would later go on to manage the Walker Brothers. The Walkers' fan club president Chrissie McCall describes King as 'small, swarthy with black greasy-type hair. Well dressed. People were afraid of him. If he said "jump" people jumped.'[8] He came, in short, with a whiff of the underworld with which Soho was then associated: the gangsters, pimps and extortionists like Jack Spot, Billy Hill and the Messina brothers, whose exploits were prime fare for the Sunday newspapers, and who would soon be succeeded by other, more ruthless operators, like a pair of East End twins called the Krays.

John and Gary of the Walker Brothers confirm the link in their joint autobiography:

> Maurice had a club off Oxford Street where we would occasionally practise in the daytime. We suspected that people would traffic in illegal goods there, which we found quite romantic. The Kray twins came down there a few times, as well as George Raft who played gangsters in the old black-and-white movies, but we never got to see any of them. And when we asked to meet the Krays we weren't allowed to. Unsurprisingly we suspected that Maurice had connections in the underworld.[9]

It may very well be in Maurice's club, then, that a picture was taken, a few years later, of Shirley with a group of men including a large American called Ed Pucci, Frank Sinatra's personal bodyguard; and a sharp-dressed East End gangster called Reggie Kray. Nor was that her only link to the twins. Some time in the early 1960s she sold them one of her many cars, a 1959 Dodge Custom Royal (registration no. SB 64). The links between showbiz figures and criminals in the 1960s have been much written about, of course. The marriage of Shirley's friend Barbara Windsor to the gangster Ronnie Knight was far from an isolated incident of such fraternisation. They often came from similar backgrounds, frequented the same clubs, liked to visit the same places on holiday.

Anyway, back in 1959, Sharp and King went out shopping for a new car for Shirley, a £4,500 little red Corvette with a TV set, picnic table and kettle in the boot, and finalised the change of Shirley's booking agent from Sullivan to their poker-playing associate, Peter Charlesworth.

Mike Sullivan, meanwhile, was quietly devastated by losing control of the woman whose career he had shaped. For the next couple of years he had, in his words, 'a Shirley-shaped hole in my heart'. He carried on hustling, managed another singer signed to Philips, Robert Earl, but his heart wasn't really in it. Then, to make some quick money, he started to run a strip club called the Keyhole in St James's.

If that sounds like a huge step down, it should be borne in mind that strip clubs, of various sorts, were big business in London at the end of the 1950s. The programme for Shirley's new show, *Blue Magic*, featured a big advert for Murray's Cabaret Club on the edge of Soho, an upmarket pickup joint where the scantily dressed showgirls would have included a young Christine Keeler. A smaller advert enticed patrons of the show to invest in sets of 'photographs taken by London's leading glamour photographer', a notorious Soho sex industry pioneer called Harrison Marks.

And, indeed, *Blue Magic* itself featured lots of chorus girls wearing very little at all.* This was very much the norm for mainstream entertainment at the time. It was a world in which a woman's role was to wear as little as possible and keep her mouth shut. Shirley Bassey's particular skill was to be aware that she lived in that world, to happily play along with it, to bump and grind and flash plenty of leg, but at the same time to make it clear to everyone that she found the whole thing something of a lark. With Shirley, for every episode of wanton rump-shaking, there's always a compensatory wink.

With *Blue Magic* assuring steady work and income for the rest of the year, Shirley and her new management team set to further overhauling her career. The one connection with the Mike Sullivan era was Johnny Franz at Philips Records. Despite Shirley's recent chart success, Johnny Franz didn't seem to be in any hurry to sign Shirley to a new contract. Peter Charlesworth saw the opportunity and had a word with Norman Newell at EMI.

Norman Newell was a chubby-faced, bespectacled East Ender, a songwriter who'd become head of EMI's A & R division in the early 1950s. He'd been responsible for putting out records by such established stars as Gracie Fields and Noël Coward, among a roster that ran the gamut from the Beverley Sisters to Paul Robeson. In the late 1950s he had had major success with new signings like the pianist Russ Conway and the young actress Petula Clark. And while his colleague Norrie Paramor was busy signing up such iconoclastic new talent as Cliff Richard and the Shadows, Norman Newell could see in Shirley Bassey an artist who was still young and fresh, but embodied the traditional musical values he understood and believed

---

* Some of them, like Morna Watson, were trained classical dancers who nevertheless had to wear next to nothing to get the job. Morna, these days a yoga teacher in Los Angeles, remembers watching Shirley from the side of the stage and marvelling at 'the way she sang with her whole body'.

in, as he told the *Melody Maker:* 'I don't think we can better the high standards set up in Britain by Philips A & R man Johnny Franz, but what I think we can do is put her on the worldwide disc ranks. I consider Shirley to be in the class of Sinatra and Nat King Cole.[10]

The deal was soon done and Shirley would go on to work with Norman Newell, on and off, for several decades, forming a far closer bond with him than she ever did with Johnny Franz. Nevertheless the changeover period between the two labels didn't do much for Shirley's chart profile. Philips released three more singles, each a reading of a standard – 'Love For Sale', 'My Funny Valentine' and 'Night And Day'.*

EMI began, rather oddly, by getting Shirley to record a couple of songs for a recording of the 1920s musical *Showboat.* Then Newell teamed Shirley up with his regular arranger Geoff Love and they got to work on her first proper album for the label.

Geoff Love was in his early forties, a dance band veteran turned orchestra leader and arranger. Like Shirley he was of mixed race. Unusually, though, he wasn't from one of the port towns, but from Todmorden in Yorkshire. His father was a black American actor and dancer, rejoicing in the name Kid Love, and his mother an English actress. In his years at EMI he provided arrangements for the likes of Russ Conway and Gracie Fields. The same year he started working with Shirley he also began making very successful light-orchestral records under the pseudonym Manuel and his Music Of the Mountains. His other major commercial triumph was his series of records with a novelty piano player called Mrs Mills. Geoff Love, it's safe to say, was not the most innovative of arrangers, and

---

* All three also appeared on Shirley's first and only full-length album for Philips, *The Bewitching Miss Bassey*, which collected together most of the singles she'd released to date.

his work with Shirley Bassey is mostly on the conservative side.

Certainly the first album they recorded together, *The Fabulous Miss Bassey*, released at the end of 1959, was aimed squarely at the Frank Sinatra-loving, album-buying audience. Like her last few recordings for Philips, the record was made up of standards and show tunes. There's a definite sense on these recordings that she's started to grow into the material, but a sense too that only part of what she could offer was being put on display.

During the recording she gave another revealing interview, this time to the *Daily Mirror*'s star reporter Donald Zec. In later years Shirley would rarely talk as frankly to journalists as she did in 1959, in her first months of freedom, living on her own and with no Svengali to guide her. Zec began by getting Shirley to consider just what she saw as her artistic strengths, starting with her physical demeanour on stage: 'It's obviously sex with a good storyline to punch it home. I clench my teeth, I use my hands like claws – I use everything a woman can use and more. I feel a complete woman when I sing – as complete as can be.'[11]

Zec wonders how complete a woman she can be at twenty-two, and Shirley assures him that 'I've been around. In show business a girl gets to know men pretty fast . . . and she grows up pretty fast too.' Then she goes back to discussing her singing:

> Sometimes I feel cool, carried along by the song. Other times I feel I want to tear down into the audience screaming like a wildcat. I'm really all mixed up inside. I'm frightened of where success is gonna take me. I've even thought of seeing a psychiatrist. A girl like me has a lot to overcome. I know I'm no beauty – my nose is too broad. I'm not exactly bosomy. But I think I've got a strong personality. Sometimes I'm terrified by the power inside me when I'm singing – it's as though the African in me is trying to get out.

It's an arresting notion . . . However, there's little sign of the African, at least not in the sense she presumably means of the primitive and unruly, in the album she was recording at the time. Nor would there be in her first single for EMI, an attempt to replicate the charm of 'As I Love You' with an English translation of an Edith Piaf ballad, 'If You Love Me (I Won't Care)', which failed to make the charts.

Indeed, once all the upheavals in her management structure had been negotiated, 1959 was a relatively quiet year for Shirley. She performed in *Blue Magic* through till September. She played Sunday shows in Blackpool. And she was involved in a couple of court cases which kept her name in the news.

In the first of these she was the victim. Some of her possessions had been stolen from her Dolphin Square apartment. The culprit turned out to be her secretary David Gilmour. However, when it came out that he had only stolen from her because he was being blackmailed over his homosexuality, Shirley publicly forgave him and he was given a conditional discharge. She even paid his court costs.

The other case was also a robbery, this time at the home of an American model called Verne Schiffman. This was a rather more dramatic case because the robber, Guenther Podola, a German immigrant, went on to shoot a policeman dead while resisting arrest and was subsequently hanged. Shirley's role in the affair was as a supportive friend, publicly thanked by Ms Schiffman.

Despite these incidents, after four manic years Shirley's life had begun to calm down just a little and she was able to take stock. Her personal life was still in flux; Shirley's relationship with Clive Sharp wasn't built to last. Her professional life, on the other hand, seemed to be going well. She didn't have Mike Sullivan scheming night and day on her behalf, but neither did she have him working her into the ground. Clive Sharp was involved in her personal management, to be sure, but when it came to the important business she could rely on her booking agent, Peter Charlesworth, doing a thoroughly professional job for her. With the London theatre run finished, Charlesworth was able to start booking Shirley further afield. While he lined up shows in Europe, Shirley set about confirming her new stability by finding a place to buy rather than rent, and fixed on a house in Stanhope Place, just up the road from the Philips Studios. She had the decorators in and was due to move in that December, as she explained to her loyal supporter Gareth Bowen in an interview for the *South Wales Echo*:

> I've finished living in hotels and furnished apartments . . . you must come and see my £12,000 house in Stanhope Place, just opposite Hyde Park. Fabulous, boy . . . refurnished and decorated top to bottom. My white Jaguar with leopard skin seats? I've graduated, Gareth. I've got a £4,000 red and cream Chevrolet sports car. My mother and sisters are living in a new house in Newport Road . . . I am so very happy.[12]

Doesn't she miss Mike Sullivan, wonders Bowen:

> Do I look as if I'm missing Mike Sullivan? He was never my Svengali – although he did help me a lot when I was coming up. You've either got that vital spark or you haven't . . . I am as you see me on the stage because I feel deep inside what I'm doing.

Clive Sharp then stepped in to wind up the interview and assure Bowen that 'Shirley's the biggest thing that ever happened in British show business' and 'my agency will project her as a huge international star'.

This wasn't just bluster from Sharp. Shirley was becoming a fixture in the British show-business firmament. Clear evidence of this was offered in the new year when she was invited to be the guest on *Desert Island Discs.* * She appeared on the show two weeks after one of her new show-business friends, Anthony Newley, and two weeks before her long-time supporter, Liberace.

Sadly, the interview has been erased by the BBC. The list of records she chose survives, though. And it's either a case of Shirley giving people what she thought they wanted, or evidence that she was a twenty-two-year-old with the musical tastes of someone twice her age. Her selections included not only Liberace but also Mantovani. Not only Frank but also Sammy. There's Harry Secombe singing Mai Jones's 'We'll Keep a Welcome', as a nod to her Welsh roots. There's her heroine Judy Garland singing 'Life is Just a Bowl of Cherries' and then, presumably to support a humorous anecdote, there's the Chipmunks singing 'The Chipmunk Song'. Finally, though, her self-confidence fully intact, she ends the show with one of her own recordings, 'A Foggy Day in London Town', from her new album.

That same month she moved into a house of her own for the first time. It was clearly a big step forward for her, as she explained to a *Daily Mail* reporter she invited over. After the journalist had been told the cost of the house – £12,000 – and the ornate door knocker – £50 – Shirley showed her the feature she was most proud of, a pale-pink sunken bath, and explained why it was so important to her:

---

* Curiously, Shirley was the fourth black woman entertainer to make an appearance on the show in its first decade (previous interviewees were Elizabeth Welch, Winifred Atwell and Cleo Laine), yet only four more have appeared in the subsequent five decades – Adelaide Hall, Jessye Norman, Joan Armatrading and Whoopi Goldberg.

We never had a bathroom at home. We used to bathe in a tin tub in the kitchen and while one used the bath someone else poured in buckets of water. One day I picked up the wrong bucket and tipped a couple of gallons of scalding water over my sister. We're a tough family and she recovered, but I cried my heart out and promised myself a bath with taps one day. A bath in a bathroom all of my own. When I saw this bath in a shop window I knew I had to have it. They had to pick me up off the floor after they'd told me the price!

Now I've got roots. I've furnished a guest room and perhaps my mother will come to stay. I'm dying to see her face when she walks in. My mother still thinks I'm the baby of the family. When I'm visiting she still says, 'Run this errand to the little shop on the corner and I'll give you sixpence for going.'[13]

The year 1959, then, had seen Shirley consolidate her position. In 1960 she would move forward again. Standing still is rarely an option in show business, but once you've reached a certain level of success the pressure for constant movement, constant reinvention, starts to lessen. Shirley had always seen being a star as a quantifiable achievement, rather like being a doctor or an astronaut. She had carried her clippings around with her to persuade herself that she was at the very least a star in waiting. But as the 1950s came to an end, she was starting to believe it. She was a star. Whether it would make her happy, this new-found status, was another matter.

SEVENTEEN

Screen Dreams

At the beginning of the 1960s Shirley Bassey was quite clear where she wanted her career to go next. She gave another interview to *Picturegoer*'s Sarah Stoddart to explain: 'I want to star in a film. You could say that's my big ambition for 1960. If I don't make it in Britain, I'll make it in Hollywood. But I'll make it.'[1]

She tells Stoddart that she's yet to receive any film offers at all, apart from the abortive business with *Tiger Bay*, but rather than put this down to racism, she prefers to believe that the British film industry is simply taking time to catch on to her charms:

> Let's say that maybe British films are now ready for me. Up to now, perhaps, my appeal has been too sexy or dynamic for our studios. But now, after *Room At The Top*, maybe I'll be offered the dramatic role I long for. Why, even musicals have become adult. *Expresso Bongo* for instance. Mm! I'd just love to make a picture like that.

At the time of the interview Shirley was hoping to be heading off shortly to New York to appear on the *Perry Como Show*. That was cancelled, but by way of compensation she spent the month of February headlining in Milan, and when she returned her new single, another dramatic ballad called 'With These Hands', was hovering around the lower regions of the charts, as it would do for most of the spring.

In April, Anthony Newley invited her to guest-star in his TV special. Newley was very hot indeed at that time. As a child actor he'd played the Artful Dodger in the David Lean film of *Oliver Twist*, and he had precisely the kind of career Shirley longed for, able to oscillate between acting and singing. That spring he was at number one in the charts with a ballad called 'Why', shortly to be chased up the charts by another number one, 'Do You Mind?'. Like Shirley he had a distinctive British style, a London-accented drawl that was to be a big influence on his great admirer, David Bowie.

Shirley seized the chance to show the world that there was more to her than big ballads and the sultry sex siren routine. Here she could show off the comic timing she'd learned over the years of starring alongside the likes of Tommy Cooper and Al Read. And so she did. The highlight of the show is a skit which shows the two stars sitting next to each other and playfully trying to outdo each other by singing short extracts from their hits, one after another. Newley has the bigger hits but when Shirley answers his rendition of 'Why' with a burst of 'As I Love You', it's a cruelly unequal contest. Newley just grins and Shirley, sporting a very chic new decade wig, lays her head on his shoulder in pretend apology. She's a natural in front of the camera, she must surely have believed her film debut could not be far away.

But as Shirley waited for the right film part to come along, she had to carry on earning a living by playing the provincial theatres, something she was starting to grow tired of. That May the *News of the World*'s Weston Taylor caught up with Shirley in Coventry and found her at a very low ebb. Partly this was because she'd just been deposed as headliner by her erstwhile support act, the comedian Ken Dodd (since that time Shirley has generally been careful to select support acts who are unlikely ever to upstage her).

Shirley starts by complaining about the food at the theatre, then says her jaw hurts. When asked what's wrong she says, 'my hypochondria pains'. When a persevering Taylor wonders if there's anything at all she's pleased about, she says, 'I don't seem to be singing so flat any more', sounding more like a grumpy teenager than a showbiz personality. Finally she elaborates as to what's bothering her:

> I guess I'm more unhappy than ever. You get so that you only live for that moment on the stage. I can't think about anything else, I put so much into that moment I'm drained. When the curtain falls and the applause dies down it's like being in the world all alone. I don't know whether I'll ever be normal again, I'm so moody. Where can I find a man in the world who'll put up with me? I change moods every two hours. I reckon I need a different husband for every mood. There is the mood where I use big words like eulogistic. Then the mood will change and I'll become a little girl again and start using three-letter words.[2]

Fortunately for Shirley's mood, the connection with Anthony Newley quickly paid dividends. Newley's new hit single, 'Do You Mind?', was written by a man called Lionel Bart, a Jewish East Ender who had made a name for himself with his songs for the cockney musical based on the writings of Soho character Frank Norman, *Fings Ain't What they Used to Be*. Now he was working on his first full-scale musical. It was to be an adaptation of *Oliver Twist*. Max Bygraves had bought the theatrical rights to the book, and the show was due to open at the end of June, with Ron Moody as Fagin and Georgia Brown as Nancy. Nancy had the show's big ballad, a song called 'As Long As He Needs Me', and thanks to some smart work by Peter Charlesworth, who would become agent and friend to both Newley and Bart (not to mention Newley's future wife Joan Collins), Shirley was given the chance to record the song before the show opened.

The recording session was set for 22 June. Norman Newell had the Abbey Road studio prepared and the orchestra booked from 2.00 till 5.30. Come two o'clock there was no sign of Shirley. Knowing his star as he did, Norman leapt to the correct conclusion: Shirley had forgotten about the session and, as was her compulsive habit, had gone to the movies. He paged every cinema in the West End and eventually Shirley got the message and turned up at Abbey Road at ten past five, just twenty minutes before the orchestra were due to pack up. She had one shot at the song. Naturally, she nailed it.

The following week *Oliver!* opened in the West End and was an extraordinary hit. On the first night the cast took twenty-three curtain calls. Later that month Shirley had her own TV special and, this time, Newley appeared as a guest star. A few weeks after that Shirley's rendition of 'As Long As He Needs Me' was released. It entered the charts at the beginning of August and stayed there for more than six months, her biggest hit yet. Already there was talk of a film version of *Oliver!* and Shirley had her heart set on playing Nancy.

By that time Shirley was in the middle of a summer season headlining at the Opera House, Blackpool. Not exactly Hollywood, or even Milan, but still the pinnacle of the British variety circuit. Meanwhile Peter Charlesworth was working hard to set up a US TV appearance for Shirley, ideally the *Ed Sullivan Show*. But as it was getting on for a year since *Blue Magic* had closed, he figured it was time Shirley had another headline stint in London.

He booked her in for a season at the Pigalle on Piccadilly. This was an upmarket supper club run by one of the big names in the London clubland of the 1950s, Al Burnett. Another of the East End Jews who were so influential in the post-war British entertainment industry, Burnett was a boxer turned comedian, impresario and inveterate gambler. His first club, the Stork Room, had become an institution. The Pigalle was a bigger venture, capable of serving a thousand customers a night. It represented a huge investment when it opened in the late 1950s, but, after initial success, it had been hit hard by the boom in strip clubs which were taking business away from the respectable kind of floor show on offer at the Pigalle. As Burnett later observed:

> More strip clubs opened every week in the West End and the public (mostly males of course) were flocking to them. In fact at one time there were over seventy strip clubs in London alone, including five or six really big ones, like Paul Raymond's Revuebar and the Casino de Paris.[3]

Burnett decided not to join in the strip-club boom but to move his operation even further upmarket. Early in 1960 he brought Sammy Davis, Jr. over from the States for the first time, getting a heap of publicity and a sold-out club, though at a considerable price. He needed another act of a similar calibre to keep the momentum going, and soon decided on Shirley Bassey. For the princely sum of thirty-two shillings and sixpence, punters could have a three-course dinner, a show featuring not only Shirley but two US comics, Marty Allen and Steve Ross, and 'the Pigalle lovelies', plus dancing afterwards. Burnett later commented:

Actually Shirley's season was better for me financially. She was a tremendous success and packed the place, and her expenses were nothing like as high as they had been with Sammy Davis. While Shirley was starring at the Pigalle, the Negro star Eartha Kitt was appearing at the rival establishment the Talk of the Town. Their rivalry became something of a battle royal, encouraged in Fleet Street. That Pigalle season was, I maintain, the making of Shirley Bassey as a great star.[4]

But while Burnett was happy to join the line of men who reckoned they were behind Shirley's success, he was oddly reticent about the incident that really had Fleet Street buzzing during Shirley's run at the Pigalle, perhaps because it exposed the fact that, while the Pigalle did have plenty of showbiz stars and high-society types attending, it was also a magnet for the rather more dubious kinds of individual who were currently making good money out of Soho.

On the Saturday night of Shirley's third week at the Pigalle, trouble broke out. A minor villain, Jack Buggy, known as Scotch Jack, showed up around midnight with a friend of his by the name of Hoey. This Hoey was having a party and Buggy got it into his head that Shirley Bassey might like to come and perform at the party. After making a drunken nuisance of themselves during Shirley's set, the two men made their way backstage. Shirley was in her dressing room talking to the actor Peter Finch and his wife who had been at the show and were paying their compliments. Peter Charlesworth intercepted Buggy and told him that Shirley was not available. Buggy and Hoey hung around anyway till a stage electrician called John Clarke told Buggy to leave the backstage area. Buggy immediately assaulted Clarke, knocking him to the ground and kicking him till a couple of waiters came to Clarke's aid. They started to escort Buggy out of the club. As they headed for the exit, a punter called Charles Reeder encouraged the waiters to throw Buggy out. Buggy then turned his attention to Reeder, picking up a plate and smashing it over his head. Reeder, a sometime all-in wrestler (known in the trade as Alf Reeder), wasn't going to sit still for this. He got up to tackle Buggy and the waiters hustled both men outside so they could settle things out of sight of the punters.

As they walked up the stairs to the exit, Buggy turned to Reeder and said 'This is going to be with tools, you know?'

Reeder told Buggy he didn't need tools, failing to understand just what Buggy meant by the term. And as soon as they were outside, he put action to words and knocked Buggy down. Buggy then turned to Hoey, who had followed them out, and said, 'Give me the tool!'

That was when Reeder discovered that the tool in question was a pistol. Buggy shot Reeder in the stomach at point-blank range, then ran off. Reeder slumped to the ground, unsure what had happened to him. Within seconds Charlesworth had hustled Shirley out of the club and into a waiting car. She saw Reeder slumped in a neighbouring doorway but had no idea what was the matter with him. The rest of the fleeing punters took no notice of Reeder either, despite the fact that he was now bleeding heavily. It was only ten minutes later, when the police arrived, that he was given any assistance. It turned out that he had been incredibly lucky. The bullet had passed through his body without causing serious damage.

Buggy nearly got away with it. Unfortunately for him, though, Maurice King, with his underworld connections, had recognised him in the club. He knew Buggy as a low-level gangster with a reputation for violence, born in the USA but brought up in Scotland, hence his nickname. Buggy had joined the American air force, then deserted and spent time working for a gang in Glasgow. Three weeks after the Pigalle incident, Buggy was arrested as he came out of a Whitechapel café and subsequently sentenced to eight years for GBH.*

Once again, Shirley had come uncomfortably close to a gunman. So it must have come as a relief when, straight after the Pigalle run, she was able to head off to New York, where Peter Charlesworth had at last succeeded in scoring a booking on the *Ed Sullivan Show*. Not only that, but they would travel out in style, aboard the *Queen Mary*.

*   *   *

Shirley took the *Ed Sullivan Show* in her stride. This was the world she knew. Ed Sullivan basically presided over a TV version of an old-fashioned variety show. On the day Shirley appeared, 13 November, her co-stars included the comics Rowan and Martin, the Broadway star Chita Rivera singing 'Spanish Rose', the film star Dick Van Dyke singing 'Put On A Happy Face' and, to end the show, a German clown act called the Le Bully Trio. The only concession to the fact this was a TV show, not a theatre revue, was a brief chat element: an appearance from John Wayne talking to Sullivan about his new film, *The Alamo*. For her part Shirley stayed close to the American songbook and performed two songs from her album, *The Fabulous Shirley Bassey*: ''S Wonderful' and 'The Party's Over'.

---

* Not that he learnt his lesson: soon after he came out, in June 1967, his body was found floating in the English Channel, bound and gagged and shot in the head. He may have been involved in a war between rival protection racketeers, or in a spin-off from the Great Train Robbery.

While they were in New York, Peter Charlesworth managed to secure a return booking: Shirley would headline a season at one of New York's top cabaret venues, the Persian Room, the following year. Back to London then, for a short break and a trip to Cardiff for Christmas with the family.

Alone in London Shirley took time to consider her situation, in particular her management situation. Peter Charlesworth's work as her booking agent she was happy with; her personal management less so. Following the gangster business at the Pigalle, Shirley had decided she had had enough of Clive Sharp and Maurice King.

Meanwhile, there had been a long-running legal battle going on ever since the split with Mike Sullivan. Sullivan was demanding £8,000 in compensation for, as he saw it, breach of contract. Early in the new year the case was due to go to court, just before a return trip to Australia: two months down under and on her own, unless she found a new manager. Let Mike Sullivan take up the story of what happened next:

At one o'clock on a cold December morning, my bedside telephone jangled me into consciousness. I groped for the handset and dragged it beneath the blankets. A small tentative voice said 'Mike?' giving the vowel sound two syllables, one high and one low, musically about a fourth apart, 'Mi-ike'.

'Yes?'

'It's me.'

Christmas was still two weeks away. It was closed season for guessing games.

'Who's me?'

'Shirley.'

'Shirley who?'

The angry yell that came over the telephone almost jerked me out of bed.

'Don't tell me you don't know who Shirley is! How many other Shirleys have you made into a star?' She said it 'Staaah', all on one long hard bright note, that only needed a backing of muted brass.[5]

That cleared up, star and ex-Svengali agreed to meet at Stanhope Place the following day. As Sullivan recalls:

A 'bing-bong' version of her hit song 'As I Love You' chimed out as I pressed the front door button to the narrow terraced house just a few yards from Hyde Park. Gerda, the German housekeeper, opened the door and I forced my feet through the deep pile of red carpeting which covered the hallway and stairs until I reached the first landing. Shirley stood at the door of the first-floor sitting room wearing an ankle-length brown robe and a haughty, man-eating expression which she subconsciously puts on to face any new or uncomfortable experience. The haughtiness melted as I reached the doorway. Her arms opened and she hugged me.

We sat five yards apart and for ten minutes we hedged. Then I said, 'Look, let's stop all the humming and hawing. What's all this about?'

It came out in a flood. 'Mickey,' she said, 'you always treated me like a child. Like a freak. You arranged things without telling me and I only used to find out about them when somebody else told me.'

However, according to Sullivan, even though Shirley had been glad to be around people who treated her like a grown-up and let her make her own decisions, she was also missing the security of having a personal manager: 'I need somebody to look after me alone. Someone who thinks I am enough. In other word, Mickey, I want you back.'

There was almost certainly another factor at play in Shirley's decision to go back to Mike Sullivan. Shirley had become very friendly with Maurice King's girlfriend, a smart dark-haired woman called Jean Lincoln. Years later she would describe Lincoln as the one true female best friend she'd ever had – 'We were like identical twins.'[6]* Lincoln was working for the agent and producer Bernard Delfont. Some time in 1960, on a night out together, the two women had discovered Kenny Lynch singing in a Soho club. Lincoln would subsequently become Lynch's manager and lover. Lynch remembers their meeting:

> I was a jazz singer singing in Rimano's on Gerrard Street, right opposite the Whisky a Go Go. Jean walked in with Shirley Bassey, just as I was singing a standard. Jean called me over said, 'You're good. Would you like to meet Shirley Bassey? We think you should be making records. Gimme your number and I'll try and get you a record deal.'[7]

Jean was as good as her word and Shirley must have been impressed with the efficiency of the Delfont agency, which by a remarkable coincidence was where Mike Sullivan now had an office. So her decision to invite Sullivan to become her manager again must have been swayed by the prospect of having her best friend involved in looking after her. And, indeed, for the next few years Jean Lincoln combined her role as an agent and manager with acting as PA to Shirley.

Andrew Loog Oldham, the Rolling Stones' original Svengali

---

* By the time she made this comment, however, Jean Lincoln was long dead. She died from an overdose of pills in 1969, shortly after moving to New York, and just before she was due to be married to the owner of the Flamingo Club, Rik Gunnell. Her death was a huge blow to Shirley.

manager, was another great friend of Jean Lincoln's. In his auto-biography he recalls the first time they met at the Delfont agency: 'When I try to recall the actual meeting,' he wrote, 'all I get is lights and action – her eyes, beauty and spirit signifying that I'd met one of the big teachers and best friends of my life.'[8] Rather more enigmatically, he told me that 'I do know that Shirley was an important part of Jean's life – as they say, somebody has to let you into the game and in Jean's case I'm sure it was Shirley.'

Meanwhile Sullivan pondered Shirley's offer to him to become her personal manager again and finally decided to give it a go. After some protracted negotiations with the Jock Jacobsen agency, an agreement was reached in early January. He would accept a reduced payment for lost earnings and henceforth would receive twenty per cent of Shirley's earnings as her personal manager. In a typical Sullivan touch he had the press come and take photos of the rapprochement, the two of them smiling and shaking hands over a cake baked in the shape of a boxing ring with little figures dressed as Shirley and himself placed on top, holding a sign saying 'A draw'.

That same month Shirley gave another hometown show, at the Gaumont Theatre, spending the night with her family in the new house she'd bought them in Newport Road, and telling a local journalist that when she came back from Australia she was looking forward to reading the script of *Napoleon and Josephine*, a new musical that Lionel Bart and Anthony Newley were writing for her.

This must have been an exciting prospect. Napoleon's wife Josephine was a Creole from the West Indies. She was actually born to white parents in Martinique but a popular myth has evolved (thanks to a misunderstanding of the term 'Creole') that she was of mixed race. The myth was good enough for Bart and Newley though, and if their Josephine was to be mixed race, then who better than Shirley Bassey to play her? It looked like being the perfect project for Shirley, written by the leading pop singer and the most successful musical dramatist around. It could have been a dream come true. Unfortunately it never materialised. In the end Bart's next musical to appear on the London stage was the Second World War set *Blitz!*, which had a conspicuous lack of suitable parts for a mixed-race heroine.

EIGHTEEN

Love and Marriage

Shirley Bassey's latest Australian tour went as well as ever, though there was friction between Mike Sullivan and her. She was no longer happy to leave all the decision-making to him. This second act of their relationship was never going to last: the clock could not after all be turned back. It didn't come as much of a surprise to Sullivan that Shirley soon found a replacement for him. What he could not have predicted was just who she picked as her next Svengali.

Shirley and Mike were stopping over in New York on their way back from Australia. It was when they arrived at their Manhattan hotel that Shirley ran into an old acquaintance, a man called Kenneth Hume who had directed some of her early TV appearances for Jack Hylton. By his own account Mike Sullivan didn't take much notice of this chance meeting.

Kenneth Hume was a TV commercial director I had seen around in London. He was homosexual, full of charm, two-faced and thoroughly detestable. I would have seen nothing wrong in Shirley talking to him. Somebody with his sexual proclivities couldn't pose any threat to a healthy, lusty girl like her. Shirley always liked her men masculine. I should have taken more notice. By our fourth day in the hotel

Hume was actively courting Shirley and she was lapping up all the fawning attention he was paying to her.[1]

As Sullivan was slowly coming to realise, Shirley's life was about to take an unexpected turn. Less than three months after the meeting in New York, Shirley Bassey and Kenneth Hume were married. That Shirley should get married after such a whirlwind courtship was not so surprising: that was the kind of thing stars did. That she should get married to Kenneth Hume was very surprising indeed.

Kenneth Hume was a decade older than Shirley, born on 22 March 1926 in London. His older brother Alan was also in the film business, an eminent cinematographer who worked on several Bond films, among much else. Now retired and living in the Home Counties, Alan and his wife Sheila were happy to talk over beer and sandwiches about Kenneth and his unlikely marriage. Alan started by recalling their family background as working-class West Londoners:

We grew up very near Putney, Roehampton. My parents were born in Fulham. We'd go to Hammersmith to the movies. My dad worked on the London Railway as his dad did, and I did when I started, but I was fortunate enough to meet someone on the trains going to Acton Works. We used to chat and I said I didn't like what I was doing, and he said well if you want to change your job, come and see me, and he worked for Olympic Film.

As for his younger brother, Kenneth:

He was all right. We used to squabble and have boxing matches which my father used to encourage, he used to get us to put on boxing gloves! We went to school together. I got involved in the Cubs and Scouts and he got involved too. We used to go camping together. When he left school he got a job at the Savoy Hotel as a sort of little lad in a uniform running around doing what he was told to do. Then he got a job operating the lift. That's how he met a lot of people.

This is perhaps something of a euphemism. Bellboys in expensive hotels were traditionally expected to be able to cater to the hotel guests' more illicit needs. If a well-heeled punter wanted a girl or boy delivered to their room, the bellboy was the person to ask. In his memoirs the publisher Anthony Blond, who later had an affair with Kenneth, recalls that, 'When he was a boy, he once told me, he had organised the pages at the Piccadilly Hotel into a union with minimum rates for pederasts.'

An ambitious young man, Kenneth soon left the hotel business, as his brother remembers:

He began to get on a bit and eventually he got into the film business. He got a job at Denham Studios as a door boy; when you're on the studio floor, enormous place, and they say, 'Red light, close the door,' he would have to put the red light on, close the door and lock it so no one came in. While he was doing that he was learning what was going on in the film studios. He used to talk to people and he got a job in the cutting room helping out and eventually he became an editor himself. Didn't take him all that long. Then he started to get involved with directing in a minor manner and eventually he made about a dozen films. I remember one I operated the camera for, a film called *Hot Ice*. He did very well.

Really, it would be truer to say that he did quite well. Kenneth directed TV shows, he made B-movies, but he never quite moved up into the first division. He did, however, became a familiar figure in London's homosexual *demi-monde* and a regular presence in memoirs written by well-connected gay men in the 1950s. Typical is a reference by the artist Donald Friend (by his own account 'a middle-aged pederast who's going to seed') to 'a nervous and fidgety young film director' visiting him in Ceylon and making facetious remarks about the garden boys.*

Kenneth Hume was not inclined to pretend to be anything other than what he was. His sister-in-law, Sheila, recalls that 'he used to bring down his chaps to see us. He thought nothing of it.' Then again, he had little choice in the matter, not after he was caught up in one of the signature homosexual scandals of the 1950s.

It began in the summer of 1953 with a house party at Beaulieu, the stately home belonging to a young aristocrat, Lord Edward Montagu. Among those present were Montagu himself, the writer Peter Wildeblood, Montagu's cousin Michael Pitt-Rivers and Kenneth Hume, all of them gay or bisexual and moving in fashionable London circles. In the course of the weekend the party went bathing at the beach on Montagu's land, along with a couple of RAF airmen that Wildeblood had brought along, and a couple of Boy Scouts who had been helping out with the tourists at Beaulieu (Montagu was a natural showman who had opened a motor museum as an adjunct to the house).

Some weeks later Edward Montagu and Kenneth Hume were arrested and accused of offences of sodomy against the two Boy Scouts. The combination of flamboyant peer and Boy Scouts was catnip to the popular press of the time and inspired a raft of jokes

---

* Hume was there to direct the pilot for a series to be called *The Adventures of an Elephant Boy*, which he had also written. Apparently the film crew encountered problems with their Sinhalese extras, who were allegedly paid in beer. Further rumour suggests that two cameramen died from snake bites during the filming.

that would became a staple of comedians' repertoires for decades to come. When the case went to court, however, the evidence of the Boy Scouts was so weak that the jury was unable to reach a verdict.*

In his autobiography Lord Montagu finally went on record with his own version of events:

> What really happened was that while I was swimming with Scout A Kenneth Hume was behaving mildly indecently with Scout B and I had later walked into the room and disturbed them. When the two Scouts returned to camp there was some jealousy from the others who had not been invited to swim. Scout B had apparently told the others what happened between himself and Kenneth Hume, provoking Scout A to say that he had had a similar experience with myself. This good-natured but stupid boasting was unfortunately overheard by the Scoutmaster, who thought it his duty to investigate. The Scouts not wishing to admit they lied ... got deeper into the mud and the accusations became exaggerated.[2]

Alan Hume went down to the court to pick his brother up and found him philosophical about the whole experience: 'I didn't suppose he was very pleased about it all, but he wasn't suicidal or anything like that.'

In fact Kenneth had, as his brother suggested, done pretty well for himself in the film and TV business. He'd worked as an editor on Carol Reed's *The Way Ahead* as far back as 1944. He'd made his directorial debut, in 1952, with a country house thriller called *Hot Ice*, and had gone on to make a series of B-movie crime dramas as

---

* There was a subsequent trial at which Montagu, Wildeblood and Pitt-Rivers, but not Kenneth Hume, were charged with offences of sodomy against the two airmen. All three were convicted and given prison sentences.

well as the bread-and-butter TV work for the likes of Jack Hylton that had brought him into contact with Shirley. At the time they met he was making a good living directing television commercials.

That he should have wanted to get involved in Shirley Bassey's career made sense. Hume was an entrepreneurial spirit. He wanted to make bigger, better films. Shirley wanted to be a film star. On that level, at least, the synergy was obvious. However, it was still a shock when they announced they were to be married, as Mike Sullivan recalls.

> Late one evening I was telephoned by John Mills, the owner of Les Ambassadeurs, a very luxurious club on Park Lane, who told me that Shirley was there and had just announced her engagement to Kenneth Hume. I asked John to send them a bottle of champagne with my congratulations and went back to sleep. The following day Hume turned up at a concert in Leicester with Shirley in a gleaming hired Rolls Royce. The matter was now becoming serious. He was getting his claws into her and to me it was a case of her money not her love that he wanted.
>
> I tried to talk Shirley out of the whole sorry affair: 'Look, it can't work. He's queer. How can you want somebody like that? You're a healthy, sexy girl. Go and find somebody who can give you what you really want. Jump into bed with them and get him out of your system.'[3]

Shirley, however, was clearly rather less of an old-school red-blooded heterosexual than her manager, as he was forced to accept:

> It did not work. Shirley was really in love with Hume. She was convinced she could change him and wanted to marry. I dared not argue any more with her. All I could do was pray that she would come to her senses. She did not and they married.

Interviewed by *Photoplay* magazine, lying on a sofa in their St John's Wood home, Kenneth Hume offered his own version of their courtship, suggesting that the meeting in New York was no coincidence but a romantic assignation:

It wasn't love at first sight for us. We first met when I was making some films for commercial television, three months before Channel 9 opened. I got a call from the Hylton office asking me to have a look at a singer who was deputising for an artiste who was sick. I went along, watched this girl Shirley Bassey and I don't mind telling you I wasn't wildly impressed. Maybe I was too tired but I wasn't keen on her. Anyway next morning I got a call from the Hylton office telling me she was to appear in the film. I had to fit her in between the Crazy Gang and a dog act. She did the show and that was that. But I remember she told me that I was too bossy and that I kept putting the camera right down her throat.

I didn't see Shirley again for about two years. In that time she became a big name. We bumped into each other somewhere in the Charing Cross Road. I'd promised to phone her but had forgotten. Well Shirley gave me her new telephone number again and I promised to ring her. I never did. Then about fifteen months ago we met in a Soho restaurant. I think she was a little annoyed that I hadn't rung. I said 'Let me have your number again and I'll ring you this time.' But she put her foot down. She wouldn't give me her number. 'What's the point,' she said, 'you say you're going to ring me but you never do!'

'All right,' I said, 'we'll make a definite date, here and now.' Which we did. I booked to go and see Antonio the Spanish dancer* with her. As I was busy I sent a chauffeur to pick Shirley up at her flat

* Presumably the great flamenco dancer Antonio Ruiz Soler.

and told him to bring her to my place. When she arrived, a little angry, I just happened to be playing one of her records – just checking up, you know. But she thought I'd planned it that way. Well, I hadn't. After that we became great friends. But just before Christmas 1960 I was taken ill and went into the London Clinic. Shirley had gone home to Wales. She found out I was in hospital and as there was no phone in her home she walked to the nearest phone box on Christmas Day and phoned the clinic. It took her quite a time to find the right number but finally she got through. It made my day.

Hume paused to light another cigarette and blow a smoke ring at the ceiling, before carrying on telling the journalist his story:

Later she went to Australia and I saw her off at the airport. On her way back from Australia she stopped off in America. I went over to see her. When I arrived at the hotel I phoned her from the lobby – she thought I was phoning from London. When we saw each other again we both realised this was it. She'd brought me a beautiful present home from Australia – a solid gold pen engraved with my initials.

I asked Shirley to marry me. But she said no. I think she was a little scared of marriage. I kept on asking her then got fed up with it. 'You ask me next time,' I said. One night at her home in Marble Arch, she gave me a present – a beautiful painting called *Guitar Blue*. I was surprised. 'What's this for?' I asked. 'It's an engagement present,' she said. I'll never forget that moment. It was one of the happiest of my life. Next day I phoned a diamond merchant friend of mine and knowing that Shirley doesn't care much for square-cut diamonds I asked if he could sell me one. When I gave it to Shirley she just stared and I waited to get her reaction. She wasn't sure what to say but I think she likes it now.[4]

This last anecdote gives some indication as to what Shirley must have seen in Kenneth Hume – someone confident enough to tease her with a diamond. Twenty years later she gave the *Sunday Mirror* her own account of her relationship with Kenneth, and it's one that dovetails surprisingly closely with his:

> Kenneth knew all the right places to go. His world was a world I knew nothing about. He taught me how to understand it. I knew nothing about paintings or furniture. Kenneth explained them to me and taught me how to appreciate them. I was fascinated with him. My other boyfriends would take me to dinner, tell me how beautiful I was and ask how soon we could get into bed. Not Kenneth. For the first three months I was seeing him he didn't romance me at all. The most I'd get was a kiss on the cheek before he packed me off home. At the time I had two other boyfriends so the lack of sex with Kenneth didn't bother me. The turning point came when I started putting off my other lovers. I liked going out with this man more than anyone else, even though he wasn't taking me to bed. It was then I first realised that sex wasn't the be-all and end-all of a relationship.[5]

However Shirley wasn't going to settle for that indefinitely, as she went on to explain:

> The first night we went to bed nothing happened. I was so upset I cried myself to sleep. And Kenneth got up, dressed and left me. I realised that my crying was a childish thing to do. It was also a big turn-off. So the next time we went to bed I decided to be very grown-up. When I found Kenneth couldn't make love to me, I calmly picked up the phone and said 'I'm ordering breakfast – would you like some?' As I did that, he grabbed my hand, put the phone down and suddenly it all happened. From that moment everything was fine between us.

And so to the engagement:

> He proposed to me six times. After that he told me 'I'll never ask you to marry me again. You'll have to ask me.' In the end I did. But the way it happened was very unexpected. I saw a painting in an antique shop. I studied it the way Kenneth had taught me. I'd never bought a painting before in my life, but I knew I had to have this one. I bought it and gave it to Kenneth. When he opened the package he was astounded: 'What's this for? You don't give expensive presents like that for no reason?' I found myself blurting out that it was a sort of engagement present. At that moment he was out of the door, saying he'd see me later. That evening when he picked me up for dinner he gave me a diamond ring. 'What's this for?' I asked. He smiled. 'It's a sort of engagement present,' he said.

The couple were engaged in May, and they went to the Cannes Film Festival together that month, Kenneth showing Shirley the world of cinema that she so desperately wanted to enter.

On Thursday, 8 June they were married at the very un-Shirley hour of 9.30 in the morning at the Paddington Registry Office, just round the corner from both Kenneth's flat in Westbourne Terrace and Shirley's house by Hyde Park. The groom arrived in a coffee-coloured Bentley – registration KH 14 – wearing a blue suit. The bride was in a pink two-piece with a fetching toque hat and veil. Eliza Jane told the newspapers that 'That's my seventh and last child married. Shirley's always been my baby. I am very happy she has found a nice husband.'

Kenneth's family were similarly delighted, not to say amazed. 'We thought she was jolly nice,' says Alan Hume. 'He should be so lucky!' His wife Sheila elaborates: 'It was a surprise when he met her. He told us straight away and then he brought her down to see us. I thought she was lovely, but then I always had – I thought her singing was marvellous, still do. I was absolutely delighted. They seemed wonderful together.'

Alan and Sheila saw a fair amount of the new couple, who would drive out to visit them at their home outside London. Alan remembers them as very happy together: 'They did get on very well. She wasn't at all starry, very ordinary, she'd come in the kitchen and wash up. She was enjoying her life, happy with what was happening with her career.'

Her career was indeed going well. She recorded two more albums that year, again largely composed of standards, and both arranged by Geoff Love and produced by Norman Newell. She had two more big hit singles, 'You'll Never Know' followed by the double A-side of 'Reach For The Stars' and the *Sound of Music* chestnut, 'Climb Every Mountain', which went to number one in the summer and stayed in the charts for months. This was the high-water mark of her career as a singles artist. A year or so later, the advent of the Beatles would remove the big-voiced balladeers from the charts permanently, but for now Shirley was the biggest female pop star Britain had yet seen.

Meanwhile, Peter Charlesworth had her booked up way in advance. All of this was, of course, good for her financially, though a cynic would point out that Kenneth Hume was a well-known gambler and Shirley's earnings were now being paid to a company, SVB Ltd, that he controlled. So it was clearly good for Kenneth to have Shirley working flat out. Never mind the fact that when they were married she had only just recovered from having her tonsils removed, and that she was laid up with laryngitis that summer during her latest season headlining in Blackpool.

That Blackpool season also saw the final chapter in Shirley's relationship with Mike Sullivan. Kenneth had made it very clear that

Sullivan's role as Shirley's manager was now redundant, with such an obvious and able replacement as himself. Rather than persuade Shirley to sack Sullivan outright, Kenneth embarked on a campaign of psychological warfare:

> Part of his campaign was to tell me that I should be standing in the wings holding a glass of water and toilet tissues for Shirley at every performance. He might as well have asked me to go on stage and do her act myself. My response to the demand that I become Shirley's skivvy was just two words. The second of them was 'off!'[6]

So when that failed Kenneth took more straightforward action and sent Sullivan a letter accusing him of being in breach of contract. Shirley was performing in Blackpool at the time so Sullivan went up there to try and resolve the issue. Hume told Sullivan that this was the end of the line. Sullivan was no longer to travel with Shirley to New York, later that year, as previously planned. Sullivan knew when he was beaten and agreed to accept a pay-off. Six years after he'd launched Shirley on the London stage their professional association was over. Shirley, meanwhile, had acquired not just a new husband but a new manager too. And while others have often criticised Kenneth Hume's management skills, Shirley herself was very happy with what he did for her:

> Before long Kenneth took over as my manager. He took over completely. He chose my numbers, decided their order, lit my act and, what is more, taught me how to do it, so that today I am technically self-sufficient. Under his guidance I developed as a television and cabaret performer. And not only was Kenneth able to handle my career marvellously, he could also handle me. I used to have terrible depressions and never found a better antidote than Kenneth's lively

optimism. If I got into a tantrum he might say something like, 'Cut, let's try that again. I didn't have the camera quite on you.' Which naturally had the effect of puncturing my balloon of temper and I would realise I was being childish and silly.[7]

Before Shirley went to New York to appear at the Persian Room, she had a series of provincial theatre dates to fulfil. Derek Johnson from the *NME* caught up with Shirley in Manchester and found a tired but determined star, eager to talk about her ambitions for a film career:

'I suppose it's the ambition of all singers to prove their worth as actors,' she mused. 'Certainly it's mine. I wouldn't mind if the film were musical or straight – just so long as it gave me a chance to act.' At this point Shirley's husband Kenneth Hume joined in. 'I honestly believe the general public will be very pleasantly surprised by Shirley's acting ability. And I'm pretty sure they will be able to judge for themselves within a year!'

Two weeks later, in early September, Shirley was in New York. Her season at the Persian Room was another obstacle hurdled with ease. The music business magazine *Billboard* announced that 'Shirley Bassey is on her way. The comely canary [!] from London made a colourful splash on the nightclub scene.' Other critics, with a similar fondness for Runyonesque alliteration, dubbed her the 'tawny tigress' and commented that 'The dynamic little British import with her stereophonic vocalising is a delight to the ear as well as the eye.'

However, there were signs of strain too, very clearly present in the interview she gave to a British journalist from *Today* magazine. The piece was headlined 'Night Is My Enemy' and began with Shirley discussing the trouble she was having sleeping:

I sing on my nerves. I always work under tension. It's my driving force. But when you live like that sleep is difficult. When I sing everything comes from inside. While I'm singing I feel fine. But that does not help much when it's time to sleep. Sometimes it's murder. I lie there for hours longing to sleep.

I haven't talked to anyone except my husband about this. But sometimes I stop and ask myself, 'What am I doing here? What the hell does it all mean? What am I trying to prove?' Do you know, I've been married for four months and I've spent precisely three weeks of that time with my husband! I'd like a baby. People say you shouldn't have babies when you're in show business because they tie you down. I don't care about that. I want to be able to settle and lead an ordinary life with a family. I'm a woman and they're natural wants for a woman. I've thought a lot about retiring in the past year. I'm not really a career girl.[8]

It's a heartfelt plea, made when she was alone, her latest Svengali thousands of miles away. And then the reality of her situation kicks in:

The money is an important driving force too. I was happy when I worked in a factory but now I've experienced other things, a different way of life – and I could never go back. I used to spend all the money I earned. Since I've been married I've saved some. I still spend a lot though. After all, what's the use of having a Rolls Royce when you're fifty? We want one now.

I can't say I'm not still temperamental. I get terrible moods – if I can't get something right in rehearsal I'll scream and shout and cry. But I'm much better than I was a couple of years ago. But I've always been like that; as a kid I was temperamental. It's a funny thing about success: if you have a temper when you're nobody you're a troublemaker. If you create when you're a star they just say you're artistically temperamental and accept it.

Even on her return to Britain her uncharacteristically inward-looking mood seems to have persisted, despite the fact that on her return Kenneth surprised her with a brand-new house for the two of them in Carlton Hill, St John's Wood. She'd been unwise enough to tell a journalist what she really thought of Blackpool, her summer base, and she'd been receiving hate mail in return, as she told the *Sunday Express*, when interviewed in her new house:

> When I said I didn't like Blackpool I got nasty letters from people berating me for being coloured – except they have another word for it which they constantly use. You know, 'nigger'. Go back to where you come from they said, it made me sick. I thought I came from Cardiff.[9]

And she goes on to make the longest statement of her public life as to her own feelings about her racial background:

> Being coloured hasn't affected me deeply. I have a white mother. I've mixed mostly with white people. Not because I wanted to, it just happened that way. Two of my sisters married white boys. My brother married a white girl. I'm married to a white boy. My mother was from Yorkshire. I don't know why we came to live in Cardiff. I never asked my mother. Isn't that strange? If my mother ever had any trouble because of marrying a West African she never told us. But somehow I have the impression that her family didn't like it. Perhaps that's why she moved to Cardiff. She and my father were divorced when I was two. I'm not hypersensitive about being coloured the way American artists are. I cannot say I think about it at all.

Does that sound too pat? Well, maybe there's an element of the disingenuous here, a suggestion of not wanting to rock the boat. But it has the ring of truth. Shirley did grow up around white people; several of her siblings did marry white people. Children don't ask their parents why they chose to live where they live. Similarly, whether or not she knew the details of her father's disgrace, she must have sensed it, must have known that this was territory best avoided. And as for not thinking about being 'coloured', she obviously didn't mean that she was unaware that her skin colour affected the way people responded to her. Rather, I suspect she meant that, culturally speaking, being 'coloured' had little meaning for her. Brought up in a white suburb by a white mother, she didn't feel culturally 'coloured' in the way that black Americans, brought up in a segregated country, couldn't help but feel.

As ever, it wasn't racial politics that were really bothering Shirley at this point in her life. Much more pressing for her, as the New York interview suggests, was the matter of whether she should carry on with her brilliant career or give it up to have children and a regular family life. And if the latter option was what she wanted, would she manage to achieve it with her curious new husband?

NINETEEN

I (Who Have Nothing)

Once you've made it as a star, life starts to take on a familiar pattern – tour, record release, another tour, TV show – and the years begin to blur into one another. For Shirley Bassey this process was well under way as 1961 turned over into 1962.

That December Shirley appeared in the *Bing Crosby Christmas Special*, filmed in London but aired on network TV across the USA, a further fillip to her profile over there. In Britain her new single, 'I'll Get By', a show tune dating back as far as 1928, made the Top Ten. She had three more hit singles in the first half of 1962, albeit only minor hits, including a particularly overwrought reading of 'Tonight' from *West Side Story* and a real oddity, a version of 'Ave Maria', which does suggest that with training Shirley might have had the stuff of a fully fledged opera singer.

All in all it would have been easy to rest on her laurels, just carry on carrying on. But Kenneth Hume was never one to sit back and let things happen. Like Mike Sullivan, he was a restless soul who always wanted to see things moving forward. So he decided to raise the game. For the previous couple of years Shirley had been using Ken Mackintosh and his band, a decent enough British outfit, for her live work. Kenneth decided it was time for an upgrade.

For her two-week run at the Palladium in May (supported by a fabulously motley crew including Mike and Bernie Winters, Lionel Blair and his twist dancers, the Temperance Seven, a magician and some Cossack dancers) he hired another British bandleader, Raymond Long. And then, upping the ante further, he decided that, for her summer theatre tour, her accompanist should be none other than the greatest American arranger in the business, Nelson Riddle, the man behind so many of Sinatra's greatest recordings (and briefly available because Sinatra had just jumped ship from Capitol Records to start his own company, Reprise).

Ken Mackintosh offers his own professionally cynical assessment of the change:

> Well, yes, Shirley was very difficult to accompany. She would snatch her words, singing them in quick phrases, and it was difficult to get an orchestra of sixteen blokes to match that timing, particularly when she would be different every night. She was always arguing with MDs. She criticised my drummer once and I stuck up for him and said, 'You're too fussy, Shirley, we did well.'
>
> It got worse when she married Kenneth Hume who was also her manager and very fussy and bossy. He wanted to get rid of me because he said that we were like a double act. He said that he was going to replace me with Nelson Riddle. Well, I shouldn't laugh. He did get Nelson Riddle in from America and they assembled a band using top musicians from the like of Ted Heath's orchestra. We were a moderately priced band and most promoters couldn't afford this extravagance. They only did a few shows as many of the dates were dropped[1].

It may have been an extravagance to bring Riddle over for the live shows, but the deal also included Riddle providing the arrangements for a new Shirley Bassey album and that was an unarguable success. Shirley's recent recordings had started to conform to a pattern: start somewhere near the top, build up and up, then a key change and go all the way over the top. With Riddle at the helm Shirley had to dig deeper, to exercise restraint and inhabit the emotional territory of the songs, rather than dragging them all onto her territory. She achieved the goal, never more so than on the album's hit single 'What Now My Love?': another song that, like so many of Shirley's signature tunes, had European roots. And, as Shirley told Russell Davies a few years ago, it was the one song that Riddle nearly didn't arrange:

The problem was that he'd already written an arrangement of the song for Sinatra and didn't want to repeat himself. Norman Newell said that was fine, he'd find another arranger for the song. Riddle's professional pride was piqued by this, and in the end he stayed up all night working on a whole new arrangement for the song, which ended up being the album's highlight.

This was a new, more grown-up, more genuinely sophisticated Shirley. Life with Kenneth Hume was clearly having its effect. In May the *Sunday Express* came to their house in St John's Wood, 'a white house in a millionaires' row surrounded by primroses in pots with an entrance mat marked S and K – Shirley and Kenneth', and found the very picture of domestic harmony:

> Downstairs in the flower-filled rooms packed with books, chosen by husband, producer Kenneth Hume, the relatives from Tiger Bay were preparing tea for Shirley's ritual four o'clock rising. 'Kenneth bought this house for me as a surprise when I was in America,' said Shirley. 'I love him. I have my own Richard Burton and Frank Sinatra rolled into one and the sooner I have a baby the better.'[3]

When the *Sunday Pictorial* interviewed the happy couple, in September 1962, the subject soon turned to Shirley's great obsession: making a film. Obviously the two of them had been frustrated in their efforts to find a suitable feature for Shirley to appear in, and they were now starting to discuss the possibility of launching the one film she would have to have a part in – her very own biopic. And the newly grown-up Shirley was clear she wouldn't want such a film to be a saccharine, airbrushed affair:

> These glossed-up phoney film life stories make me sick. I don't want a biography with all the murkier moments in my life skated over. Audiences would tumble to its deceit in a second. It must be more on the lines of Lillian Roth's film *I'll Cry Tomorrow** – she told everything.[4]

Then Kenneth takes over and gives the reporter a pitch for the movie he envisions:

> Let me tell you about the film. It opens in the most sordid house of a sordid slum. The doctor has just delivered a stringy-looking coloured child with the words, 'Oh well, here's another one of them.' The baby yells and gradually the squawking modulates into Shirley singing the theme song. We go through her childhood, including the tragic episode of her first love. She was eight and idolised a boy of ten. One day he told her why he didn't want to see her again, because she was dirty. She was dirty, but the shock of finding it out like this caused the obsession she still has for cleanliness.
>
> The story goes on to tell how she had a baby at sixteen and yet was so naive that she didn't know about it till she was six months

---

* A 1950s MGM melodrama in which Susan Hayward was Oscar-nominated for her part playing the real-life Broadway star Lillian Roth, as she battled an overbearing mother and a drink problem.

pregnant. There'll be the shooting affair when a gunman barricaded himself in with Shirley in a London hotel. And we'll dwell on Shirley's continual fight against ill omens and her own temperament.

It would have been an extraordinary film to make in early 1960s Britain, and, of course, as with most extraordinary ideas, it didn't come to pass. Instead the restless Hume started to develop something called *The Secret Keepers*. This was to have been a TV comedy series starring Alma Cogan as a private eye. Hume would appear to have shot a pilot episode, though one that seems never to have been broadcast. However, the *Daily Mail* ran a story about the show, illustrated with location photographs. One of these stills features Shirley holding up a sign saying 'Husband and 4 agents to support'.

According to the supporting text the show featured Alma Cogan's PI hunting down a runaway husband played by Frankie Howerd. In the course of her search she bumps into Shirley who plays a street busker (thus the sign). Alma Cogan offers her a penny for a song and Shirley responds by throwing a brick through her office window.

It's a definite shame that this appears to have vanished without trace. The casting of Shirley as a busker is another example of the playfulness that seems to have characterised the Bassey–Hume relationship. Which makes it surprising that only two months later, on Saturday, 24 November, the papers were full of the story of their marriage breaking down. 'All over, says Shirley', was the splash on the cover of the *Daily Mirror*, while in the *Daily Mail* Shirley told a young Barry Norman that 'I won't go back to him. My marriage is over. I have given my wedding and engagement rings back to my husband. My belongings are packed ready to be taken away at our house.'[5]

So what had happened between August and September to cause this breakdown? Well, this undated anecdote from Mike Sullivan may explain matters:

> Early one evening I took a telephone call from her home in West London. She was hysterical and distraught. She had caught Hume in bed, making love to her chauffeur. I told her to come to me immediately. Shirley almost fell out of the taxi that stopped outside my flat. She was in a terrible state, screaming, sobbing and shaking, and I took her in and tried to comfort her.
>
> 'Mickey, I really thought he was out of all that,' she croaked. 'How could he?'[6]

Before Sullivan could provide a reasonable answer to this imponderable, Kenneth Hume arrived, also distraught. And after a while Sullivan sent Shirley home, then gave Kenneth a talking to: 'If she does call me again and you are the cause of her trouble I will break your fucking neck.'*

The damage, however, was done. As Shirley made very clear to Barry Norman: 'I am going to America on Monday and soon after that to Australia. When I come back I shall look for a new home.'

Before she could go Kenneth took an overdose of sleeping pills. He survived. Shirley left for New York, sadder and wiser.

*   *   *

---

* This was the last time Mike Sullivan figured in Shirley's career. They met once or twice over the succeeding years but were never close again. Sullivan died in May 1995. He was wheelchair-bound and living in straitened circumstances, but happily married to his fifth wife, the French actress Dany Robin, when a fire swept through their Paris flat killing them both – a sad end for a much-loved, if not always trusted, man, and the person most responsible for Shirley Bassey's success.

Shirley's second season at the Persian Room built on the success of her previous visit. On 4 December, to coincide with the start of her run, she appeared on networked TV, on the *Garry Moore Show*, singing 'As Long As He Needs Me' and 'I Could Have Danced All Night'. The society folk came out in force to see her perform, among them none other than the new First Lady, Jacqueline Bouvier Kennedy.

The leading Black American magazine *Ebony*, clearly fascinated by this oddity, this black British singer who seemed so at home in the white world, made her their cover star and devoted seven pages to pictures of her. She also came to the attention of the Broadway lyricist and producer Richard Adler, who was charged with assembling a bill for a gala concert to celebrate the end of JFK's second year in office. He invited Shirley to perform and she arranged to extend her stay in the US. How could she resist? Marilyn Monroe's performance for the Press at his inauguration was already the stuff of legend. And JFK's new Camelot was at its height, as the Washington society columnist Betty Beale observed when previewing the gala:

Life in Washington under the Kennedy administration is one spectacular after another . . . A dazzling extravaganza on the eighteenth to mark the end of the President's second year in office. It's going to be such a colossal collection of talent it will out-glitter the Madison Square Garden show for JFK last spring. The $100 per ticket Democratic gala at the Armoury will be preceded by a $1,000 per person dinner in honour of the Kennedys. The diamond dining will take place in Washington's new International Inn, and, in case you would like to toss your own $1,000 dinner at home, this is what they will be having. Avocado pear stuffed with lobster, crab and shrimp, green turtle soup amontillado served with cheese sticks, poached fillet of

English sole, glace Veronique, hearts of palm salad with rolls, and Cherry Blossom International (which means a bowl of vanilla ice cream covered with cherry herring* and black cherries and topped by an American flag sitting in a bigger bowl of dry ice over which boiling water is poured). The patriotic effect will be of an American flag waving above rising mists of steam. And if the artistic effort's in vain guests can drown their disdain in dry champagne.[7]

The gala was emceed by Gene Kelly and Kirk Douglas. The stars included Judy Garland, the opera singer Joan Sutherland, comedienne Carol Burnett, actress Diahann Carroll, the new folk singing sensations Peter, Paul and Mary, plus the 'part Negro Welsh girl' Shirley Bassey. A little continental flavour was added by Yves Montand and, oddly enough, Antonio and his Flamenco Dancers, as seen by Shirley on her first date with Kenneth Hume.

Performing for JFK was one of the undoubted highlights of Shirley's career. She'd already performed before the British royal family, but neither Prince Philip nor Prince Charles could exactly match up to the President in the charisma stakes. As she observed years later: 'When he shook hands with me, it was like being hit by a bolt of lightning. It was sheer magic and the first time I realised political power was sexy. Oh yes, he could have left his shoes under my bed any time.'[8]

From the US, Shirley headed back to Australia for another summer season down under. The first thing she had to deal with was some unfinished business. On her visit the previous year she had set in motion a libel action against a magazine called *Pix* which had given a lurid account of her private life, focusing on the Pepe

---

* Not quite as alarming as it sounds; this is actually a kind of cherry brandy; aka cherry heering.

Davis affair. The matter came to court shortly after Shirley arrived back in Sydney.

It was a curious action for Shirley to bring. The *Pix* piece was pretty run-of-the-mill, just a rehash of the press cuttings from Davis's trial. However she was duly awarded damages of A£3000 against the magazine's publishers.

Shirley arrived back in the UK in March and went straight into a string of provincial theatre dates. When in London she stayed at the Mayfair Hotel but gradually she and Kenneth Hume began to resume their relationship. The two of them were seen together eating out at the White Elephant Club. On 10 March he drove her back from a show in Southend and stayed over in her suite, waking up in the middle of the night to find an intruder going through Shirley's possessions. Hume chased the thief away and made an appearance in the following day's papers when he announced, regarding Shirley, that 'We are playing it by ear.' Shirley's lawyer, Walter Lyons, added that 'Miss Bassey and her husband Kenneth Hume are reunited to the extent that they are again on friendly terms. But Miss Bassey has made no decisions about her future.'

Walter Lyons was a busy man that year as one of his other clients was a woman who was making headlines: Christine Keeler. The Britain Shirley had returned to after her months on tour was one suddenly caught up in change: the Profumo scandal was all over the news and a new group, recently signed to Shirley's record label, EMI, were all over the charts. They were the Beatles, and it's worth noting that, for all the obvious differences between the Tiger Bay Tigress and the Fab Four, there were similarities too. Like Shirley, the Beatles came from a port city and got a head start from the black American records that the sailors brought in. But where Shirley had had her dockland rough edges care-fully smoothed off by her variety training, the Beatles had had theirs sharpened by their time in another, rougher yet, port city: Hamburg.

On 4 April Shirley did make it onto the front pages of the newspapers. 'I'm Having A Baby Says Shirley Bassey' was the headline in the *Daily Mail*. Shirley went on to elaborate:

> Kenneth and I parted towards the end of last year. But we were reconciled when I got back from my Australian tour and we have been deliriously happy ever since. I would like a girl but he wants a boy. Some people who are cynical about our reconciliation will be dumbfounded. But our true friends will be thrilled.[9]

This was undoubtedly wishful thinking. The cynics were able to figure out that the timing was mighty tight for Shirley to have returned home from Australia, reconciled herself with Kenneth, and discovered her pregnancy. But if Kenneth was concerned about that, he kept it to himself. When the newspapers asked him how he felt, he came up with the wonderfully enigmatic reply that he was 'pleased, although a little baffled'.

Only Shirley herself can know what private agreement was arrived at between the two of them. Kenneth must, at the very least, have had his suspicions that the baby would not turn out to be his. Why did he close ranks and assume the role of the prospective father with apparent enthusiasm over the coming months? The possible explanations run the gamut from the idealist – that he loved Shirley so much that he didn't care whether or not he was the biological father of her child – to the cynical, that he loved Shirley's money so much he was determined to remain married to her.

Either way, the Humes returned to married life in St John's Wood. In April, Shirley appeared at the London Palladium supported by fellow balladeer Matt Monro. In June she had to rest up at a London clinic after pulling out of an ITV *Live at the Palladium* show.

By now it was time for Shirley to return to the recording studio. It was a year since she'd made the album with Nelson Riddle. There was no chance of working with him again, so Shirley and Kenneth decided to go with another of the regular EMI arrangers, Tony Osborne, who had arranged the B-side of 'What Now My Love?' And to further freshen things up, they decided that this time the producer would not be Norman Newell, but the man behind the Beatles' run of hits, George Martin.

All that remained was to choose the song. The one they came up with was another European translation. The Italian singer Joe Sentieri had had a hit called 'Uno Dei Tanti' in 1960. The great US writing and production team, Jerry Leiber and Mike Stoller, picked up on it and, unusually for them, translated it into English. 'I (Who Have Nothing)' was a US hit for Ben E. King early in 1963. Their British publisher, Cyril Shane at Bernstein, Shapiro and Co., knew just where to take it. So sure was Shane that this was a Bassey vehicle that he gave the lyrics a sex change before presenting it to EMI.

It was George Martin who finally picked the song from a choice of eight contenders to be Shirley's next single: 'The Italian song stuck out a mile,' he told the *Daily Mirror*.

The song was indeed perfect for Shirley. If she couldn't get a part in a film, well, here was a song as full of drama as any movie. She might not be able to show her dramatic talents on screen, but here was the opportunity to give a supremely theatrical vocal performance. And so she did, aided by state-of-the-art production from George Martin and a wonderfully melodramatic arrangement from Osborne: 'I wrote that in 5/4 which enabled us to put a big tympani beat in it. Shirley wouldn't have known if it was 5/4 or 10/4, but it didn't matter as she was somebody who could feel an arrangement and knew when to come in.'[10]

The song was recorded by a heavily pregnant Shirley on 6 September 1963. Tony Osborne was in charge of the recording: 'The session with Shirley took from 2.30 to 3.50 p.m., which is comparatively short. We only made three complete takes. She sang naturally, I didn't try to compress the voice.'[11]

Shirley too was happy with the result: 'It came very easy except for the timing on the breaks. Maybe I would come in too soon. I just sang it naturally – just the way I felt it. And I liked it so much.'[12]

Two weeks later the song was in the charts. It's an extraordinary record, one that elevates Shirley from being just one more singer to being – there's no other word for it – a diva.

Shirley's life over the previous decade since her debut in *Memories of Jolson* had been one of non-stop drama and now her art was starting to reflect that. From this point on, she joined the company of Judy Garland, Edith Piaf et al. women whose music was inseparable from their turbulent lives. In 'I (Who Have Nothing)' Shirley the woman and Shirley the singer are indistinguishable. We know it from that first dramatic syllable – 'I' – and, from here on in, neither she nor her audience would be in any danger of forgetting it. 'I (Who Have Nothing)' is, if you like, her masterpiece; a gaudy, sentimental and magnificent statement of pure ego.

TWENTY

A Knight in Shining Armour

Though she was seven months pregnant when she recorded 'I (Who Have Nothing)', Shirley's schedule still wouldn't let up. She went back into the studio with George Martin to record her next single, 'My Special Dream', which was also her first movie theme, used in a film called *The Victors*.* She even carried on performing live. Tony Osborne, who had now taken over as her stage pianist, recalled accompanying her at a club in Majorca:

> Shirley was eight months pregnant at the time and I honestly thought she was going to have the baby right there on stage. For her opening number she used to come on, point to the massive bulge in her dress, and sing 'I Should Have Danced All Night' . . . it brought the house down.[1]

In September the *Daily Sketch* interviewed Shirley and Ken together, both apparently thrilled at their impending parenthood, and Shirley doing a good job of seeming to believe that the baby

---

* *The Victors* was the one and only feature film directed by the blacklisted Hollywood screenwriter Carl Foreman. A powerful Second World War movie, based on Alexander Baron's great novel *The Human Kind*, it was too bleak to chime with the public mood.

was indeed Ken's. She discussed what they were going to call the child:

> Christopher if it's a boy and Samantha if it's a girl. I know I want him so much to be fair and have my bone structure in his face and the colour of Kenneth's eyes. Look how blue they are. And we shan't allow anyone to call him Chris. And he must have a really good education so he will never be lost for words like I am. I've engaged a fair, plump nanny for him. She's twenty-nine and worked for ten years in one of the Barnardo homes.[2]

Asked if she was hoping for a boy, she replied 'I don't really mind if it is a girl, because this time I can keep her.'

In October, taking her place amongst the great and good of London society, she went to see the first night of Peter O'Toole's epic rendition of *Hamlet* at the new National Theatre. A few weeks later, on 8 November, she gave birth to her second child, a girl called Samantha.

Samantha was born at the London Clinic in Harley Street. 'Now I have everything', Shirley told the press. That Christmas, Sharon came to stay in London and meet her little sister. Sharon had recently been told by Iris that her Auntie Shirley was in fact her mother. She'd been up to visit Shirley before, but this time she decided she wanted to stay on permanently.

'I've always wanted to have Sharon back', Shirley told the *Daily Mirror*. 'Now I know what perfect family happiness is.' And indeed she looks radiant in the photos of her posing with her two daughters that appeared in all the newspapers that January.

However, the two months since Samantha's birth were all the time out Shirley was going to be able to take. On 4 January she played a show at the Leicester Square Odeon and afterwards threw a party, a couple of days before her twenty-seventh birthday, with music from the pre-Procol Harum beat group the Paramounts and a guest list that ranged from Tommy Steele to George Martin to the music business lawyer Allen Klein.

After that, she was straight off on tour. This time her accompanist was John Barry plus his group and an orchestra. She was due back in the recording studio in the first week of February to record a song called 'Gone', written for her by Tony Osborne, to be produced once again by George Martin. The week after that she would be off abroad again: New York, Australia, Hong Kong. Her initial plan was to take her baby with her, but when Samantha came down with bronchitis, she was advised to leave her behind in the care of her nanny.

As for Sharon, Kenneth was hardly the person to look after a presumably somewhat confused nine-year-old, but his brother Alan had children, so Alan's wife Sheila was called in to help: 'I had four kids and Shirley was going away somewhere and they asked me to have Sharon. I did that several times when they went away, she was the same age as my youngest.'

And so it was that, less than three months after Samantha was born, Shirley was on her travels again. First stop was New York, where she was booked to appear at the Carnegie Hall, an extremely prestigious event.

When she arrived in New York, though, it was in the wake of the first landing of the British invasion. Her upstart label-mates the Beatles were also playing at Carnegie Hall, three days before Shirley. They'd landed in New York on 7 February and the city had gone famously nuts. Rather than sulk at being upstaged, Shirley went along to see what all the fuss was about: 'I went to their Carnegie Hall show and it was a terrifying experience. After a while I stopped watching the Beatles and started watching the audience.

I think they were still cleaning the place up when I appeared there the following Saturday night.'³

Shirley was only three years older than John Lennon, but it was very clear that she belonged to a different generation. While the Beatles filled the hall with screaming teenagers, Shirley was entertaining their parents. That said, though some way from a sell-out, her Carnegie Hall appearance was a triumph too. As the veteran American agent Sidney Bernstein, who had booked both acts, recalled: 'Shirley's concert in a half-filled Carnegie Hall was an artistic triumph. Her thrilling voice, beauty and incredible stage presence evoked memories of a young, dynamic Judy Garland. The audience showered her with flowers.'⁴

Shirley was happy with it too, as she told the *NME* a few weeks later: 'The atmosphere is fantastic, and although I was rather nervous at first the audience was marvellous to me. I'll remember that night for the rest of my life.'

Thirty years later a recording of the show was released. After some initial nerves, this is Shirley at her most refined. There's little of the burlesque that would feature in her later shows, no 'Kiss Me Honey, Honey' and no 'Big Spender', just a passionately delivered set, mostly made up of standards. This is Shirley the classicist, paying her respects on the stage where all her idols had performed.

There was drama offstage, too, as Kenneth Hume used the moment of one of Shirley's greatest triumphs to sack her agent, Peter Charlesworth, whose hard work had set up the show. Kenneth was determined to solidify his power as Shirley's manager, even if his role as her husband was in question.

Back to Australia then for yet another season. The *NME* caught up with her there and reported that 'Shirley's opening night at Sydney's Chequers was a repetition of a now familiar scene. The overbooked club packed to suffocation; ecstatic audiences and reviewers left searching for new superlatives.' As for the star herself, she was enjoying the winter warmth, though finding it hard to be separated from her baby. 'I miss her very much, but she has a very capable nanny,' she told the reporter.[5]

However, Shirley didn't have much more time to spend with her baby when she returned to the UK in April. She was straight off on a further theatre tour with John Barry. She'd known Barry for a while. His group, the John Barry Seven, had had a run of instrumental hits at just the time when Shirley was becoming a regular in the charts. He had also provided the arrangements for the TV show *Drumbeat* and for some of EMI's acts. And he'd very quickly made the leap into films. He'd provided the score for Adam Faith's 1960 film *Beat Girl*, and worked on the soundtrack to the first of the James Bond films, *Dr No*. Then, when Lionel Bart was employed to write the score for the second Bond film, *From Russia With Love*, only for the producers to discover he couldn't read or write music, Barry had been called in to provide the know-how.

Barry was also a well-known ladies' man. His first marriage had recently ended in divorce, following his affair with their Swedish au pair, Ulla, with whom he'd had a child. Eventually Ulla had gone back to Sweden and Barry was footloose and fancy-free once more.

Shirley too, if not actually divorced, was clearly no longer viewing her marriage to Hume as a monogamous affair. As she told the *Daily Mail* years later, 'I had other men in my life and Kenneth was never jealous of any of them.' So it was hardly surprising when Bassey and Barry got together. Vic Flick, the man responsible for the classic 'James Bond Theme' guitar riff, was in John Barry's group for the tour, and he offers a succinct assessment of the situation: 'Shirley had married this real strange queer guy, he used to follow her around.'

The Shirley Vic met was a woman starting to become very aware of her star status and not much inclined to fraternise with the troops: 'I never had any one-on-one conversations with her. She had a little bit of an above-it-all attitude. She knew she was good and she played on it.'

One of the places they went to on the tour was Cardiff. It was a city in flux. That year, while its most famous ex-resident had been off touring the world, the planners had started to knock down the old Tiger Bay. The grand houses of Loudon Square and the mean surrounding terraces alike, all succumbed to the wrecker's ball. It was not, as is often claimed, the end of Tiger Bay: a community, in the end, is made up of people, not buildings. A new council estate was built and housed many of the former residents. But it was clear evidence that the community was no longer what it had been. And, again, that was not necessarily a bad thing. Where once the old Tiger Bay had been an isolated outpost of multicultural life, now all major British cities were starting to incorporate populations from the former colonies.

Nor did it impinge on Shirley much. In fact she spent as little time as possible in Cardiff. There's an amusing clip from a Welsh TV news programme covering her visit. The reporter ends by asking Shirley, 'Are we likely to see you back in Cardiff fairly soon?' Shirley looks horrified at the idea and says 'Not fairly soon, I shouldn't imagine.'

Even the bonds of her Cardiff family were no longer as strong as they had been, not now she had Sharon living with her. As her sometime manager, Vic Lewis, remembered:

When we went to Cardiff we used to pass her mother's house. So I used to say, 'Shirl, let's pull over and go and see mum.' 'Oh no, no, she'll come down tonight, they'll all be there tonight.' She meant all her sisters and their families. I said, 'Well, of course they will.' 'Well then,' she'd say, 'can you look after them? I don't want to see them before the show.' On a couple of occasions even after the show I shouted up to her, 'Shirley, your family's here!' and she'd shout down, 'Tell them I'll see them next week!'[6]

Back in London, the affair with Barry carried on until one night Shirley bumped into the Australian actor who'd been in her dressing room at the Pigalle on the night of the shooting: Peter Finch. As Shirley later recalled:

I met him first when I was appearing in cabaret at the Pigalle. He was dining with his wife and sent a message asking to meet me. I had been accepted as a star for some years, but I was overcome at the prospect of talking to such an actor. I hardly knew what to say.

Some years later we met in a fashionable restaurant when I was going out with John Barry, the composer. Peter was appearing in *The Seagull* with Vanessa Redgrave on the West End stage, and amiably invited John and me to the theatre.

Unfortunately John couldn't go. My press agent said I couldn't go alone. 'You're a big star,' he said. 'You should have a male escort!' So he sat in the stalls with me and my secretary. Naturally I went backstage to congratulate Peter and he took me to supper. And that's how it really began between us, an unbelievably beautiful affair.[7]

Peter Finch was a big deal in 1964. He'd been born in London in 1916 to well-off but dysfunctional parents and had mostly been brought up by his Australian grandmother, first near Paris, then in India and finally back in New South Wales. Australia formed him but it was when he returned to London that he made his name, initially as a theatre actor. Laurence Olivier helped him and Finch became close to the Oliviers, eventually embarking on a long affair with Laurence's wife, the actress Vivien Leigh.

Finch went on to make a name in movies as a rugged but smart Richard Burton type. His role in *A Town Called Alice* made him a genuine star. He went on to receive a string of BAFTA nominations for now more-or-less forgotten films – *Windom's Way*, *The Nun's Story*, *The Trial of Oscar Wilde*, *No Love for Johnnie*. When he met Shirley in the spring of 1964 he had just finished filming an adaptation of Edna O'Brien's *The Girl with Green Eyes* alongside Rita Tushingham, and was making a much-heralded return to the West End stage in Chekhov's *The Seagull* alongside Vanessa Redgrave and Peggy Ashcroft.

He was living with his second wife, a South African actress called Yolande Turner, in a house in Mill Hill, north London. However, most of his time was spent in Soho propping up the bar in Gerry's Club, drinking and unashamedly whoring. Yolande accepted his behaviour up to a point, enjoying the thrill of attempting to tame a bad boy, a struggle graphically described in her notably frank book about their life together:

> It seemed to me he'd had every woman in London, including the ladies of the night, who never failed to give him a wave from the pavements around Mayfair as we sailed by in a taxi. 'Allo Finchy.' 'Ow you doing then?' He'd thrust his head out of the window and call, jerking a thumb in my direction, 'Got her now.' I felt quite proud till one night he went decidedly too far.[8]

That was the night he brought Yolande along to watch him have sex with two hookers they'd bumped into while driving through the West End. This was the point when it became clear to her that Finch wasn't going to let marriage tame him. He liked hookers too much, particularly black hookers and preferably two at a time. Yolande, unsurprisingly, soon became sick of this behaviour, not just because of the infidelity, but because of what it revealed about Finch.

Finchy also suffered from the embarrassing delusion that blacks hung from the trees. When, in his mind, I started to get above my station, he would snap that a woman shouldn't think and what he wanted was 'one that hung from the trees'. When I asked 'Like who?' he answered me with, 'A peasant, a geisha, a black girl. They never give you any lip.'

'You chauvinist.'

'That's right and that's why I like hookers and black girls.'

'You don't know a thing about black people, Finchy. I'm more black than you'll ever be.* You're a patronising pig.'

As soon as Finchy saw a black man or woman, he would make such a performance, clasping them in his arms like a long-lost relative and calling them mate. It embarrassed the hell out of them at first. They'd look mystified at his indiscriminate love: then, not to hurt his feelings, which were genuine if misplaced, they'd pat him on the back and walk off shaking their heads.[9]

It's unsurprising that Finch should have fallen for Shirley, then. Though it's hard to imagine that she'd be delighted at being thought of as a kind of sexual animal, akin to a hooker. But if Finch's – at best – naive enthusiasm for black culture may not have been much of a pull for Shirley, he did have a lot of other things going for him. He was just her type of man: extremely good-looking, older than her, an autodidact who loved to talk about literature and

* By this she's referring to the fact that she was largely brought up by black servants in South Africa.

philosophy, and also an action man. Above all he was a genuine movie star, and she was a woman who wanted, more than anything else, to make it in films.

In the first flush of her love for Kenneth Hume she'd described him as a mix of Frank Sinatra and Richard Burton. Well, Peter Finch filled that description a whole lot more convincingly than Kenneth ever did. And she fell for him hard: 'He was a knight in shining armour. He was so handsome, so knowledgeable. I would curl up and listen to him for hours.'[10]

Their affair played out across London that spring and summer. Shirley was headlining at the Talk of the Town for a season and each night, after the show, they would go out together. Yolande was oblivious, on holiday in Italy with their children, already wondering whether to divorce Finch. Finch himself moved out of Mill Hill and stayed at his mother's place in Bury Walk, Chelsea. For a while the two lovers holed up together in the Carlton Towers Hotel in Knightsbridge. It was from there that, at 3 a.m. one night, Finch called his agent, Laurie Evans, to say, 'I'm with Shirley Bassey. We want to do a play together. Can you think of one?' Half asleep, Evans did his best:

> Othello. No, wait a minute I've got it the wrong way round. Let's see, there was a good American play that had some success a while back called *Deep Are The Roots*. No, that's the black man and white girl too. What about *Antony and Cleopatra*? I'm going back to sleep.[11]

No more was heard of this project, unsurprisingly. Shirley might have had potential as an actress but she certainly wasn't ready for Shakespeare. Meanwhile, the tabloids got wind of the affair, which was not difficult as the pair were making little attempt to hide it. Yolande was doorstepped in Italy and asked what she thought about it. She was shocked, of course. Finch went out to try and calm her down, but failed. Yolande took a half-hearted overdose. She survived and determined on divorce. Finch came back to Shirley.

It wasn't only Yolande who was unprepared to accept the situation; the normally easy-going Kenneth Hume was also disturbed by it. He had spent the early part of the year putting together a bizarre project called *Mods And Rockers*. This had started off as a stage show, a ballet set to the music of the Beatles. Hume had made it into a short film which he directed. The action involved groups of teenagers clad as mods and rockers having a *West Side Story*-style balletic rumble while an effeminate black teenager watches from afar, when not staring lovingly at a statue of a naked gladiator. None of it makes any sense except as a dreamlike homoerotic fantasy. The film ends with the black boy walking off arm in arm with one of the rockers. All of this was accompanied by a band called the Cheynes (featuring a young Mick Fleetwood) covering a selection of Beatles songs. Hume turned this unpromising fare into a feature film by padding it out with film clips of assorted British beat groups. If its homoerotic heart didn't make it a hard enough sell, its release was swiftly curtailed when the Beatles took exception to the fact that the advertising gave the misleading impression that the group themselves featured in the film.

On the face of it, then, Hume would seem to have gone back to his old gay life and accepted that Shirley too was back to her single ways. But while he had tolerated her previous dalliances, the relationship with Finch thoroughly upset him: 'When Finchy came along he saw him as a threat. He put a detective on us and everywhere we went we were followed. We could trust nobody. When we stayed in hotels I always used to put the sheet over my head when the waiter came in to serve us breakfast.'[12]

This put the Finch–Bassey relationship under considerable strain and by the time Finch headed out to Israel in July, to make a film called *Judith* with Sophia Loren, the cracks were already starting to appear. The flaws in Finch's character, his excessive drinking and his self-obsession, were starting to reveal themselves. But the respite did at least allow Shirley to pay some more attention to her career. Her last single 'Gone' had not been the success she'd hoped for, barely making the charts. She went back into the studio with George Martin to record her next single, 'Who Can I Turn To?' Oddly, her song titles had started to mirror her life.

And on 23 July she was back at the Palladium for a remarkable show, the latest *Night of a Hundred Stars*. Shirley – and this shows how much of a name she was – co-headlined the show with the Beatles. The true star, though, was Shirley's enduring heroine, Judy Garland.

Garland was not officially billed as appearing, but when the second half of the show opened she was one of a number of stars seated at a table at the side of the stage. Shirley dedicated one of her songs to Garland and went over and embraced her at the end of it. The audience were determined that the legend would sing for them and when the MC, Richard Attenborough, tried to end the show, he was drowned out by the calls for Judy. Sure enough Ms Garland, a trouper to the last, but now already in the decline that would see her die just five years later, stepped forward and stole the show with renditions of 'Swanee' and the inevitable 'Over the Rainbow'.

For Shirley, seeing this must have been both an inspiration and a warning. She was as addicted as Garland to the passionate impersonal love of the audience, but she didn't want their pity. Shirley didn't want to be known for the wreckage of her life. At heart she was, like her mother, a survivor.

A few days later Kenneth Hume served notice of his intention to divorce Shirley, and to cite Peter Finch as the co-respondent. Shirley resolved to fly to Israel and sort things out one way or the other with Peter Finch, to start to get her life back under her own control.

TWENTY-ONE

The Man With the Midas Touch

Judith, the film Peter Finch was making in Israel, was pure hokum. Like many of the movies he made, it took a serious subject – in this case the formation of Israel after the war – and trivialised it. Sophia Loren was never going to convince as the Jewish wife of a Nazi war criminal who becomes a freedom fighter on an Israeli kibbutz while wearing some very short shorts.

The *Daily Express* sent a reporter out to get Finch's reaction to the news of Kenneth Hume's divorce petition. Finch obliged with some characteristically actor-ish thoughts on the meaning of life:

> I once read a marvellous criticism of an actor's performance in Russia. It said that this actor had built many bridges – and then was unable to decide which one to cross. I've thought about that quite a bit. It's the truth about everybody, really, isn't it? Which bridge will you cross? Which bridge will I cross? Which bridge will any of us cross? There are so many, so many in all our lives.[1]

A few days later Shirley arrived in Israel, at the coastal town of Nahariya, a little way north of Haifa. She spent five days there, during which time she discovered that she was not cut out to be an actor's consort. She couldn't play second fiddle and she wouldn't live with a man whose drinking was as out of control as Finch's. A Judy Garland might have stayed. Shirley Bassey left.

Peter Finch stayed on and went out with the crew and got roaring drunk and lamented that 'I've been set too many traps in my life! Emotional traps! Traps set by women! That's all they want to do. Take everything and give nothing. But not any more! I want to be free!' He also complained that his career was suffering in the States 'because I've had an affair with a coloured girl. They've given me up because of my affair with Shirley Bassey!' No question he was still doing his best to feel the black man's pain while receiving the white movie star's salary.

Finch continued to chase after Shirley for a while but was repeatedly rebuffed. He would tell anyone who would listen how he was pining for her, including the actress Sarah Miles, in this case while trying to make a pass at her:

> He poured his heart out while I poured out the whiskey. What a lonely man he was. He shared his grievances with me, his unrequited longing for Shirley Bassey and how he couldn't live without her. The only thing as repetitive as his broken heart was his determination to get his lips onto mine or his hand up my skirt.[2]

Years later Shirley told the *Sunday Mirror* how she coped with Finch's behaviour: 'In the end I couldn't take any more. I ran away. I hid from my knight in shining armour. And it hurt him terribly. He came after me and tried to find me. But as far as I was concerned it was over.'[3]

This is probably a bit of an oversimplification. The affair seems to have limped on into the following year. As late as April 1965 Shirley was photographed saying goodbye to Finch at London airport, as he was heading off to the States to make a film called *The*

Flight of the Phoenix. That was the definitive end to the affair though as there, while making the film, Finch found a new lover, a black American woman called Florrie Christmas. They stayed together for a while and then, in April 1966, following a serious illness, Finch decided to move to Jamaica, where he owned a beach house. There he met a young local woman called Eletha Barrett whom he declared 'a true primitive.' Having finally found what he was looking for, he settled down with Eletha: they had a child together and married in 1973. Three years later he died of a heart attack, shortly after completing his final film, *Network*, for which he would win his single posthumous Oscar.

Back in the UK, Shirley did her best to settle back into life with her two children. While she'd been caught up in her affair with Peter Finch, her former beau John Barry had been hard at work on the score for the third Bond film, *Goldfinger*. By all accounts he hadn't spent any time moping after Shirley, and the following year he would get married for the second time, to a seventeen-year-old Jane Birkin. By August he was working on the title song, and he needed someone to write the lyrics:

> I called up Anthony Newley, who I knew casually, and said would he do this and he said, 'Well, I'm usually the composer and Leslie Bricusse writes the lyrics.' I said, 'Well, I'm the composer here.' And he said, 'OK. I'll write the lyric with Leslie.'[4]

Leslie Bricusse picks up the story:

> (We) arranged to meet Barry at his Cadogan Square apartment at eleven the next morning. We arrived promptly and John proudly sat down to play us his melody. After the first three notes Tony and I both instinctively sang, 'Wider than a mile', which went down like

a ton of lead.* But we loved the melody, took it home with us and went straight to work.

Now I have written some pretty unlikely lyrics but that one ranks high on the list.[5]

There was only one singer John Barry could imagine delivering this extraordinary tale of the man with the Midas touch: Miss Shirley Bassey. She'd barely returned from Israel when he gave her a call:

I had seen some of the title sequence. It was kind of over-the-top and bizarre and Shirley could be over-the-top and bizarre too. I knew her very well and she said she'd do it. She didn't know anything about it. She said what's Goldfinger? I said he's the villain, Shirley, you're singing about a bad guy. She had a terrific range, a very powerful singer.[6]

The recording took place on 20 August. Norman Newell was nominally the producer but Barry was in charge of the session. It's one recording date that Shirley still remembers very well:

I tell you, I just heard those opening bars and I got goose pimples. It was an experience to do that in a studio with sixty musicians. They had an enormous film screen in the studio and I had to sing 'Goldfinger' to what was happening on the credits. And when it came to 'the kiss of death' with the famous Bond car it was very sensuous you know, and then I got to the end and the credits didn't seem to end and I had to hold this note it seemed for ever, and I was looking

---

* That's the second line of 'Moon River'. Barry's flatmate Michael Caine thought exactly the same thing when Barry played him the music on its own.

over at John going G-o-o-o-o-o-o-ld. I nearly passed out. They gave me water. It's a cruel business, show business![7]

Vic Flick, who played guitar on the session, adds a little gloss to this:

I remember when she was doing the 'Goldfinger' thing, John Barry wanted this long note held. He said do it again and she said she couldn't but then there was a rustling noise and suddenly this bra comes over the top of the vocal booth. And then she really let it go.

Barry was more than happy with the result: 'She belted the hell out of it. Shirley was good because she didn't ask too many questions. She didn't intellectualize it. I mean, you didn't want to think about it too much.'[8]

The producer, Harry Salzman, hated the song but the director liked it and anyway there wasn't time to come up with an alternative. And so the song that has come to define the most successful movie franchise ever only just made it into the final cut. Strangely, it wasn't a big hit on initial release in Britain, but it was hugely successful in the States. It became Shirley's only significant chart success there, and the accompanying soundtrack album went to number one in the US, right at the height of Beatlemania.

If there's one song that the casual listener associates with Shirley Bassey, it's this one; the story of the man who loves only gold. It's brassy, irresistible, and as camp as it's bizarrely sincere. Its power is such that Shirley Bassey, this disembodied voice singing the theme tune, is a more memorable film presence than any of the Bond girls themselves. They're all putty in Bond's hands while Shirley is entirely cynical and unreachable.

Shirley singing 'Goldfinger' is a rebuke to all the directors and producers who had never cast her in a film, who never would cast her in a film. It's not black or white, European or American. Her voice is that of a woman who seems actually to live in the world of the Bond films, a fabulous place of glamour and mystery, sex and sophistication, a world whose key locations are West End London, Switzerland and Monte Carlo, nightclubs and casinos, ski slopes and marinas, fast cars and yachts. It's the dream landscape of the star; it's the world Shirley wanted to inhabit from the first time she felt her foot on the ladder.

In reality, of course, the world of the star had its drawbacks. Shirley certainly had an inkling of the price she was paying to inhabit it when she gave an interview to the *Daily Express* two weeks after recording 'Goldfinger'. She's interviewed in her latest home, a house in Belgravia where she was living with Sharon and Samantha, following her split from Hume. She started by enumerating her reasons for not marrying Peter Finch:

> Just now I am not ready for marriage to anyone, I feel I have to be free. I am a terribly selfish person and until I can overcome that selfishness I'd make a lousy partner for anyone. It's like I have only so much love to give and I tend to give it all out in one go. But I don't want to be trapped. You fall in love with a man and he wants to put a fence around you, keep you all to himself.[9]

Then her train of thought is interrupted by the sound of Samantha crying and she launches into a remarkably honest summary of her life to date and a presentiment of her life to come.

> There are the children. They need a father. They need the discipline of a man around the house. I suppose the trouble with my life is that my talent has got in the way of my happiness. It is a big talent,

I know that. And every time I walk on stage I am following myself. Trying to top my last performance. Dammit, I'm twenty-seven years old but I'm still a child woman. I haven't grown up – and I don't really want to. Being Shirley Bassey is a tough way to run a life.[9]

TWENTY-TWO

The Second Time Around

The soundtrack to *Goldfinger* was an instant hit. By December 1964 it was the number one album in the USA and Shirley's title song was in the singles charts on both sides of the Atlantic. Shirley herself, however, was in a bad way. Two days before her divorce hearing she collapsed and was taken to the London Clinic where she was reported to have undergone three stomach operations. Kenneth was a regular visitor to her bedside, and moved back in to look after her and the children over the new year.

The newspapers speculated that there might be a reconciliation, but it was not to be. On 24 February Kenneth's petition for divorce went through uncontested. Kenneth Hume brought along the sensational revelation that he had had a blood test and he was not Samantha's father. He named two men as having had adulterous liaisons with Shirley. They were Peter Finch and another Australian, John McAuliffe, who had booked some of Shirley's shows there. Shirley has never named Samantha's father, and so speculation as to his identity has tended to focus on these two men. Since her relationship with Finch only started after Samantha's birth, that leaves McAuliffe as the more likely candidate.

Shirley wasn't there to comment. She'd been out to New York in early February to capitalise on her new-found American success by appearing on the *Danny Kaye Show*. Danny performed a James Bond skit as 'James Blonde' and Shirley sang a couple of songs. Then the two of them duetted on a version of 'A Spoonful Of Sugar'. Then, the day before her divorce hearing, Shirley arrived in Sydney for her now traditional Australian visit. On arrival she told the press how happy she was to be back and let slip that she was hoping to appear in a musical based on the life of Josephine Baker – another project that seems to have vanished into the ether.

Having started brightly, with 'Goldfinger' reverberating around the world, 1965 should have been a big year for Shirley. Instead it was oddly flat. Without Kenneth's personal management she just carried on playing shows around the world – Singapore, Kuala Lumpur, Barcelona, Cannes, Beirut, London, etc., etc. – efficiently booked by Vic Lewis, but without any great sense of purpose or forward momentum.

In April, the month she finally said goodbye to Peter Finch at London airport, she released a defiant version of Edith Piaf's 'No Regrets' that scraped into the bottom reaches of the charts. She recorded an album, *Shirley Stops The Shows* which, as its title suggests, was a collection of show tunes. None of it felt especially relevant to a British music scene in the grip of the beat boom. 'Goldfinger' had given her a shot at appearing alongside the Rolling Stones and Dusty Springfield, but *Shirley Stops The Shows* seemed to accept that she was after all essentially a cabaret artiste.

Perhaps she was relying on the next James Bond soundtrack to help keep her in the charts. The new Bond film was *Thunderball*. John Barry initially despaired of writing a song with that title and instead wrote (with Leslie Bricusse) a song called 'Mr Kiss Kiss Bang Bang'. He recorded it with Shirley singing and she must have assumed she had another hit on her hands. Unfortunately for her, Barry wasn't happy with the song and he decided to re-cut it with the much more restrained Dionne Warwick as the vocalist. Shirley was furious, so much so that she took unsuccessful legal action to try to force the Bond producers to use her song,* but then came a further twist as the studio decided that the title song should after all be named after the movie. So Barry and Bricusse managed to write a song called 'Thunderball' and gave it to the only man capable of pulling off such a ridiculous title – Shirley's compatriot Tom Jones.

Shirley must have been worried by this drift in her career because that August she got back in touch with Kenneth Hume and asked him to manage her again. What may also have influenced her decision was the fact that, while they'd been apart, Hume had managed to direct a feature film, a piece of sub-Cliff Richard fluff called *I Gotta Horse*, starring Billy Fury and produced by Hume's friend, the flamboyantly gay pop Svengali Larry Parnes.

Kenneth immediately put Shirley's career into overdrive. Like Mike Sullivan, he loved a publicity stunt. Shirley was due to play a season at the Pigalle to be recorded for a live album. On the opening night Hume delivered a thousand red roses to the club. And midway through her set Shirley made a special announcement: 'Now I'd like to sing a song for the man I'm going to marry. He happens to be my ex-husband.' And with that she launched into 'The Second Time Around'.

The newspapers loved it. Front-page coverage all over the place. Shirley posed with her new square-cut diamond engagement ring and told the press that they were both 'much more mature' and 'very much in love'.[1] Shirley's run at the Pigalle lasted till November when she appeared at the Royal Variety Performance along with

---

* All was presumably forgiven and forgotten by the time she recorded 'Diamonds Are Forever' in 1971.

Pete and Dud and commercial folk sensations Peter, Paul and Mary.*

Meanwhile, Kenneth made plans. First on his list was for Shirley to make a concerted effort to make it in the USA. She'd played New York and Las Vegas and she'd done a few TV shows, but she was far from a household name. *Goldfinger* had provided an opening and Kenneth was determined to exploit it: 1966 would be Shirley's American year.

To this end he needed to find a musical director for Shirley who would be prepared to spend much of the year abroad. That ruled out the dance-band veterans like Alyn Ainsworth who had conducted the Pigalle show. They were generally too booked up at home. He decided on a younger man, a pianist called Kenny Clayton, who had already been working with Shirley on and off for the past year.

Today, Kenny Clayton is a Soho fixture. Petula Clark's musical director for many years, he can still be found playing around the jazz clubs and bars of the West End. I met him at one of the last old-school Soho hangouts, Gerry's Club in Dean Street, the place where Peter Finch used to prop up the bar. Kenny's a dapper and funny man with the youthful yet hard-bitten mien of the show-business survivor. He remembers his first impressions of his new employer – 'Stunning looking, of course, marvellous Welsh accent.'

He was less impressed by Kenneth:

I don't think he liked himself very much. What do you do with a bisexual who thought he was the greatest thing on earth but basically underachieved? He dabbled a bit with films, with this and that.

---

* The Queen spoke to Mary Travers of Peter, Paul and Mary after the show: 'I liked your guitars very much,' she said. 'I prefer them to the electric sort.'

I think he married Shirley because it made him look better. Kenneth used to tell her that she must wake up every morning and go straight to a full-length mirror, look at herself and say 'I'm a star.' So that's what she did. She believed it and everyone else did. It probably did help her. You have to bear in mind where she came from – you need a bit of help, bit of encouragement.

And on meeting Shirley herself, Clayton soon realised that her musical director had quite a job to do:

The difference between Shirley and myself is that I started studying classical music at the age of seven, and by seventeen I was almost ready for the concert platform, except I knew people who were even better than I was, I probably didn't have the discipline. So I got into a more comfortable side of the profession. But Shirley didn't have any of that at all. Shirley was pure instinct. She'd had no training, couldn't read, couldn't count, couldn't pitch, couldn't do anything, but she had that 'I'm going to do it' attitude. So she needed help with arrangements. If you're in this business and you can't actually read the notes . . . well, she used her ears, but she needed coaching. And she had the instinct for it. And of course she's not the only one like that: Errol Garner, one of my favourite piano players, taught himself. Fantastic.

Before they went off on tour, Kenneth Hume secured Shirley a prime-time in-concert show on the BBC. One of Kenny Clayton's tasks was to arrange the opening number, a Tony Newley song called 'On A Wonderful Day Like Today'. He quickly discovered that music was not the first thing on Shirley's mind at this point in her career:

She said I want to do this song. I said fine, I'll come round and do a rehearsal. She had a mews house in Belgravia. I go over there and sit down at the piano. I brought out my manuscript paper and my pencil and said 'OK, how would you like it to go?' She said, 'Like this, but in my key,' and handed me a 45 of Johnny Mathis singing the song. I said, 'Well, I always like treating something differently.' She said 'No!' That was how she liked to learn a song, putting it on the record player before she went to bed.

During the TV rehearsals Shirley's relationship with Kenneth Hume was soon back to its hot-tempered norm. Matters came to a head as they ran through a frenetic arrangement of 'La Bamba'. Frustrated by her inability to get the dance steps right as she sang, Shirley, not a great believer in patient application, declared that she hated this 'La Bamba' crap and stormed off to her dressing room. Kenneth stormed after her and demanded she get back out there. Shirley is very fond of telling the story of what happened next. It's a precise example of what she loved about Kenneth:

> He was ranting at me and I was stamping my foot saying, 'I won't do it!'. I said to him, 'How dare you talk to me like this? – I am a *star*.' He stared at me and said: 'Twinkle, fucking twinkle' – and walked out.[2]

At the time she didn't find it funny. Instead, she claimed illness and retired to the London Clinic for what was becoming an annual visit. Rehearsals were resumed after Christmas, though, and the televised concert is one of the best surviving visual documents of Shirley's early career.*

---

* Unfortunately the BBC have never seen fit to release it commercially, though clips can be seen in various documentaries about Shirley.

The show was broadcast in February, by which time Shirley was in Australia again, warming up for the US. For this trip she took her children with her for the first time, along with their nanny Thelma; tour manager Bernard Hall, an old friend; and Kenny Clayton. On arrival in Sydney she announced that she had after all reconsidered her plan to remarry Kenneth. 'We are much better friends as we are,' she said, confirming the suspicions of those who had speculated that the whole remarriage business was just one of Kenneth's publicity stunts.

In April, Shirley played the Royal Box cabaret room at the Americana Hotel, which celebrated her appearance by flying a home-made Welsh flag from the roof. The following month she was at the Sahara in Las Vegas. Playing Las Vegas was now a much bigger deal than it had been in the El Rancho, Lili St Cyr days. Shirley had to be content with second billing to Roger 'King Of The Road' Miller. At her best under pressure, Shirley duly stole the show on a nightly basis. When she came back to London at the end of May, sporting the most enormous pair of bell-bottoms ever seen, she was able to announce that she had secured a half-million-dollar contract for a series of headlining shows at the Sahara over the next three years. And this wasn't the only piece of good business Kenneth had done in the US. Shirley's contract with EMI was at an end, and he'd negotiated her a lucrative new deal with the American label United Artists – not bad for an artist whose last couple of singles had failed to chart altogether.

Back in London the schedule didn't let up. In July, she followed Barbra Streisand into the Prince of Wales Theatre with her own show, *Shirley Bassey Entertains*. This was a popular success, but the critics were starting to complain that here was a singer whose act was becoming more than a little formulaic. Michael Walsh in the *Daily Express* commented that: 'Miss Bassey has added a sense of comedy to her more obvious talents. But I fear she has lost a little heart. And I wasn't entirely won over when, amidst the flowers and the cheers, she brought on her two children to share in the applause.'[3]

There were similar thoughts from the *Times* critic: 'Miss Bassey does have a very good voice and excellent musical backing but both are used to provide such melodramatic climaxes and contrived contrasts that the effect palls very soon for the uninitiated.'[4]

Kenny Clayton, the man responsible for the excellent musical backing, had some sympathy with this point of view:

> Well, for me Shirley's voice was always better when the doctor had told her, 'You're shouting too much, you need to look after the nodules in your throat.' And for a couple of nights she'd produce the most lovely sounds and you'd see the way she could have, if she'd cared to, moulded all that potential she had. But after a couple of nights she'd go back to shouting. Of course she's one of the greatest shouters in the business.

And of course, the truth of the matter was that Shirley's audience loved the melodrama. As *The Times* also observed, she had by now established a devoted following all of her own:

> Miss Bassey was given a tumultuous acclamation by a packed house. This reception probably represents an adult version of the ritual enjoyed by the Beatles, with standing ovations instead of screaming and flowers instead of jelly babies. The audiences had obviously come to adore Shirley Bassey and adore her they did.

The *NME*'s gossip column spelt it out clearly when it observed that 'There were more queens at Shirley Bassey's Prince of Wales opening than a royal wedding.' The idea of a camp audience was not yet familiar to the mainstream press in these immediately pre-gay-liberation years, but increasingly this is what Shirley attracted then, and has done ever since. There's an enormous amount to be said for it from a performer's point of view. There's no audience so loyal. The downside is that your personal suffering becomes an essential part of your act, and over time your life becomes indistinguishable from your stage performance. It's a phenomenon implicitly acknowledged in the title of Shirley's 2009 comeback album, *The Performance*, and detailed in its title track, the Pet Shop Boys' composition 'The Performance Of My Life'.

TWENTY-THREE

Napoleon and Josephine

Having done the necessary deals to ensure Shirley's future as a recording and touring artist, Kenneth turned his attention back to their shared dreams of stage and screen success. In the autumn of 1965 he'd taken an interest in a musical called *Please Sir* about the early life of Dr Barnardo. This was co-written by a young Welshman called Gil King, with whom he was having an affair. King had written the lyrics while the music was composed by another young Welshman, Michael J. Lewis. Lewis had quit his job as teacher in a North London comprehensive to make it in the music business. He'd been introduced to King by the composer and bandleader Cyril Ornadel and together they'd written the musical. King had then brought the project to Kenneth Hume. Based for many years now in the US, Michael J. Lewis has since had a very successful career as a composer for film and TV, but he's still happy to credit Kenneth Hume as the man who gave him his start in the music industry:

> Ken was a great guy. He and I were complete opposites – I was this beer-swilling, rugby-playing Welshman writing this music. I mean I was dedicated but every night I was down the pub. Ken was a fly boy all right. He was as fast as they come, and I'm sure he tried to swindle

me more than once, but I don't have any bad memories of him. It was Gil who led me to Ken. There was some liaison between Gil and Ken which I wasn't party to. When I met Ken he said 'I want to get behind your show.' I used to go over there, to his flat in Westbourne Terrace, and play the songs, and he would bring out these great big glasses and fill them up with champagne and brandy and ice. It was high living all right.

Ken devoted a considerable amount of his own money to developing the project. He began by paying out for demo recordings of some of the songs, Not simple demos either, but full-scale productions orchestrated by Ivor Raymonde and sung by Vince Hill and Shirley herself. The young Michael Lewis was enormously impressed.

> Shirley did him a big favour by doing three numbers for the demo and she was absolutely great. None of us could believe what was happening, that we had this major star doing a demo. We did the recordings at IBC on Upper Regent St. on 15 Dec 1966. It was my first recording session – the first time I walked into a recording studio, and there they were, playing my music! That was a turning point in my life. I knew I was home – the studio's been my life ever since.

The demos Shirley recorded have never seen the light of day but they helped the project move forward. By September 1966 Kenneth was able to announce that *Please Sir* would soon be opening in the West End. By then he'd brought in the well-established writer and director Bryan Forbes to write the book and direct. Forbes's friend Richard Attenborough was slated to star, and Bernard Delfont to co-produce.

Shirley herself was not slated to appear in *Please Sir*. There was

no obvious part for her. Instead, while she headed back to the States
that autumn for an extended tour, Kenneth decided to enlist the
help of Lewis and King in reviving an old project, the *Napoleon
and Josephine* musical that Lionel Bart had once expressed an interest
in writing. Kenneth was sure this was the ideal vehicle for Shirley,
and that winter he worked away on writing the script in collabo-
ration with the screenwriter and novelist Gavin Lambert, a smart
gay British writer who had made it in Hollywood.* Lewis and King
got on with writing the songs.

Meanwhile, Shirley was in the States almost constantly from September 1966 till the following March. She made her Los Angeles
debut in September at the Cocoanut [*sic*] Grove. She played the
Sahara's sister casino resort in Lake Tahoe in October and then
went back to LA where Kenneth, together with his assistant Leslie
Simmonds, had arranged a series of TV appearances for her. As
they were going to be there for a while, Shirley rented a house in
Beverly Hills, on Coldwater Canyon, and had Sharon and Samantha
come out to stay. Kenny Clayton was there too and remembers it
as a very happy time:

> We were doing TV things for a week then we had two weeks not
> doing anything. We had this house, Shirley's two daughters were there.
> Tony Newley and Joan Collins were just up the road. I ended up
> babysitting for Shirley and Joan Collins. Shirley would say, 'Let's go
> out shopping' and Joan would say, 'What about the kids?' and Shirley
> would say, 'Don't worry, Kenny will look after them!' I used to take
> them to the park. There was an English girl called Judy Carne who
> was out there. I took her to a party in Coldwater Canyon and met a

---

* A very interesting choice of collaborator: Lambert had just written the screenplay
for an adaptation of his classic Hollywood satire *Inside Daisy Clover*.

guy called Carlos who was a scriptwriter and his wife Julie who was a singer, and they said we're having a pool party, would you like to come? I said 'Oh, I'm staying down the road with Shirley,' and they said, 'D'you think she'd like to meet Sidney Poitier?' So I said, 'Shirley, d'you want to come out to this party?' 'Oh, no, I'm too tired.' 'Sidney Poitier will be there.' 'I'm just getting dressed!'

In November Shirley filmed the *Andy Williams Show* and by December, when she showed up in a white mesh dress over white tights to a 'British style mod party'* that Vanessa Redgrave and David Hemmings gave to welcome Antonioni to LA, she is referred to in the press as part of 'Hollywood's English colony'.

Christmas 1966 was spent back in Las Vegas for another season, this time supported by an early incarnation of the Osmond Brothers. In January she appeared on the *Dean Martin Show* and filmed a one-hour special in which she appeared alongside the Count Basie Orchestra. It was Kenneth Hume's idea; he figured correctly that the networks would go for the 'Bassey Meets Basie' catchline.

Kenny Clayton, a dedicated jazzman, was thrilled by the prospect of working with one of the all-time greats, but a little embarrassed by the context. He couldn't imagine that the Count would be looking forward to working with the British pop singer:

I think for Count Basie it was anathema, but he managed to find enough songs to make it work. Shirley had a week to prepare. Count

---

* The party sounds hilarious: a remarkable roster of acting talent, ranging from Warren Beatty to the doomed Welsh actress Rachel Roberts via Rock Hudson and Natalie Wood (the star of *Inside Daisy Clover*) were forced to listen to what the reporter describes as 'ear-splitting music by a rock and roll group called the Gordian Knot'. Rock Hudson, apparently, wasn't dancing: 'I can't dance to this music unless I'm high,' he said.

Basie had one day in between shows in San Francisco and New Orleans to come in and do the music. So there we were rehearsing Basie's band with Bassey's music! Well, we did it. Then the producer said, 'Look, we've got to have a song when you're on together.' Well, we did have a good arrangement of 'Sing a Happy Song' so we decided to do that. Afternoon rehearsal, the producer said, 'We're going to do 'Happy Song' now.' I said, 'OK'. The producer said, 'Bill Basie will be playing the solo – will you show Bill Basie what you want him to play?' So I run it through. We've got this double piano bench, the two of us, and we get to the solo and I do my best. It's only about sixteen bars and around bar fourteen Basie leans over and says 'Don't play all that shit!'

That was great, for Bill Basie to tell you not to play all that shit! He was the past master of less is more. It was such a privilege to spend six hours with the best band on the planet. And, even though the music wasn't quite to their taste, they played so well it was fantastic.

It had been a great few months for Shirley but then, late that January, she had a major setback. Ever since the production of a film version of *Oliver!* had been announced she'd been desperate for the role of Nancy. Lionel Bart had said he wanted her to play the part. The film's director Carol Reed had agreed. It was the break she had been working towards for years. And then, on 17 January 1967, the studio announced that they had cast Nancy and she would be played by Shani Wallis.

Shani Wallis was another of Jack Hylton's protégées, another client of Mike Sullivan's too, but her career had been very quiet for years. And yet she had got the part over Shirley. What had gone wrong? Eventually the word came back that the US financiers had overruled Carol Reed. They would not tolerate a black

Nancy (laughably, the reason given was that black American audiences might not take kindly to a black Nancy dying – nothing to do with white American audiences objecting to seeing a black woman married to a white man, of course). In the end, the situation was brutally clear: Shirley Bassey, this woman whose life and art had flourished through simply ignoring the whole business of 'race', had had her greatest ambition thwarted by the simple, inescapable matter of her skin colour.

In the wake of this bitter disappointment, Shirley had another month's engagements to fulfil in the US, including a stint in Miami Beach, before returning to England in March. On her return Kenneth did his best to cheer her up by persuading her that they would throw themselves into *Napoleon And Josephine*, now simply to be known as *Josephine*. No sooner had she arrived back in the country than Kenneth brought Michael Lewis round to play her the songs he'd written for the show:

I went to her place, she'd flown in from New York that morning, she'd gone to bed, had a nap, so I met her late afternoon. I remember her coming down this winding staircase – no make-up, no wig, looked like just another girl – and she bawled out 'Where's that bloody Welshman?' So I played her these songs and this was a major education for me. She goes, 'Love your songs, Welsh boy, but I can't sing them.' I was confused. I'd been brought up with this classical background where a soprano is a soprano – they go from middle C up two octaves. That's what sopranos did. But pop singers, and Shirley was a quintessential pop singer, they sing about a fifth or even a sixth lower than legitimate sopranos. They sound high because their top notes are in fact quite low and the whole tessitura is so much lower than a legit soprano. Shirley wanted me to play these songs down a sixth. I had to go away and transpose the songs down. I had to learn that classical and pop singers were two different breeds, their voice production and phrasing. Shirley was the one to teach me that.

A few days later, on 16 March, Kenneth invited the press round to Shirley's house to officially announce the project. The next day the *Daily Express* splashed the story on the front page: 'Shirley – the £110,000 Josephine' and repeated Kenneth's claims that the show would be produced that autumn in the West End with a budget of £110,000 and would then transfer to Broadway before being made into a film. So committed was Shirley to the project, he announced, that she would be cancelling a series of lucrative contracts to sing in Las Vegas in order to appear in the show.

The *Western Mail* report gives an insight into just how much this meant to Shirley:

'I have never done a musical before and it is a great challenge,' said Miss Bassey. 'I hope that this will lead to my becoming a film star. This is my main ambition.' She said she had been waiting ten years for the right part for her to start her acting career and it had taken Mr Hume to find an authentic story and make it right for her.[1]

That same month Shirley had her first high-profile British TV appearance for a while when she appeared alongside an array of largely Welsh talent including Tom Jones, Stanley Baker and Harry Secombe in a show called *The Heart Of Show Business*. This was a charity affair to raise money for the people of Aberfan, the Welsh mining village where 116 schoolchildren had been killed by a collapsing coal tip the previous autumn ('buried alive by the NCB' as an anguished father cried out at the inquest). Shirley Bassey talked to the press at a drinks party to promote the show, but she's obviously uneasy talking about such a politicised issue:

I flew straight back from the States when I heard about it. Suppose, being Welsh, I hadn't. God, I would have been barred from Wales forever. Everybody has made the effort in so many ways to help Aberfan. Yes, I'm sentimental but also truthful. For instance nothing dramatic happened [when I heard the news], like my crying my eyes out in Hollywood because of my family in Cardiff. I left Wales such a long time ago. Oh there's heart all the time in whatever I do, but people just don't know when Shirley Bassey* is showing her real heart.[2]

It's not the most coherent response to the horror of Aberfan that you can imagine. A charitable interpretation would be that Shirley was trying to make the point that she was hardly personally involved in the tragedy, and wasn't going to pretend she was, just to garner publicity for herself. And before long the interview moved on to the matter of her upcoming musical:

I'm restless and ambitious. That's why I'll be playing Josephine in a stage musical about Napoleon this year. We've got plenty in common, Josephine and I.[3]

The reporter wonders whether, if Shirley is Josephine, Kenneth might be Napoleon. Shirley is delighted to agree. 'I even call him the same name,' she says and calls out, 'Napoleon, Napoleon Bonaparte,' across the room. Sure enough Ken responds with a smile.

In April, Shirley gave a bizarre interview to the *Sunday Telegraph* which gives some idea of how the musical was going to approach the character of Josephine. Her answer takes the form of an extraordinary rant.

---

* A worrying early instance of the star referring to herself in the third person.

Napoleon and Josephine – behind every great man there's a woman? Rubbish! Behind every great man there's a woman getting him to do aggressive things he doesn't really want to do. And that's evil. Because all women are evil. Why don't men understand this, the evil in women?

Napoleon. You've got to understand about Napoleon in the bedroom if you want to understand Napoleon. Evil. Starts right there in the boudoir. Little whispers. 'No, you can't have my body today.' Josephine probably told Nap something like that. So he rushes out of the bedroom. 'Then I'll capture Egypt today!'

Women are to blame for all the evil in the world. I understand about these things. I should have been a psychiatrist. I want Dudley Moore to be Napoleon for me. Everybody laughs. He's just a funny little man. But that's Napoleon. Set Europe on fire because he was such a funny little man and Josephine goes titter titter titter. She got Napoleon to attack Russia.* Wasn't that bad? And that's in all women. Look at that woman who started all the trouble in this country. What's her name? Mrs Pankhurst, that woman. 'Get back to the kitchen where you belong,' some man should have told her. And you know, that's what all we women really want. Get put back in the kitchen where we belong. We don't want emancipation. Josephine – people got killed all over Europe because of that woman. She used men for gain and for pleasure. Men shouldn't have women tied to them. Especially great men. They should take their pleasure with women – and dump them!

Anyway at the end of the musical *Josephine*, she's been laughing at this Dud Moore style Napoleon, making him start wars to compensate. Funny little man titter titter titter! But, now she sees he's such a conqueror, she falls in love with him. And that's when he

* No she didn't, but never mind.

dumps her. And she crumbles. 'Au Revoir'. That's the song I sing at the end. That's when Josephine goes. And that's it. The End. This *Josephine*, it's not just Napoleon and Josephine's story. It's everybody's story.[4]

Quite what provoked this outburst is unclear, as is her state of mind while delivering it. Whatever the circumstances, though, it's an exceptionally, if unintentionally, revealing rant.

First off there's the pervasive sense of sexual guilt that must underpin all the 'women are evil' stuff. Shirley surely knew what it was like to exert that power over men. Hadn't Pepe taken her hostage at gunpoint? Hadn't Peter Finch told everyone who'd listen about his broken heart? Sex is perhaps the ultimate power without responsibility but Shirley was all too well aware of the havoc that could be unleashed by its indiscriminate use.

Secondly there's the matter of getting back into the kitchen – 'that's what all we women really want.' On the face of it, this is absurd. Who, after all, would mistake Shirley Bassey for a natural-born homemaker? But at the same time, it's a cry from the heart. Some part of her must very much have wanted to set show business aside, to be a wife and, particularly, a mother; to lead a domestic life and not tour the world leaving her kids in the care of nannies and relatives.

Finally, there's Napoleon, the funny little man. Kenneth Hume was her Napoleon, of course, and even if her hold over him wasn't simply sexual, she could see that he was working himself into an early grave, trying to advance her cause across the globe. Overall, then, the whole rant suggests a woman deeply at odds with herself and the choices she's made.

A week after the interview Shirley went back into Regent Sound to demo half a dozen songs for *Josephine*,* including the one called 'Au Revoir' that she referenced in the interview. All seemed set fair for the Bassey–Hume partnership. *Please Sir* was still on course, though it was now going to be a film rather than a stage musical. *Josephine* had the star power of Shirley behind it and a producer, Kenneth, who was never going to sack her for being the wrong colour.

The only trouble was that Kenneth wasn't well. He'd lived a fast life and he worked obsessively and it was all catching up with him. He was a very heavy smoker and had suffered from repeated bouts of pneumonia. But his physical afflictions were less severe than his mental troubles. Kenneth was a manic depressive. His physician Dr Victor Ratner (a Harley Street doctor-to-the-stars type who would later die from a self-prescribed methadone overdose) had been treating Kenneth for depression for the past three years. He'd prescribed him antidepressants, which he topped up with an array of sleeping tablets. On 18 June Ratner was called in when Kenneth couldn't be woken. Ratner managed to revive him and Kenneth told him he'd taken a number of pills plus 'a large helping' of alcohol. 'He told me it was really all too much,' Ratner said later, 'and he could not bear the thought of disintegration. He felt very depressed and thought it was not all worthwhile.'[5]

Ratner ensured that Hume had a live-in male nurse, a man called John Coffey, from then on, plus regular visits from a psychiatrist, but a week later, on Sunday, 25 October, Hume was once again found unconscious and this time Ratner was unable to revive him.

Kenneth Hume was forty-one years old when he died. Oddly,

* These were called: 'Martinique', 'King of Hearts', 'Goodbye', 'Au Revoir' and 'Josephine and Bonaparte'. Once again these have vanished into the vaults, though Michael Lewis told me that he recycled 'Martinique' for his soundtrack to the 1975 Thomas McGuane film, *92 in the Shade*.

Ratner would later tell the inquest, he appeared to have taken a smaller dose of pills than the week before. Just three or four barbiturates had been enough to kill him, due to an undiagnosed coronary problem.

Shirley was called immediately and rushed around to the flat, where she remained for an hour. Her long-time secretary and good friend, Jean Lincoln, described her as 'extremely upset'. Then the nearest relative, Kenneth's brother Alan, was called in:

> When he died he'd been ill and he had someone looking after him, a male nurse. One day we got a phone call to say he'd died. So we went straight over there to where he was living, to find out what had been going on. Apparently the nurse had gone out and it sounded like Ken had taken an overdose of paracetamols or something. I don't think it was suicide but I don't know. He was younger than me and it's a pity he's not here today.

The next day the papers reported Kenneth's death. They evidently had some difficulty finding anyone prepared to eulogise him. The best the *Mirror* could come up with was the producer and pop Svengali Larry Parnes, who offered this decidedly lukewarm tribute: 'He did have a tendency to upset people but those of us who knew him well found a lot in him.'[6]

Was it suicide? The inquest was inconclusive. On the one hand Kenneth was described as having been very depressed. On the other hand he had not mentioned suicide and the amount of barbiturates he took would never have killed a healthy man.

The funeral was in High Wycombe, where Alan and Sheila now live. Sheila's father, a funeral director, made the arrangements. Shirley came, brought a single red rose and laid it in Kenneth's coffin. She was thirty years old and a part of her life was over.

With Kenneth dead, the *Josephine* project was doomed. Just a day after he died Shirley's publicist, Howard Kent, was quoted as saying, 'I do not know what will happen now. He was the lynchpin of this show.' The truth was that *Josephine* was all about Kenneth's vision for Shirley, and without his manic energy it was no more than a dream, or rather, the end of a dream.

Twenty years later Shirley paid him this tribute:

> He was the one big love of my life, even though we were divorced when he died. Ken had emphysema and it would have killed him. But he chose to end it all. He didn't want to sit around, he wasn't the type to be an invalid. For two years [after his death] I thought he'd died of cancer. Then finally the truth came out that he'd committed suicide. I hadn't been told because everyone thought I wouldn't be able to cope with it. My father left my mother when I was about two, and for a long time I was looking for a father figure.[7]

From now on there was no more talk of films or musicals for Shirley. Kenneth had run himself into the ground trying to make it happen and he had failed. *Oliver!* had passed her by. She would never again tell a journalist that her main ambition was to be a film star. From now on she would simply consolidate what she already had: her career as a recording artist and, above all, as a concert performer.

And that, for me, is where the story ends. Obviously it's not where Shirley Bassey's story ends. But what comes after is too familiar to need rehearsing here; it's the Shirley Bassey of the public imagination, the larger-than-life Shirley Bassey of endless tours and TV specials and chat-show sofas. That Shirley Bassey is curiously constant through the seventies and eighties and nineties and noughties. From the outside she seems to have changed hardly at all. On the inside, no doubt, things are different: but the Shirley

Bassey of subsequent decades is far more private, more heavily defended, than the young woman who used to pour her heart out to passing journalists.

The public Shirley Bassey is a deliberately exaggerated construction, rather like Dolly Parton in that way, a showbiz diva of flamboyant moods and extravagant outfits. Her music too is exaggerated, its emotional content deliberately larger than life. And much of it has its roots in Kenneth Hume's posthumous bequest to her: the album they recorded together in the USA just before he died, a record with the oddly prophetic title *And We Were Lovers*.

Two songs from the album were released as singles, at either end of 1967. The first, released in March when Kenneth was still alive, was a reading of 'If You Go Away', rendered terribly autobiographical by his death. The second, released that autumn, was a show tune called 'Big Spender'. It was taken from the musical *Sweet Charity*. Kenneth spotted it and suggested that Shirley record a faster, more emphatic version. The result was her first hit since 'Goldfinger'. The song quickly became the highpoint of her stage show. It's brassy and indomitable, camp and knowing.

Together these two songs offer the road map for everything that was to come. Somewhere between the tragedy of 'If You Go Away' and the irrepressible energy of 'Big Spender' lies the subsequent life of Shirley Bassey.

Eight days after Kenneth's death, Shirley opened at the Talk of the Town. The season had originally been billed by Kenneth as Shirley's 'Farewell To Cabaret' before she launched herself as a star of stage and screen. Now it was her tear-stained return. On the first night, when she reached the line 'this is where our story ends' from the song 'I Wish You Love', she collapsed on stage, struck down by grief. But still, the next night she carried on.

After the Rain

And so to the Roundhouse, north London, forty years later. Sold-out show, TV cameras here to record her for the BBC. It's part of the relaunch that Dame Shirley Bassey is currently undergoing. There's a new record called *The Performance*, her first collection of new material in twenty years. Oddly enough, it's the first time in her career that she's had an album of songs custom-written for her.

The record's not out yet. So far I've heard only one song on the radio, a number called 'The Girl From Tiger Bay' written by the Welsh rock band the Manic Street Preachers. On first hearing it's OK: anthemic if a little cheesy. Its assertion that Shirley will 'always be the girl from Tiger Bay' is more than a little simplistic, of course.

Still, it's good to see Dame Shirley getting this kind of proper attention. It's years since she had a major record label behind her, years since she's had this kind of TV and radio attention. It's as if the world at large, or Britain at least, has suddenly woken up to the fact that there aren't many genuine old-school stars left and that we should treasure the ones we have.

There's been a fashion for this kind of thing in the last decade or so: ageing legends getting a makeover and a relaunch. Shirley's compatriot Tom Jones was one of the first to get the treatment; the late Johnny Cash perhaps the most successful. Oddly – significantly even – I can't think of a major female star who's had this kind of re-branding operation. But then who are the other enduring female stars? There are a few Americans – Barbra, Aretha, Liza – but none of them has a career as long as Dame Shirley's. And, as for Britain, who else is there – Lulu? Petula Clark? – showbiz troupers, for sure, but not really superstars.

So there's no road map for the Shirley Bassey relaunch, no obvious point of comparison. As far as the men go, she's certainly closer to Tom Jones than Johnny Cash. Her voice is still in good order, and her instincts defiantly showbiz. Unlike the Man in Black, she won't be croaking through Nick Cave songs like a dead woman walking, will not be here to show off her war wounds.

And then the lights go down and there's the TV chat-show host Paul O'Grady walking out onto the stage to introduce the star attraction. Orchestra swells and Dame Shirley makes her entrance. She stands still at the back of the stage for what must be a full minute, a trick for gaining the audience's attention she first learned at the Glasgow Empire half a century ago. Finally she comes to the front of the stage, the band launches into 'Diamonds Are Forever' and we're under way. And from the first note it's clear that she has us. Fifty-six years into her career, her voice has lost none of its power and command. The song itself is as cartoonish as ever but it does its job perfectly, reminding us all of just who Shirley is and how much a part of our collective memory.

When it ends she goes with barely a pause into her second number, a Stephen Sondheim ballad called 'I'm Still Here'. And this is where I realise that this show is something more than just a good-time trawl through the greatest hits. It's not the song, really, sung in the persona of an ageing showbiz trouper looking back over her life of ups and downs; it's the fact that when she reaches the defiant refrain 'And I'm still here', it's as potent a demonstration of the power of popular music as can be imagined. She's still here, we're still here, and we're all of us grateful for that.

It's the first of the night's several moments of grace. When the song finishes she talks to the audience for the first time, mentions her appearance at the Glastonbury festival a couple of years earlier, the show that led indirectly to this relaunch. In between songs she's visibly nervous: it's obvious how much this occasion means. Then she plays the first of the night's songs from her new record. It's 'The Apartment', written by Rufus Wainwright. It's a slight letdown. Shirley's singing is fine but, like much of Wainwright's material, there's too much cleverness, too little tune.

A couple more hits soon raise the temperature again. First there's her 1970s beat ballad 'Never Never Never', before a rollicking 'Kiss Me Honey, Honey, Kiss Me' sees the Dame showing off her dance moves with great good humour. Then a bearded thirty-something singer-songwriter called Tom Baxter shuffles on stage and the band starts playing another of the new songs. This one's called 'Almost There'. It's a big ballad, and this time you can see she's feeling it, a sad song full of loss, a story of dreams and loves that didn't work out. For a moment the spectre of her first husband and the love of her life, poor dead Kenneth Hume, hangs in the air.

Better still is the next song. Another singer-songwriter, Richard Hawley, comes on stage, plugs in his guitar and waits for the pianist to lead the band into one of the most restrained and affecting ballads Shirley has ever sung, 'After The Rain'. It's another reflection on things lost, loves ended, and its refrain, 'This girl just can't take it any more' is startlingly poignant. And it ends for once on a sigh, not a crescendo.

There's more after that: a swinging 'Lady Is A Tramp'; another big new ballad, 'The Performance', from the Pet Shop Boys, a burlesque romp through 'Big Spender'; all before the inevitable 'Goldfinger' sends us off into the night, covered in the remnants of the shower of gold confetti released at end of the song.

Somewhere along the way, perhaps it was during the version of 'The Girl From Tiger Bay', accompanied by a big screen showing snapshots from Shirley's early career, I receive a text from a friend of mine elsewhere in the crowd. It says simply, 'How could you?'

I know what he means, of course – we'd been talking earlier about Shirley's life and some of the facts that I'd uncovered in my research, in particular her father's crime that had overshadowed the family for years – and I'm wondering the same thing. How could I write this book? In an interview to promote the new album she says that this record is her autobiography, she has no need to write a book now. So why not go along with that? Why not allow her to reduce the hardships of her childhood to the platitudes of 'Girl From Tiger Bay'? Why rake up all the muck?

I hope I have an answer to that. I hope that this book, which does indeed rake up a certain amount of difficult muck, does not do so for titillation but because I tend to think that acknowledging truths, even hard truths, is in the end helpful to all concerned. And I would hope it's the case that whoever reads this – and even Shirley herself – will come away thinking more of her, rather than less.

That's certainly been the case for me. When I started writing this book I was fascinated by Dame Shirley's life, but somewhat agnostic about her talent and her character. I certainly wasn't at all sure that I would end the book liking her. But that's what happened. I both like and admire the woman who emerges in this book. And more than that, I'm sure I was not alone during her concert at the Roundhouse in being profoundly moved by her skill, her courage and, above all, her spirit.

DISCOGRAPHY

Singles

1956

'Burn My Candle (At Both Ends)' b/w 'Stormy Weather'
'The Wayward Wind' b/w 'Born to Sing the Blues'
'After the Lights Go Down Low' b/w 'If You Don't Love Me'

1957

'Banana Boat Song' b/w 'Tra La La'
'If I Had a Needle and Thread' b/w 'Tonight My Heart She Is
    Crying'
'Fire Down Below' b/w 'You, You Romeo'
'Puh-Leeze! Mister Brown' b/w 'Take My Love, Take My Love'
Live EP: Shirley Bassey At The Cafe De Paris, London

1958

'As I Love You' b/w 'Hands Across the Sea'
'Kiss Me, Honey, Honey, Kiss Me'

1959

'Love for Sale' b/w 'Crazy Rhythm'
'My Funny Valentine' b/w 'How About You?'
'Night and Day' b/w 'The Gypsy In My Soul'
'If You Love Me (Really Love Me)' b/w 'Count On Me'

1960

'With These Hands' b/w 'The Party's Over'
'As Long as He Needs Me' b/w 'So in Love'

1961

'You'll Never Know' b/w 'Hold me Tight'
'Reach for the Stars' c/w 'Climb Ev'ry Mountain' (double A-Side)
'I'll Get By' b/w 'Who We Are'

1962

'Tonight' b/w 'Let's Start All Over Again'
'Ave Maria' b/w 'You'll Never Walk Alone'
'Far Away' b/w 'My Faith'
'What Now My Love?' b/w 'Above All Others'

1963

'What Kind of Fool am I?' b/w 'Till'
'I (Who Have Nothing)' b/w 'How Can You Tell?'

1964

'My Special Dream' b/w 'You'
'Gone' b/w 'Your Love'
'Who Can I Turn To?' b/w 'To Be Loved By A Man'
'Goldfinger' b/w 'Strange How Love Can Be'
'Now' b/w 'How Can You Believe?'

1965

'No Regrets' b/w 'Seesaw Of Dreams'
'It's Yourself' b/w 'Secrets'

1966

'The Liquidator' b/w 'Sunshine'
'Don't Take the Lovers from the World' b/w 'Take Away'
'Shirley' b/w 'Who Could Love Me'

1967

'The Impossible Dream' b/w 'Do I Look Like A Fool'
'Big Spender' b/w 'Dangerous Games'

Albums:

Born To Sing The Blues 1957
The Bewitching Miss Bassey 1959
Show Boat (Various Artists) 1959
The Fabulous Shirley Bassey1959
Shirley 1961
Shirley Bassey 1961
Let's Face The Music 1962
Shirley Stops The Shows 1965
Shirley Bassey At The Pigalle 1965
I've Got A Song For You 1966
And We Were Lovers 1967

Recommended Compilations

Burn My Candle – The Complete Early Years 1956–58
The Complete EMI Columbia Singles Collection
Bassey – the EMI/UA Years 1959–1979 (Box set which includes
    a live album from Carnegie Hall 1964)

APPENDICES

1 A Short History of Tiger Bay

Cardiff's rise to industrial prominence began at the start of the nineteenth century. Its initial success was predicated on the iron industry and on the vision of a family of Victorian entrepreneurs, the Crichton Stuarts, aka the Marquesses of Bute. Iron had been discovered in the valleys north of Cardiff, around Merthyr Tydfil. A canal, the Glamorganshire, was dug out to bring the iron ore down to the sea at Cardiff.

Despite the fact that by 1830 Cardiff was the major iron-exporting port in Britain, however, it still lacked anything very much in the way of dock facilities. The major local landowner, the Second Marquess of Bute, decided to take a gamble. He commissioned the building of the West Bute Dock, which opened in 1839. The investment was huge; to pay for it the Marquess had to mortgage some of his substantial estate, but, as he said to his solicitor, 'I am willing to think well of my income in the distance.'

He wasn't wrong, His timing, in fact, was perfect: two years after the dock opened there was a new railway line to serve it, the Taff Vale, designed by Brunel himself and running alongside the canal from Merthyr to Cardiff. And soon its iron cargo began to be supplanted by the South Wales valleys' other great natural resource: coal. In 1840 Cardiff exported just forty thousand tons of coal. By 1862, the figure was two million tons. By 1913 this had risen to ten million.

By the middle of the century, Cardiff was a boom town. Soon the small settlement that had already existed a mile or so upstream spread south towards the new docks. They called this new area between the docks and the old town Butetown, after the man whose coffers it was filling. And from the beginning, the arrangement of the railway lines, the Bristol Channel and the river was such that there was a natural division between Butetown and the rest of Cardiff.

In those early days Butetown was the heart of Cardiff. Mount Stuart Square, at the entrance to the docks, was the city's commercial hub, and Loudoun Square, in the heart of Butetown, was among the city's smartest addresses, boasting a Young Ladies' Seminary as well as providing a home for shipwrights, builders, master mariners and merchants, the new aristocrats of a seafaring city.

The second half of the nineteenth century saw Cardiff expand at a breathtaking rate. By the end of the century it was one of the world's biggest, busiest ports. The sheer number of ordinary seamen using the port forced changes in the area's make-up. The smart houses of Loudoun Square were converted into seamen's lodging houses, and the merchant classes retreated into the main body of the city, which soon sprouted bourgeois northern suburbs. The seafaring supremos, the ships' captains and so on, congregated around the southern tip of the island, in smart streets like Windsor Esplanade.

By now Butetown was home to a fair cross-section of the world's seafaring peoples – Chinese, Lascars, Levantines, Norwegians, Maltese, Spaniards et al. A wild and licentious community was emerging, finding worldwide fame as Cardiff's own 'Tiger Bay'. Black seamen too, both from East Africa and the West Indies, were a part of this cosmopolitan mix, the first of them arriving as early as 1870, and by 1881 being numerous enough to have their own Seamen's Rest. By the time of the First World War, there were around seven hundred coloured seamen in Cardiff. A fair percentage of these would have been a transient population of men without families, but others had put down roots. Some of the area's most notable musicians, including the Deniz brothers and Don Johnson, were born into mixed-race families in Cardiff in the years before the war. Don Johnson was born in Grangetown, the new dockland suburb over the river from Butetown, precisely because his father, a West Indian sailor, didn't want his children to be brought up in Tiger Bay.

The arrival of war made a big difference to the community. Many of Tiger Bay's citizens joined the war effort. Seamen went into the navy and merchant navy. The *Western Mail* reported, in 1919, that fourteen hundred black seamen from Cardiff lost their lives in the war. Others joined the army, the West Indian regiments or the Cardiff City Battalion.

Conscription into the army also left a huge gap in the domestic labour force, and, at the same time, East African trading ships were being requisitioned for the navy, leaving a pool of unemployed sailors. So in Cardiff, as also happened in Liverpool, factory jobs were opened up to the seamen. Unsurprisingly, now that they were based in Cardiff for a substantial period of time, more and more sailors began to put down roots and to make the first moves towards an integration into the wider community – one aspect of which was the forging of relationships with local women. This last development foreshadowed the GI bride phenomenon of the Second World War, except for the crucial distinction that this time the exotic suitors were not intending to whisk their brides across the ocean, but were planning to stay put in Butetown.

Trouble came with the war's end. The soldiers returned from overseas and unemployment loomed. Black workers were thrown out of their factory jobs, and seafaring work was likewise in high demand. Black unemployment rapidly became serious, while general white unemployment became one of the key issues of the day. In some cities, notably Glasgow where John MacLean, 'the British Lenin', held sway, the whiff of communist revolution was in the air, and the government was briefly terrified. In seafaring cities like Cardiff and Liverpool, however, the racial minority was fitted up for the role of scapegoat.

Racial tensions first began to appear among the returning soldiers. Peter Fryer, in his groundbreaking history of the black presence in Britain, *Staying Power*, tells the awful tale of an incident in a veterans' hospital in Liverpool in which five hundred white soldiers set upon the fifty black patients, many of whom were missing at least one limb. A pitched battle was fought with crutches and walking sticks as the principal weapons (though not all the white soldiers sided with the racists: a contemporary account, in the *African Telegraph*, records that 'When the [military police] arrived on the scene to restore order, there were many white soldiers seen standing over crippled black limbless soldiers, and protecting them with their sticks and crutches from the furious onslaught of the other white soldiers until order was restored.')

If the Belmont Hospital affair had an element of cruel farce, much of what followed was tragic. In the summer of 1919, in South Shields and Liverpool and Cardiff, Britain's first race riots of the modern era broke out. The post-war slump provided the conditions for these mass outbreaks of racist violence – and Fryer clearly demonstrates that the riots consisted of white mobs randomly attacking blacks – but it was generally sexual jealousy that provided the flashpoint. The returning troops could easily be goaded into believing that 'their' women were being stolen. Whites would repeatedly claim, as justification for assault, that blacks had been 'making suggestive remarks to our women' or some such. And the newspapers were swift to follow this line. Fryer records a *Liverpool Courier* editorial pontificating that: 'One of the chief reasons of popular anger behind the present disturbances lies in the fact that the average Negro is nearer the animal than is the average white man, and that there are women in Liverpool who have no self-respect.'

The 1919 race riots were not simply regrettable occurrences in far-off days but rather the crucible in which Britain's subsequent racial pathology was formed. The cry for tribal solidarity to protect their jobs from these 'outsiders' was overlaid with sexual hysteria. This hysteria presumably arose from a combination of black people having long been caricatured as apelike or bestial, and the legacy of Victorian prudery that regarded sex as a bestial activity. Certainly what was created was the potent combination of blackness as both an economic and a sexual threat.

According to Fryer the flashpoint of the Cardiff riot on 11 June 1919 was, ironically enough, 'A brake containing black men and their white wives, returning from an excursion, attracting a large and hostile crowd.' However, an account written by a policeman present at the time, Albert Allen, gives a rather less genteel and more detailed account:

'I was the only PC on duty at the Wharf when it started and I was on duty the whole time it lasted in the Docks area. First of all I would like to point out the cause. In Cardiff there were quite a number of prostitutes and quite a number of pimps who lived on their earnings.

When conscription came into force these pimps were called up. Then a number of prostitutes went to the Docks district and lived with these coloured people who treated them very well. When the war finished the pimps found their source of income gone as the prostitutes refused to go back to them. The night the trouble started, about 8.30 p.m., a person who I knew told me to expect some trouble. I asked him why and he explained that the coloured men had taken the prostitutes on an outing to Newport in two horse wagons and that a number of pimps were waiting for their return.

Next, by Allen's account, the pimps attacked the wagons near the Monument – at the edge of the city centre and fifty yards or so from the Bute Street bridge which signals the beginning of Butetown – and a pitched battle ensued before police reinforcements dispersed the crowd and attempted to cordon off Butetown. What was by now an angry white mob, including many armed demobilised soldiers, then proceeded to rampage around the town looking for blacks to assault. Some managed to get past the police lines and into Butetown, where they smashed the windows of Arab boarding houses.

This initial disturbance petered out around midnight, but the rioting was to continue for several more days. On the second day a Somali boarding house in the centre of town was burnt down and its inhabitants badly beaten. More boarding houses were then burnt down in Bute Street, and an Arab beaten to death. On the third day, a white mob gathered once more in the centre of town and prepared for another assault on Butetown.

This time, however, Butetown was ready for them. If its position on an isthmus at the bottom of the city made Butetown a convenient ghetto, it also made it a fortress. There was only one easy way in from the town centre, via Bute Street itself, and the other approaches, from East Moors and Grangetown, could be easily watched, so armed sentries were posted – the blacks too having brought their weapons home from the war – and the community waited. As a South Wales News reporter saw it on 14 June 1919:

> The coloured men, while calm and collected, were well prepared for any attack, and had the mob from the city broken through the police cordon there would have been bloodshed on a big scale . . . Hundreds of Negroes were collected, but these were very peaceful, and were amicably discussing the situation amongst themselves. Nevertheless, they were in a determined mood and ready to defend 'our quarter of the city' at all costs . . . Long-term black residents said: It will be hell let loose if the mob comes into our streets . . . if we are unprotected from hooligan rioters who can blame us for trying to protect ourselves?

Their defence was successful and the rioting died away over the next few days, leaving in its wake three dead and many more injured, but a decisive corner had been turned. The authorities' only response to the troubles was to offer to repatriate the black community. Around six hundred black men took up the offer within the next few months, though many of the returning West Indians went back with the express intention of inciting anti-British feeling. And, indeed, within days of some of the Cardiff seamen returning to Trinidad, fighting against white sailors broke out, followed by a major dock strike.

The majority, however, decided to stay on, to make a permanent home on this ground they'd fought for. From this point on, Butetown was not simply a conventional ghetto or a colourful adjunct to the city's maritime life, but effectively an island. It was not simply a black island: the area had always had a white Welsh population and continued to do so. There was an Irish presence too, as well as

Chinese, Arab and European sailors, and refugees from successive European conflicts as well. And as the black or coloured population was initially almost exclusively male, Butetown rapidly became a predominantly mixed-race community, almost unique in Britain, the New Orleans of the Taff delta, home of the Creole Celts. But this integration was firmly confined to Tiger Bay: above the Bute Street bridge you were back in the same hidebound old Britain.

This was the place where Henry Bassey decided to settle in during 1919 and where his daughter Shirley was subsequently born.

2 Bute Street and Its Cafés

Let's start with Kenneth Little's description of the geography of Bute Street around the time of Shirley's birth:

> The wide thoroughfare, traversed by a double tramway track with overhead wires, connects the Pier Head with the uptown area, a distance of over a mile. A large part of the east side of the road contains no shops or buildings, and virtually all pedestrian traffic proceeds along the west or Loudoun Square side past the almost innumerable 'cafés' for which Bute Street is famous or infamous, and the only slightly less numerous boarding houses and public houses. There are also shops, mainly clothiers', who sell a great variety of garments, from seafaring equipment, such as firemen's suits, naval uniforms, seaboots, wire belts (used because their elasticity is not affected by sweat), etc., to smart lounge suits and felt hats; a number of general stores, and a few jewellers and tobacconists. There are no multiple stores, either here or in Loudoun Square.[1]

The most profitable businesses on Bute Street were not the respectable daytime establishments, but the ones that came into their own after dark and specialised in catering to the desires of visiting sailors. These were the so-called 'cafés'. Little again:

> The notorious Bute Street café, as well as its proprietor and his 'staff', have all a certain uniformity of characteristics. Through windows, sometimes partially boarded up, are displayed fairly ostentatiously one or two articles of food, perhaps a few bottles of mineral waters, and sometimes a price list. The outside appearance of the place is essentially drab and unprepossessing, and is enlivened but little by

the exotic name scrawled over the window. The door at the street admits into a room of varying size and shape, and of various degrees of cleanliness, wherein are a few small tables, chairs and usually one or two couches or settees of battered leather. A strong smell of cooked or cooking food pervades the air, and a wireless set, usually a radiogram, is in full blast in an adjoining room at all times of the day. Apart from light refreshments, such as tea and lemonade, groceries and food can sometimes be bought, and during the daytime a certain amount of this 'legitimate' business is carried on. Sometimes there are large mirrors on the wall in such apposition as to reflect the entrance of visitors to the café into an inside room; a usual feature of the establishment; to this room entrance is gained through a doorway, sometimes screened, at the back of the café. Here, 'callers' can lounge in a greater degree of seclusion, waited upon and chatted to by one or two of the female attendants. Café proprietors are mostly Maltese, but there are other nationalities in the business, such as Indians, Jews and Africans. In several cases the premises are actually owned by the person running them, and, although there are exceptions, there is no doubt that most of them are what the police are in the habit of terming 'alleged brothels', which come into service after dark.

A contemporary police report on the Bute Street cafés gives a flavour: 'The keepers of the premises are of low moral character. All the cafés are frequented by the wives or paramours of alien or coloured seamen away at sea, who live either on or near the premises. Young attractive girls are induced to work in the cafés as servants and later cohabit with the keeper or one of the misfrequenters.'[2]

Little takes up the theme:

The procedure appears to be somewhat as follows; by virtue of their possessing a food licence, these cafés are able to keep open for 'refreshments' till 11 p.m., i.e. one hour later than the public houses close. This enables alcoholic drinks to be served after hours to those who require them, and full advantage is taken both of the thirst of the customer and of his lack of sobriety. For example a number of concoctions are sold at enhanced prices. In some cases, it is merely diluted whisky at 7/6 per cup: in other cases, when more of a 'kick' is required, a mixture of Australian wine and methylated spirits is supplied. Near beer and hop beer are also available at a cost considerably above their flagon price . . . In some cases the methylated mixture is supplied deliberately for the purpose of stupefying a customer. A more usual purpose is that of solicitation. The café proprietor himself may act as the pander on some occasions.[3]

At this point the girls themselves would take over, perhaps with the initial accompaniment of musicians like Don Johnson or the Deniz brothers, helping to get the sailors into the mood. Interestingly, however, the girls themselves were always from outside the community:

The 'café girls' themselves are invariably white. Some of them are old hands at the profession, and may even specialise in coloured men. Others are comparatively new at the art, and more or less in process of being 'broken in'. Most of these women are fairly young, and some are quite attractive in appearance and smartly dressed. During the day they are to be seen occasionally at a café door, usually wearing an apron, which appears to be a badge of their occupation as 'waitresses'. Their terms of engagement vary. Usually, however, they appear to work on a commission basis with the café proprietor at whose establishment they live. They sleep upstairs in a room which contains a large double bed and a few articles of furniture.

Perhaps most of these girls, however, drift into the Bute Street milieu directly or indirectly through sheer economic necessity. Particularly during the depression in the South Wales coal trade, young girls were forced into such cities as Cardiff to work in some cases practically for their keep alone. After long hours of tedium and drudgery they readily accepted the invitation of other girls like themselves to find relief in the cosmopolitan excitement of dockland and in a life where, as they speedily discovered, they could earn more money in half an hour than was previously produced by a month's drudgery. Added to this is the opportunity for the first time in their lives to wear expensive, even fashionable clothing.[4]

By 1937, when Shirley Bassey was born, the pubs and cafés of Bute Street had passed their heyday, and the advent of war would hasten their decline. By 1940, when Mass Observation sent a team of writers to report on the state of Tiger Bay, the area was starting to become depressingly seedy rather than excitingly so. Their report deals witheringly with the neighbourhood pubs:

The public houses in Tiger Bay are mostly shabby and out of date, of a poor type, and showing a higher degree of intensive drinking than anywhere else we have ever observed. A few pubs have the character of an ordinary British pub with 'regulars' and strong social ties; but most cater simply for selling drinks to seamen, often stimulated by the girls sitting around in nearly all the bars.[5]

Even the girls themselves get a bad press from the cynics of Mass Observation:

Many of the girls are very shoddily and poorly dressed and do not attempt any glamour. Like the pubs which are shabby, and like the cafés themselves, they do not have to compete with anything else in

Tiger Bay to keep up their standard; and their main customers are men to whom anything is glamorous after weeks or months spent fighting the Battle of the Atlantic.[6]

A final note, then, from the Mass Observation report, a little coun-terbalance to the temptation to romanticise the old Tiger Bay:

It would be a mistake to suggest that these cafés are dens of iniquity: they are feeble and insipid compared with their parallels in foreign ports. The atmosphere is crude, but without much virility; the tempo slow, but without much pulse or beat to it. Where there are facilities for dancing, they are used half-heartedly.[7]

3 A Short Account of Mahmood Mattan and the Murder of Lily Volpert

In 1952, when Shirley Bassey was fifteen years old, there was a murder case in the Cardiff docklands that demonstrated all too clearly how the black people of Tiger Bay were seen by the outside world.

Volpert's store was a fixture at number 203 Bute Street, a few yards down the road from Shirley Bassey's birthplace above the Canadian Café. Located amongst the sailors' pubs and the cafés, it was one of the principal reasons for the respectable folk of Butetown to venture onto the main drag. The Volperts were Jews, part of the substantial Cardiff Jewish community who'd arrived over the previous century, fleeing the pogroms of the east (legend has it that many of those who'd embarked in Tallin or Riga thought they'd booked a passage to New York, only to be dropped off in Cardiff by unscrupulous ships' captains).

The Volperts' store was a haberdashers – 'The only time we went on Bute Street was to go to Volperts to get elastic or pins,' says Patti Flynn – but under Lily Volpert's direction it expanded to sell clothes to the local girls, as Maureen Ombull remembers: 'Yes, we used to get our clothes from Lily. She always stood outside the shop and she'd say come in and have a look and so we'd go in and have a look at the dresses and we'd choose one and pay in instalments.'

More profitably, Lily Volpert also offered moneylending, pawn-broking and cheque-cashing services to the sailing fraternity. Her interest rates were high, as they always are in such businesses (after all, it's a high-risk activity, lending money to such peripatetic folk). Some resented her for it, but, like them or not, the Volperts and their shop were a keystone of the Butetown community. They didn't just work there; Lily and her sisters also lived up above the shop.

So the events of 6 March 1952 came as a considerable shock to the community. That evening, sometime after eight, as Lily and her sisters ate their dinner in the back room of the shop, having recently closed for the evening, someone knocked on the door. Lily went to see who it was. Presumably she must have known the caller, as she didn't call or cry out to her sisters. Instead, she was reaching for something from a shelf when her visitor, acting with rare speed and certainty, put one hand over her mouth to stop her from screaming, pulled out a razor with the other hand, and cut her throat with a single motion. He then laid her down on the floor and went over to the till, from which he took almost £100 – a small fortune then, and left. All without disturbing the sisters in the back room. It was only when another visitor arrived a few minutes later that Lily's murder was discovered.

There was outrage and disbelief in the community. For all Tiger Bay's lurid reputation, murder here was a rarity. The Volpert family announced a reward of £200 for evidence leading to the arrest of the killer. Then a West Indian named Harold Cover stepped forward and told the police that he'd seen a Somali man acting suspiciously outside the shop just before the murder.

The police soon came up with a couple of plausible suspects. One was a big gold-toothed man called Tahir Gass, known locally as 'the Crazy Somali', due to his history of eccentric behaviour. The other was Mahmood Mattan, a sometime sailor and steelworker, at that time unemployed, who was known to have gambling debts and to be in hock to Lily Volpert.

Ignoring the fact that Cover had mentioned a gold tooth in his description of the Somali outside the store, the police decided to arrest Mattan. Mattan was married to a Welshwoman, a girl called Laura Williams, from the Valleys, who'd been just seventeen when they met. They'd had three children in the five years they'd been together, had moved up to Hull for a while in search of work, but were back in Cardiff now, living in two separate houses in the same street in Adamsdown – in separate houses allegedly because of the racism they experienced there. Why in such circumstances they stayed in Adamsdown – on the other side of the railway tracks, close to the centre of town and in the shadow of the prison – rather than return to Butetown, remains mysterious.

Whatever the reason, Adamsdown is where they were, and when the police raided Mattan's house they found a broken razor and shoes with microscopic traces of blood on them. Never mind that the razor was clean and the shoes were second-hand, it was evidence enough for the police to arrest him. Mattan was charged with murder.

The trial, in Bob Dylan's phrase, was a pig circus. The evidence against Mattan was flimsy in the extreme. All the police could come up with was the bloodstains on his shoes and the unreliable evidence of Cover who, by the time the trial began, had changed his story to suit the police case and damn Mattan. Any decent lawyer would have pulled the prosecution apart. But Mattan didn't have a decent lawyer; his defence barrister was a clown who called his own client 'a half child of nature, a semi-civilised savage'.* The jury duly convicted the bad black man and in September 1952 Mahmood Mattan became the last man to be hanged in Wales.

Mattan's family never stopped protesting his innocence. His

---

* If you want to know who Mahmood Mattan was there's a photograph by Berth Hardy in a *Picture Post* from 1950. It's in a photo story on Tiger Bay and Mahmood is pictured sitting in the Somali-run Berlin's Milk Bar in the Bay. He's wearing a flash suit and an even flashier tie; he has a ready smile and weakness around the eyes. It's a gambler's face, the kind of face that always finds a woman ready to mother.

widow Laura, alone at first, and then joined by her three sons, Omar, Mervyn and David. The struggle to clear Mahmood's name overshadowed their lives. Like the Basseys, the children grew up fatherless, shame hanging over them.

The evidence to support their case mounted up quickly. In 1954 Tahir Gass, the Crazy Somali, was arrested after stabbing to death a wages clerk called Granville Jenkins. He was found not guilty by reason of insanity and sent to Broadmoor, before being shipped back to Somaliland.

And if that wasn't enough, in 1969 Harold Cover, the iron witness, was convicted of the attempted murder of his daughter. He slashed her across the neck with a razor, in an obvious echo of Lily Volpert's murder. But the Home Office weren't prepared to allow an appeal. It took until 1998 for the case to be reopened. By then there had been a whole slew of miscarriages of justice acknowledged in the courts, from the Birmingham Six to the Cardiff Three. The Mattan case could no longer be ignored. When the case did finally come to court the three appeal judges swiftly struck out the conviction on the grounds that Cover's evidence was thoroughly unreliable. It took another four years, though, before the family were awarded some financial compensation for their loss. It didn't help, anyway. A year after the money came through Omar Mattan drowned himself off the coast of Scotland. Four years later Mattan's widow Laura died of cancer.

Back in 1952 the meaning of the Mattan case for the non-white people of Cardiff was obvious. Don't mess with the world outside the Docks. If you do there'll be trouble. Down here people may see you as a whole human being. Out there, if you're not careful, you'll be 'a half child of nature, a semi-civilised savage'. It's hardly surprising that Shirley Bassey and many of her contemporaries got out at the first chance they had.

4 A Short History of Minstrel Shows

It's ironic that Shirley Bassey's show-business debut should have been in a minstrel show, *Memories of Jolson*. It's a tradition that, for obvious reasons – the negative stereotyping of black people, either by white actors blacking up or by black actors caricaturing themselves – has fallen into disrepute. The strength of anti-racist feeling in Britain ensures that the Black and White Minstrel Show and its ilk will never again appear on our TV screens, and no budding black female star today will make her debut in a revue starring a blacked-up white man and featuring songs from the old plantation.

By and large this is a good thing, a sign of how far we've come as a society, etc., etc., but it's worth looking a little deeper into the history of the minstrel show before condemning it out of hand as a celebration of unbridled racism.

The minstrel shows and their use of blackface are part of a tradition going back to the early nineteenth century. There are records of blacked-up minstrel troupes appearing in the US in the 1830s. They started in the northern states and presented the supposed sound of the plantation – in fact a mishmash of British and Irish folk music with some American innovations – along with some broad and, indeed, racist comedy, all of it performed by a troupe of blacked-up white men.

These shows became immediately successful, and, by the middle of the nineteenth century, were the most popular form of mass entertainment in the US. They would usually feature songs, dance routines and comedy. What's striking, though, is how full of contradictions they were. At the same time as these shows ridiculed the American Negro, they also celebrated him. They could simultaneously incorporate viciously racist and misogynist humour, the elegant parlour songs of Stephen Foster, and some more or less authentic African American dances. As the writer Eric Lott suggests in his book on blackface, there's a powerful mixture of mockery and admiration at play here: 'to put on the cultural forms of "blackness" was to engage in a complex affair of manly mimicry . . . To wear or even enjoy blackface was literally, for a time, to become black, to inherit the cool, virility, humility, abandon, or *gaîté de coeur* that were the prime components of white ideologies of black manhood.'[1]

To further complicate the picture, by the 1840s actual African Americans had started their own minstrel troupes. They generally billed themselves as freed slaves (whether or not they were) and provided a slightly more authentic version of plantation culture, though still for the delectation of a white audience. They even stuck to the convention of blacking up.

The advent of the Civil War and the abolition of slavery, unsurprisingly, impacted on the popularity of the form. Romancing life on the slave plantations was no longer an option. The shows started to become more highbrow and included spirituals and choir singing. But by the early part of the century the minstrel show tradition was almost dead. Vaudeville had adopted most of the key elements of the minstrel shows, but removed the racial aspects. The few black minstrel shows that carried on performed mostly to black audiences.

The blackface tradition, however, refused to die out completely. Crucially, Al Jolson, the great singing star of the early twentieth century, blacked up for several numbers in *The Jazz Singer*, the first talkie and one of the most successful films ever made. Here was a sincere attempt to bring the black jazz tradition to a white audience, yet it was done by a white man in blackface, whose shtick nodded unmistakably back to the minstrel tradition with its undeniably racist history. This is not to say that Jolson himself was a racist: far from it, he was a Russian Jew who believed firmly in equality. Meanwhile popular radio and TV comics like Mack and Moran and Amos 'n Andy were white comedians playing crude black stereotypes for laughs.

What we must bear in mind is that the shows appealed to common folk, both black and white, who simply thought them funny. The intellectual classes may have deplored such shows as demeaning, but the people who were being demeaned often took them less seriously.

Which leads on to the enduring popularity of blackface minstrel shows in the UK. Strangely, given the fact that the British never had any onshore slave plantations, the blackface craze caught on almost immediately. The first blackface entertainers started to appear in Britain in the 1830s, given impetus by an 1836 Royal Command Performance for Queen Victoria in which the American vaudeville performer and Negro impersonator Thomas Dartmouth 'Daddy' Rice sang and danced his character 'Jim Crow', a caricature of a plantation slave.

The initial wave of enthusiasm resulted in such bizarre cultural artefacts as an 1850s song called 'Niggermania', celebrating the new blackface minstrel show phenomenon. As its historian, Michael Pickering, observes:

> The 'nigger' phenomenon was manifest not only on the professional stage, but also as an amateur form of street entertainment. Throughout the century blackface acts could be found at virtually every venue or popular gathering, from the seaside to galas, festivals, town fairs and mops, agricultural shows, charity shows, club days, pantomimes and so on. The 'nigger' minstrel remained a ubiquitous figure in British entertainment until the end of the century.[2]

All this in a country in which black people were virtually unknown. What was the appeal? It's hard to be certain as to the popular taste of the Britain of a century and a half ago, but here goes anyway. Firstly there's the rustic humour: much of the merriment at the expense of the blacked-up pretend darkies is the same as the amusement occasioned by portrayals of rural hicks across the world. The minstrel darkies are no distance from the hayseeds of the Grand Ol' Opry or the Wurzels of the Shepton Mallet agricultural show. Secondly there's the songs: these were often the familiar ballads of the British folk tradition, but now with added transatlantic gloss. And finally there's the dancing – the minstrel shows always offered choreographed dance routines.

So while, in Britain, the minstrel shows never became the dominant part of the entertainment industry, they did have an enduring popularity. And, as in the US, the coming of the mass media gave them a new lease of life. In 1933, the BBC started a radio show called *The Kentucky Minstrels*, a weekly compendium of classics from the minstrel tradition. One difference from the American shows was that this British tribute was an integrated affair. White British comedians and singers worked alongside a smattering of black Americans who'd found their way over to London to work.

What this points to is the profound naivety of the whole project. As far as the British audience was concerned these minstrel shows were an authentic rendition of life in this far-off place called Dixieland. So, if they featured some actual black Americans, well then, that would make the whole thing even more authentic. The black Americans themselves, being entrepreneurial types who had already got themselves to Britain, saw what was wanted and did their best to deliver the very best yessir Dixie stereotypes they could manage. Call them Uncle Toms if you like, or just see them as black showpeople struggling to make a living a long way from home.

The Kentucky Minstrels radio show was a sizeable hit. It ran for seventeen years and featured a revolving cast of guests around a core of three black Americans: Ike Hatch, Shirley's future co-star in *Memories of Jolson*; plus Harry Scott and Eddie Whaley, who had worked together as a comic act touring the United States, and had arrived in the UK as far back as 1909. In 1934, there was a spin-off movie made from the series, also entitled *Kentucky Minstrels*, which starred Scott and Whaley alongside the pioneering black actress Nina Mae McKinney, and was the first British film to feature black stars.

The radio show finally ended in 1950, but there were regular theatrical revues in a similar vein, amongst them *Memories of Jolson*. In 1958 an outfit rejoicing in the name 'Whitaker's Nigger Minstrel Troupe' were touring the northern clubs. And that same year, as television took over from radio as the nation's mass medium, the BBC launched the rather more tastefully named *The Black and White Minstrel Show*.

This show became both the genre's greatest ever popular success and its last hurrah. It ran for twenty years and regularly attracted audiences of over fifteen million. Its spin-off stage show ran in the West End for twelve years. Unlike *The Kentucky Minstrels*, all the cast were white (at least until the comedian Lenny Henry appeared in a late 1970s series). The female performers didn't black up, but the men almost always did.

Today the show is seen as a straightforward embarrassment. The BBC refuses to reissue any of the shows on video or DVD. It's held up as a paradigm of the bad old days when Britain was a nation of racists. Again, though, this is somewhat oversimplified. I'm old enough to remember *The Black and White Minstrels*: they regularly blighted the Saturday evenings of my childhood. My grandmother was very fond of the show. I wasn't. It wasn't the blackface that put me off, though, it was the hideously old-fashioned nature of the whole enterprise: the dreadful corny songs, the hideously perky dance routines, the unfunny comedians. To me at the age of nine or so, the blackface seemed no more offensive than the canes and top hats and straw boaters and so on and so on. It was a nostalgic show for a generation of older white people who knew little of black people and probably didn't care to know much more. Did it inspire a generation of racists? I don't think so. Did it confirm an older generation in a patronising attitude to black people? More than likely.

Watch it now, though, and what's most striking is the incredible naivety of the show. Its offensiveness lies not in any malicious intent but rather in the sense that all concerned clearly didn't think of black people as real people who might be offended by this blackface nonsense, at all. The other aspect that's striking is how professional it is: the singing and dancing are of consistently high standard. As you watch you're seeing highly skilled artists working in a dying medium. It's sad in many senses of the word, and for any number of reasons.

At least part of the sadness is in seeing the end of a tradition – not just of minstrel shows, but of vaudeville and variety, of acts honed by endless touring, of the traditional entertainment of the working people. As much as it reflects a culture which treated black people with prejudice and condescension, it was also the culture out of which came stars like Shirley Bassey, themselves creatures of variety and vaudeville and, yes, minstrelsy.

5. A Short History of British Striptease

One thing I wasn't expecting, when researching the showbiz world of the 1950s, was the central role of nudity or near-nudity in the stage shows of the time. Much of the appeal of the touring revues Shirley Bassey appeared in as a teenager was the appearance of scantily clad dancers. The second of these shows, *Hot From Harlem*, was produced by Paul Raymond, who would go on to become Britain's leading impresario of titillation.

Even when Shirley made it to the West End in the late 1950s, the supporting attractions would always include plenty of near-nudity. Take the show *Blue Magic*, in which she co-starred with Tommy Cooper in 1959. The programme is full of pictures of dancing girls clad only in shiny knickers and pasties to cover their nipples. It betokens a distinctive interpretation of 'family entertainment' in which the show, rather than attempting to entertain all the family at once, seeks to entertain them one at a time. Thus there are dance routines for mum, acrobats for the kids, and girls with hardly any clothes on for dad.

It's all rather more risqué than the conventional vision of the 1950s allows, but in fact striptease, in one form or another, had been a feature of the British theatrical world since the 1930s. That was when a wealthy widow called Lauren Henderson took over the Windmill Theatre in Soho and was having trouble attracting an audience. Plays, films and conventional revues all flopped. Henderson wanted to copy the Parisian cabarets like the Folies Bergère and the Moulin Rouge with their artful striptease shows but, as far she could see, the British censorship laws forbade any such thing. Then her business partner, Vivian Van Damm, spotted a loophole in the laws. As long as the girls didn't move, there was no law against them appearing nude on stage. Motionless nudes were artistic; moving nudes were pornographic and illegal.

So the Windmill started to present shows that alternated variety acts with *tableaux vivants* of naked girls, often imitating a famous painting to prove their artistic credentials. The shows were immediately popular and became all the more so during the war years, when servicemen on leave in London showed a ready appetite for such entertainment. The Windmill prided itself on never closing throughout the war, even during the Blitz, and it began to gather its own mythology as a centre of metropolitan licentiousness. Its ban on audience members turning up with opera glasses or similar meant that places at the front of the auditorium were much sought after, and, as soon as anyone left their chair, there would be the unedifying spectacle of fellow connoisseurs of the female form performing the 'Windmill steeplechase', leapfrogging over the seats in front to get closer to the action, or rather inaction, on stage.

Producers of touring revues soon took a leaf out of the Windmill's book. By the late 1940s striptease artistes like Phyllis Dixey or Chrystabel Leighton-Porter, aka Jane of the *Daily Mirror* (Jane was a cartoon character, beloved of servicemen, who was forever losing her clothes in the course of her adventures), became big stars of the touring circuit. By the beginning of the 1950s a nude act or two was pretty much de rigueur, as Paul Raymond discovered when he was having trouble booking his first variety bills:

I was at the Queen's Park Hippodrome Manchester – the manager said he would book the show if I put in some nudes. The two dancers we had on the bill agreed to take off their bras for an extra ten shillings a week each; they did a single posing act each in the first half, and a double posing act in the second half. So the show, which had been called *Vaudeville Express*, overnight became *Festival Of Nudes*. We took twice or three times what we'd been taking in normal circumstances . . .[1]

Raymond got the message and embarked on the career that would see him become one of Britain's richest men (mostly, in the end, through his property portfolio, which included much of Soho, but also from his succession of strip clubs and soft-core porn magazines).

Gradually the proportion of nudes to legitimate variety acts in the touring revues increased. This growing emphasis in titillation eventually alienated mixed audiences and is often given as the reason for the downfall of the touring revues, which were all but extinct by the end of the 1950s. The truth of the situation, though, was that it was television that killed variety. The public could see better-quality acts in their living rooms than were available in the cold and tatty Hippodromes of provincial Britain. It was actually the strip show – offering something that certainly wasn't available on the telly – that kept the format going for as long as it did. What killed the nude revues, meanwhile, was a change in the interpretation of the law from the late 1950s onwards, which allowed the girls to actively strip, as long as they did so in the privacy of a members' club. And so the nude revues vanished and strip clubs like Paul Raymond's Revuebar started to proliferate instead.

NOTES

One

1 Interviewed by Danny Stradling for *Musical Traditions*
www.mustrad.org.uk/articles/staithes.htm

2 Stan Hugill, *Sailortown* (Routledge & Kegan Paul, 1967)

Two

1 Stan Hugill, *Sailortown* (Routledge & Kegan Paul, 1967)

2 Michael Banton, *The Coloured Quarter* (Cape, 1955)

3 Interviewed by Val Wilmer for National Sound Archive oral history of jazz in Britain

4 Ibid.

5 Ibid.

6 Ibid.

7 Neil M. C. Sinclair, *The Tiger Bay Story* (BHAC, 1993)

Three

1 K. L. Little, *Negroes in Britain* (Kegan Paul, 1947)

2 Ibid.

3 Ibid.

4 Ibid.

Four

1 Court records from the Glamorganshire Assizes, found in the National Archives
2 Report in *Western Mail*, 1938
3 Report in *South Wales Echo*, 1938
4 *Empire News*, 19 February 1956
5 Ibid.
6 Interview with Deborah Ross, *Independent*, 15 September 1997

Five

1 *The Slate*, TV documentary, BBC Wales, 1993
2 Muriel Burgess, *Shirley* (Century, 1998)
3 *The Slate*, TV documentary, BBC Wales, 1993
4 Interview with Dennis Holman, *Reveille*, 15 January 1972
5 *After Dark* magazine, January 1972
6 http://www.bbc.co.uk/wales/southeast/sites/streetsofcardiff/pages/stories_splott.shtml
7 Interview with Dennis Holman, *Reveille*, 15 January 1972
8 *Empire News*, 19 February 1956

Six

1 TV interview with Russell Harty, 1984
2 http://www.bbc.co.uk/wales/southeast/sites/streetsofcardiff/pages/stories_splott.shtml
3 *Sunday Express*, 6 December 1970
4 *National Tattler*, May 1970
5 BBC radio documentary on Tiger Bay, 1964
6 *The Slate*, TV documentary, BBC Wales, 1993
7 Interview with Dennis Holman, *Reveille*, 15 January 1972
8 *Empire News*, 19 February 1956
9 *The Age*, 2003
10 *Wales on Sunday*, 11 October 1998
11 *The Slate*, TV documentary, BBC Wales, 1993
12 Interview with Deborah Ross, *Independent*, 15 September 1997

13 Ibid.

14 *Wales on Sunday*, 1989

15 The *People*, 1958

16 Interview with Deborah Ross, *Independent*, 15 September 1997

17 Norman Dennis, Fernando Henriques, and Clifford Slaughter, *Coal is Our Life* (London, 1956)

Seven

1 David Rayvern Allen, *John Arlott* (HarperCollins, 1994)

2 *Melody Maker*, 1958

3 As quoted in Wendy Webster, *Imagining Home: gender, 'race' and national identity, 1945–64* (UCL Press, 1998)

4 *Empire News*, 26 February 1956

Eight

1 *Empire News*, 26 February 1956

2 Ibid.

3 Roy Hudd, *Roy Hudd's Cavalcade of Variety Acts: A Who Was Who of Light Entertainment, 1945–60* (Robson Books, 1998)

4 *Empire News*, 26 February 1956

5 *This Is Your Life*, 1972

6 *Empire News*, 26 February 1956

7 Ibid.

8 *This Is Your Life*, 1972

9 The *People*, 25 January 1958

10 *Daily Mail*, 17 January 1998

11 The *People*, 25 January 1958

12 Joe Collins, *A Touch Of Collins* (Columbus, 1986)

13 Ibid.

14 Roy Hudd, *Roy Hudd's Cavalcade of Variety Acts: A Who Was Who of Light Entertainment, 1945–60* (Robson Books, 1998)

15 www.nutsandboltscomedy.com/cyril_lagey.html

16 *Empire News*, 26 February 1956

17 Joe Collins, *A Touch Of Collins* (Columbus, 1986)

18 BBC Radio 4, *Woman's Hour*, 1957

19 Muriel Burgess, *Shirley* (Century, 1998)

20 Ibid.

21 *Jet*, 26 August 1954

22 Interviewed for National Sound Archive oral history of jazz in Britain

23 The *People*, 25 January 1958

Nine

1 *National Tattler*, May 1970

2 *Empire News*, 26 February 1956

3 *The Age*, 2003

4 Michael Sullivan, *There's No People Like Show People* (Quadrant, 1984)

5 *Empire News*, 4 March 1956

6 Michael Sullivan, *There's No People Like Show People* (Quadrant, 1984)

7 Ibid.

8 *Empire News*, 4 March 1956

9 The *People*, 25 January 1958

10 *Daily Telegraph* letters page, 3 December 1968

11 Michael Sullivan, *There's No People Like Show People* (Quadrant, 1984)

12 Ibid.

13 Ibid.

14 Ibid.

15 Ibid.

16 Ibid.

17 Ibid.

18 Ibid.

Ten

1 *Empire News*, 4 March 1956

2 Michael Sullivan, *There's No People Like Show People* (Quadrant, 1984)

3 Ibid.

4 *Empire News*, 4 March 1956
5 Michael Sullivan, *There's No People Like Show People* (Quadrant, 1984)
6 Ibid.
7 Ibid.
8 Ibid.
9 Donald Auty, *Twilight of the Touring Revue* www.arthurlloyd.co.uk/Twighlight.htm
10 Michael Sullivan, *There's No People Like Show People* (Quadrant, 1984)
11 *Daily Mail*, 24 June 2006
12 Ibid.
13 Michael Sullivan, *There's No People Like Show People* (Quadrant, 1984)
14 Ibid.
15 Ibid.
16 Ibid.
17 *Empire News*, 19 February 1956
18 Michael Sullivan, *There's No People Like Show People* (Quadrant, 1984)
19 Pamela W. Logan, *Jack Hylton Presents* (BFI, 1995)

Eleven

1 Anthony Reynolds, *The Impossible Dream* (Jawbone Press, 2009)
2 Al Read, *It's All in the Book* (W.H. Allen, 1985)
3 *Evening Standard*, December 1955
4 *Sunday Dispatch*, 18 December 1955
5 *South Wales Echo*, January 1956
6 Ibid.
7 Ibid.
8 *South Wales Echo*, 13 October 1957

Twelve

1 *Sunday Mirror*, 19 September 1982
2 Ibid.
3 Michael Sullivan, *There's No People Like Show People* (Quadrant, 1984)
4 Ibid.
5 *Sunday Pictorial*, 12 February 1958
6 Ibid.
7 Ibid.
8 Michael Sullivan, *There's No People Like Show People* (Quadrant, 1984)
9 Ibid.
10 Tommy Steele, *Bermondsey Boy* (Michael Joseph, 2006)
11 Michael Sullivan, *There's No People Like Show People* (Quadrant, 1984)
12 *Sunday Pictorial*, 12 February 1958
13 Michael Sullivan, *There's No People Like Show People* (Quadrant, 1984)
14 Ibid.

Thirteen

1 Michael Sullivan, *There's No People Like Show People* (Quadrant, 1984)
2 Ibid.
3 *Las Vegas Sun*, February 1957
4 *New Musical Express*, February 1957
5 Michael Sullivan, *There's No People Like Show People* (Quadrant, 1984)
6 Ibid.
7 *Picturegoer*, 17 January 1959
8 *Sunday Express*, 17 December 1961
9 Michael Sullivan, *There's No People Like Show People* (Quadrant, 1984)
10 Ibid.

Fourteen

1 *Saturday Evening News*, 28 April 1957
2 *Evening News*, 6 January 1957
3 *Daily Sketch*, 14 May 1957
4 *Empire News*, 28 July 1957
5 Michael Sullivan, *There's No People Like Show People* (Quadrant, 1984)
6 Ibid.
7 *Sunday Pictorial*, 12 February 1958
8 *Daily Sketch*, 11 November 1957
9 *South Wales Echo*, 13 November 1957

Fifteen

1 The *People*, 26 January 1958
2 The *People*, 2 February 1958
3 The *People*, 9 February 1958
4 The *People*, 25 May 1958
5 Michael Sullivan, *There's No People Like Show People* (Quadrant, 1984)
6 *New Musical Express*, 26 December 1958

Sixteen

1 *Daily Mail*, 19 November 1958
2 *South Wales Echo*, 26 November 1958
3 *Picturegoer*, 10 January 1959
4 *TV Mirror*, 10 January 1959
5 *Daily Sketch*, 26 January 1959
6 Michael Sullivan, *There's No People Like Show People* (Quadrant, 1984)
7 Ibid.
8 Anthony Reynolds, *The Impossible Dream* (Jawbone Press, 2009)
9 The Walker Brothers, *No Regrets* (John Blake Publishing, 2009)
10 *Melody Maker*, 25 April 1959
11 *Daily Mirror*, 31 August 1959
12 *South Wales Echo*, December 1959
13 *Daily Mail*, 16 December 1959

Seventeen

1 *Picturegoer*, 2 January 1960

2 *News of the World*, 8 May 1960

3 Al Burnett, *Knave of Clubs* (Arthur Barker, 1963)

4 Ibid.

5 Michael Sullivan, *There's No People Like Show People* (Quadrant, 1984)

6 *Wales on Sunday*, 5 May 1991

7 Andrew Loog Oldham, *Stoned* (Secker, 2000)

8 Ibid.

Eighteen

1 Michael Sullivan, *There's No People Like Show People* (Quadrant, 1984)

2 Lord Montagu, *Wheels Within Wheels* (Weidenfeld, 2000)

3 Michael Sullivan, *There's No People Like Show People* (Quadrant, 1984)

4 *Photoplay*, April 1962

5 *Sunday Mirror*, 19 September 1982

6 Michael Sullivan, *There's No People Like Show People* (Quadrant, 1984)

7 Interview with Dennis Holman, *Reveille*, 15 January 1972

8 *Today*, November 1961

9 *Sunday Express*, 17 December 1961

Nineteen

1 Interviewed by Spencer Leigh www.jazzprofessional.com/interviews/ Ken_Mackintosh%20Interview.html

2 BBC Radio 2 interview, 25 May 2003

3 *Sunday Express*, May 1962

4 *Sunday Pictorial*, 30 September 1962

5 *Daily Mail*, 24 November 1962

6 Michael Sullivan, *There's No People Like Show People* (Quadrant, 1984)

7 *St Petersburg Times*, 13 January 1963

8 *Daily Record*, 1 November 2009

9 *Daily Mail*, 4 April 1963

10 *Independent*, 3 March 2009

11 *Daily Mirror*, 19 October 1963

12 Ibid.

Twenty

1 Quoted in profile by David Ades for the Robert Farnon Society
www.rfsoc.org.uk/tosborne.shtml

2 *Daily Sketch*, 9 September 1963

3 *New Musical Express*, March 1964

4 Sid Bernstein, *It's Sid Bernstein Calling* (Jonathan David, 2001)

5 *New Musical Express*, March 1964

6 *The Real Shirley Bassey*, Channel 4, 1990

7 *News of the World*, 5 April 1970

8 Yolande Finch, *Finchy* (Arrow, 1980)

9 Ibid.

10 *Sunday Mirror*, 19 September 1982

11 Elaine Dundy, *Finch Bloody Finch* (Michael Joseph, 1980)

12 *Sunday Mirror*, 19 September 1982

Twenty-One

1 *Daily Express*, 5 August 1964

2 Sarah Miles, *Serves Me Right* (Macmillan, 1994)

3 *Sunday Mirror*, 19 September 1982

4 *The Real Shirley Bassey*, Channel 4, 1990

5 Leslie Bricusse, *The Music Man* (Metro, 2006)

6 *The Real Shirley Bassey*, Channel 4, 1990

7 *The Slate*, TV documentary, BBC Wales, 1993

8 *The Real Shirley Bassey*, Channel 4, 1990

9 *Daily Express*, 15 September 1964

Twenty-Two

1 *South Wales Echo*, 13 September 1965
2 *Hello* magazine, 2007
3 *Daily Express*, 20 July 1966
4 *The Times*, 20 July 1966

Twenty-Three

1 *Western Mail*, 17 March 1967
2 *News of the World*, 27 March 1967
3 Ibid.
4 *Sunday Telegraph*, 2 April 1967
5 *South Wales Echo*, 5 July 1967
6 *Daily Mirror*, 26 June 1967
7 *Wales on Sunday*, 1988

Appendices

Appendix 2: Bute Street and its Cafés

1 K. L. Little, *Negroes in Britain* (Kegan Paul, 1947)
2 1930 police report found in the Glamorgan Record Office
3 K. L. Little, *Negroes in Britain* (Kegan Paul, 1947)
4 Ibid.
5 *Mass Observation Report: Tiger Bay* (Mass Observation, July 1941)
6 Ibid.
7 Ibid.

Appendix 4: A Short History of Minstrel Shows

1 Eric Lott, *Love and Theft: Blackface Minstrelsy and the American Working Class* (New York, Oxford University Press, 1993)
2 Michael Pickering, *John Bull in Blackface* (*Popular Music*, 16 February 1997)

Appendix 5: A Short History of British Striptease

1 Roger Wilmot, *Kindly Leave The Stage! The Story of Variety 1919–1960* (Methuen, 1985)

ACKNOWLEDGMENTS

Writing a biography like this, concerning the life of a woman as a famous as Dame Shirley Bassey, I have found help and information in any number of places. There's hardly a Cardiffian of a certain generation without a story to tell. And, in the age of the internet, there have been any number of anonymous bloggers and amateur historians who have provided invaluable titbits of information. My thanks to all of them.

In writing the early, historical, sections of the book, I am enormously indebted to the pioneering work of Val Wilmer, Britain's foremost historian of both the jazz world and the black British presence, who has been unstintingly generous with her time and her contacts.

For assorted assistance along the way I would like to thank Maureen Ombull, Kenny Clayton, Neil Sinclair, Louise Freeman, Wyn Calvin, Marion Konyot, Morna Watson, Michael Lewis, Alan and Sheila Hume, Carri Munn, Nick Nicholas, Richard Mills, Max Decharne, Nigel Algar, Mark Ainley, Patti Flynn, Anthony Brockway, Vic Flick, Cathi Unsworth, Big Jim Sullivan, Anthony Reynolds, Richard Thomas, Jim Tucker, Dan O'Neill, and Paul Daniels. I would also particularly like to thank Paul Willets for his invaluable research tips, and Liz Allan for her help at IPC. Thanks also to the staff of BHAC, Cardiff local history library, Glamorgan Records Office, The National Archives, the V&A Theatre Archives, and of course, the indispensable, soon to be closed, Colindale Newspaper Library.

As ever, my wife, Charlotte Greig, was my first and most demanding reader; without her particular brand of editorial tough love this would be a considerably less readable book.

Thanks to my agent, Abner Stein, to my screen agent Lesley Thorne, to Jon Riley, Josh Ireland, Lucy Ramsey and everyone at Quercus, and to Rachel Wright for her meticulous copy editing.

Finally I'd like to acknowledge the financial assistance offered by a Writing Bursary from the Academi, that invaluable resource for Welsh writers.

PICTURE ACKNOWLEDGMENTS

1

Top *Private Collection*
Bottom right *Photo by Associated Newspapers/Rex Features*
Bottom left *Photo by Southampton City Council*

2

Top *Pratt/Keystone Features/Hulton Archive/Getty Images*
Bottom left *Photo by John Pratt/Keystone Features/Hulton Archive/Getty Images*
Bottom right *Photo by Associated Newspapers/Rex Features*

3

Top left *Photo by Mirrorpix*
Top right *Photo by Mirrorpix*
Bottom left *Photo by Popperfoto/Getty Images*
Bottom right *Photo by Popperfoto/Getty Images*

4

Top left *Photo by Keystone/Getty Images*
Top centre *Photo by Len Cassingham/Daily Mail/Rex Features*
Top right *Photo by Bill Howard/Associated Newspapers/Rex Features*
Bottom *Photo by Larry Ellis/Express/Getty Images*

5

Photo by Daily Sketch/Rex Features

6

Top *Photo by Jack Manwaring/Daily Sketch/Rex Features*
Middle Shirley's *Photo by Bentley Archive/Popperfoto/Getty Images*
Bottom *Photo by George Freston/Fox Photos/Getty Images*

7

Top left *Photo by Daily Mail/Rex Features*
Top right *Photo By John Twine/Daily Mail/Rex Features*
Centre right *Photo by Bentley Archive/Popperfoto/Getty Images*
Bottom *Photo by Evening Standard/Hulton Archive/Getty Images*

8

Photo by Tophams/Press Association Images

TEXT ACKNOWLEDGMENTS

Material from *Shirley: Appreciation of the Life of Shirley Bassey* by Muriel Burgess, published by Arrow. Reprinted by permission of The Random House Group Ltd

Material from the *News of the World* © News of the World/nisyndication.com

Material from the *Mirror* and *Sunday People* © Mirrorpix

Every effort has been made to contact copyright holders of material reproduced in this book. If any have been inadvertently overlooked, the publishers will be pleased to make restitution at the earliest opportunity.

INDEX

Adelphi 117, 118–19, 120, 134,
    140, 147
Adler, Richard 247
After Hours 191
'After the Rain' 298
Alleyne, Pankey 86
'Almost There' 298
And We Were Lovers 295
'The Apartment' 298
Arlott, John 61
Arnold, Eddie 141
'As I Love You' 189–90, 191
'As Long As He Needs Me' 215,
    247
Astor, Berkeley Square 112–13,
    115–16
Attenborough, Richard 264, 283
Australia 171, 176–8, 182, 185,
    225, 248–9, 256–7, 274, 279
Auty, Don 108

'Banana Boat Song' 149–50, 161,
    163

Barber, Chris 88
Barry, John 255, 257, 259, 268–70,
    274–5
Bart, Lionel 214–15, 223–4, 257,
    284, 286
Basie, Count 189, 285–6
Bassey, Edith Grace (later Biami –
    sister) 17, 29, 36–7, 40, 44,
    66
Bassey, Eileen (sister) 29, 36–7,
    41, 44
Bassey, Eliza Jane (née Start –
    mother) 4, 9–14, 17–18,
    28–31, 41, 70, 86–7
   Henry's court case 33, 35
   marries Bobo Mendi 44–5
   Mendi court case 131–2
   Shirley's contract 120
   Shirley's memories 38
   Shirley's voice 47
   Shirley's wedding 234
   WWII 36–7
Bassey, Ella (sister) 29, 44, 79

Bassey, Henry (father) 14–18, 22,
    28–32
  child abuse 32–5
  deportation 37
Bassey, Henry Jr (brother) 29, 44,
    51
  music 59–60, 63
  wedding 167
Bassey, Iris (later Denning –
    sister) 29, 44, 131–2, 167
Bassey, Marina (sister) 29, 41, 44,
    51
Bassey, Samantha (daughter) 255,
    257, 271–2, 284
  birth 254
  father 273
Bassey, Sharon Eileen (daughter)
    79–80, 89, 95–6, 100, 102,
    131, 255, 271–2, 284
  birth 91–2
  Daily Mail article 196–7
  and Iris 167
  moves in with Shirley 254
  newspaper articles 178–82
  and Pepe 139
Bassey, Verona (sister) 29
Baxter, Tom 298
Beale, Betty 247–8
The Beatles 249–50, 255–6, 263,
    264
Beaujolais (poodle) 193–4, 197
Belafonte, Harry 149, 153, 163
Benjamin, Louise 'Lulu' (later
    Freeman) 25–6, 49–51,
    68–9, 74–5, 77–8, 80

Jersey 96
  and Mike Sullivan 99–100,
    101–3
  Shirley's pregnancy 90
  war 38–9
Berde, Lily 148, 151, 177
Beresford Clarke, Leonard &
    Sylvia 186, 193
Bernstein, Sidney 256
Bestic, Alan 176
Biami, Edith Grace (née Bassey –
    sister) 17, 29, 36–7, 40, 44,
    66
Biami, Victor 40
'Big Spender' 8, 295, 299
Bing Crosby Christmas Special 241
'Birth of the Blues' 152, 189
Blond, Anthony 227
Blue Magic 199, 204–5, 208, 326
'Born To Sing The Blues' 143
Bowen, Gareth 133, 176, 209
Bricusse, Leslie 268–9, 274
Buggy, Jack 217–19
Burgess, Muriel 87
'Burn My Candle (At Both Ends)'
    3, 114–15, 117–18, 121–2,
    129, 130, 136, 141, 143
Burnett, Al 216–17
Burns, Sydney 81, 106
'By the Light of the Silvery Moon'
    79, 96

Café de Paris 144–6, 147–9, 164
Calvert, Eddie 189
Calvin, Wyn 48, 63–6, 91

Canadian Café 29–31, 58
Caribbean Heatwave 96
Carnegie Hall 255–6
Casa Blanca Club 60–1
Charlesworth, Peter 202, 204,
    205, 209, 215–20, 235, 256
Ciro's 150, 159–61
Clarke, John 217–18
Clayton, Kenny 276–8, 279, 280,
    284–6
'Climb Every Mountain' 235
Coffey, John 292
Coles, Shirley 52
Collins, Joan 160, 215
Collins, Joe 81–2, 86, 106
Columbia Records 151–2, 153–4
Cooper, Helen 136–7
Cooper, Tommy 2, 199, 326
Craig, Eddie 61
Curran's factory 53–4, 56–7, 60

Daniels, Dusty 84
Daniels, Maxine 187
Daniels, Paul 14
Davies, Beryl 31
Davies, Russell 243
Davis, Gloria 163, 168, 172
Davis, Mahala 72
Davis, Sammy Jr 152, 153, 158,
    216
Davis, Terence Pepe 134, 136–40,
    146–7, 163, 170–7, 180
  Pix libel action 248–9
  trial 182, 184–5
Dean Martin Show 285

Dearing, Michele 165–6
Delfont, Bernard 222–3, 283
Deniz, Antoni 24
Deniz brothers 58, 305, 313
Deniz, Frank 22, 24
Deniz, Gertrude 24
Deniz, Joe 22, 24
Deniz, Laurie 24
Denning, Bill 44
Denning, Iris (née Bassey – sister)
    29, 44, 131–2, 167
Desert Island Discs 210
Dhery, Robert 117
'Diamonds Are Forever' 275n,
    297
Dodd, Ken 214
Don't Be Shy, Girls... 108–9
Durrant, Pat 43, 46

'Ebb Tide' 85, 87, 97
Eckstine, Billy 59–60, 155
Ed Sullivan Show 219
Edwards, Jimmy 117
Embassy Club 140
EMI 205–6, 279
Empire, Glasgow 110–11
Ennis, John 163–4
Evans, Laurie 262

The Fabulous Miss Bassey 207,
    219
Fields, Gracie 92
Finch, Peter 259–68, 271, 273,
    274
'Fire Down Below' 170

Flick, Vic 257–8, 270
Flynn, Patti 49, 60, 316
Forbes, Bryan 283
Ford, Mary 31
Forsyth, Bruce 191
Frank, Elizabeth 127
Franz, Johnny 123–4, 141, 142, 143, 149, 154, 161, 164, 189–90, 205–6
Freeman, Beryl 51
Freeman, Iris 70, 72, 84, 87
Freeman, Johnny 49
French, Louis 30
French, Walter 48–9, 50–1
Friend, Donald 228

Garland, Judy 97, 210, 248, 252, 264
Garry Moore Show 247
Gill, Chris 74
Gilmour, David 208
'The Girl From Tiger Bay' 296, 299
'Goldfinger' 3, 268–71, 273, 274, 276, 299
Gollin, Ed 152, 153
Gomez, Eddie 58, 60–1
'Gone' 255, 264
Gordon, Bruce 177
Gordon, Cliff 69–70, 72, 73
Grade, Leslie 161, 162, 186
Grant, Ian 145
Green, Bertie 112–13

Hall, Angus 200–1

Hall, Bernard 279
Hall, Tom 12
Hamilton, Barry 146–7
Hancock, Tony 117
'Hands Across The Sea' 189
Harry, Ifor 42, 87
Hartford-Davis, Robert 135, 136
Hatch, Ike 73–4
Hawley, Richard 298
The Heart of Show Business 288–9
Heliwell, Arthur 180
Henderson, Lauren 326–7
Henshall, William 79
Hill, Vince 283
Hippodrome, Keighley 108–10, 112
Hippodrome, London 161–2, 168, 169–70
Holness, Harold 85
Hot From Harlem 71, 81–91, 326
Hover, Herman 159–60, 161
Hudd, Roy 73, 83
Hugill, Stan 19–20
Hull, Tom 154
Hume, Alan 226–7, 229, 234–5, 255, 293
Hume, Kenneth (husband) 6–9, 225–37, 241–5, 262, 263, 264–5
    And We Were Lovers 295
    death 292–4
    divorce 265, 266, 273
    fatherhood 253–4
    as manager 236–7, 275–9, 282, 287–92

marriage breakdown 245–6
reconciliation 249, 250
sacks Charlesworth 256
Shirley in hospital 273
Hume, Sheila 6, 226, 228, 234–5, 255, 293
Hylton, Jack 116–21, 124–5, 140–1, 145

'I Could Have Danced All Night' 247
'I (Who Have Nothing)' 251–3
'I Wish I Had a Needle and Thread' 154, 164, 170
'If You Go Away' 295
'I'll Get By' 241
'I'm Still Here' 297–8
Innocent, Mal 61

Jack Hylton Presents 120–1, 123
James, Sydney 99, 110
Jarrett, Bertie 83
Jemmett, Maureen (later Ombull) 49, 50–1, 68
Johnson, Ben 69, 74, 78, 93–4, 95, 96–7, 105
Johnson, Derek 237
Johnson, Don 21–2, 23, 58, 305, 313
Johnson, Iris (half-sister) 14
Johnson, Pamela 74, 77, 78
Johnson, Samuel 14, 44
Jones, Mai 64–6, 210
Jones, Tom 2, 275, 296
Jones, Vivian 54

Josephine 6–7, 223–4, 284, 287–92, 294

Katleman, Beldon 156, 157
Kaye, Danny 274
Keeler, Christine 204, 249
Kellond, Betty 91, 92, 116
Kennedy, John F. 247–8
Kent, Howard 294
King, Dave 119
King, Gil 282, 283, 284
King, Maurice 198, 201, 202–4, 218–19, 220
'Kiss Me Honey, Honey, Kiss Me' 190, 191, 298
Kitt, Eartha 97, 145, 160, 217
Konyot, Marion 126, 127, 128, 131, 134
Kray twins 203–4

Lagey, Cyril 83–4
Lambert, Gavin 284
Lane, Naida 84, 88
Las Vegas 150, 154–9, 279, 285
Lee, Benny 113
Lee, David 120
Levy, Hilary 80n
Lewis, Michael J. 282–3, 284, 287
Lewis, Vic 258–9, 274
Liberace 148, 210
Lincoln, Jean 222–3, 293
Link, Terry 84
Little, Kenneth 27–8, 311–14
Loew, Arthur Jr 160
Loftus, Peter 96–7

Long, Raymond 242
Los Angeles 159–61, 284–5
Love, Geoff 206–7, 235
Lynch, Kenny 222
Lyons, Walter 249

McAuliffe, John 273
McCall, Chrissie 203
McGarvey, Paddy 128–31
Mackintosh, Ken 241, 242
Marriner, John 92–3
Martin, George 251, 253, 255, 264
Mattan, Mahmood 316–19
Meadows, Bertie 171
Meek, Joe 141–2
Memories of Jolson 69–78, 79–80, 82, 324
Mendi, Joseph 'Bobo' (stepfather) 44–5, 47, 86–7, 131–2, 133
Metcalfe, Alfred 12–13, 18
Metcalfe, Florence (half-sister) 13, 133
Miller, Mitch 151–2, 154
Mills, Richard 202–3
minstrel shows 73, 320–5
Mods and Rockers 263
Mollia, Lawrence 29–31
Montagu, Lord Edward 228–9
Monte Carlo 168–9
Morecambe & Wise Show 87
Morley, Angela 143
'Mr Kiss Kiss Bang Bang' 274–5
Muller, Robert 193–7
'My Body's More Important Than My Mind' 145, 187

'My Special Dream' 253
Myers, Stanley 94

Napoleon and Josephine see Josephine
'Never Never Never' 298
Neville-Willing, Major Donald 144, 145, 148
New Theatre, Cardiff 162, 167
New York 150–4, 255–6
Newell, Norman 205–6, 215, 235, 243, 269
Newley, Anthony 210, 213, 214–15, 223–4, 268, 277
Night of a Hundred Stars 187–9, 264
Nightingale, Benny 74
Norman, Barry 245, 246

Oldham, Andrew Loog 222–3
Oliver! 214–15, 286–7
Olivier, Lawrence 187, 259–60
'On A Wonderful Day Like Today' 277–8
Onassis, Aristotle 168
Osborne, Tony 251–2, 253, 255

Pacter, Trudi 135
Paris 150
Parker, Beryl 84
Parker, Ross 113–15, 116–17, 118, 145
Parker, Victor 'Narker' 58
Parry, George 61–2
Paul, Les 145, 189

Pavlou, Maria 117
The Performance 281, 296
Perrick, Eve 176
the Persian Room 220, 237, 247
the Pigalle 216–19, 259, 275
Pix libel action 248–9
Please Sir 282–4, 292
Podell, Jules 153
Podola, Guenther 208
Presley, Elvis 122n

Quinton, Peter 173–6

Rainbow Club 48, 51, 66, 68,
    162–3, 166, 167
El Rancho 150, 154–9
Ratner, Dr Victor 8, 292, 293
Raymond, Paul 81, 326, 327–8
Raymonde, Ivor 283
'Reach for the Stars' 235
Read, Al 124–8, 187
Reed, Carol 286
Reeder, Charles 218
Regan, Maggie 83–4
Reindeer, Eddie 73, 75–6, 78–80,
    96
Reynolds, Anthony 124
Richmond, Val 84
Riddle, Nelson 242–3
Robeson, Paul 25, 205
Roundhouse 1, 5, 296–9
Russ, Simmie 84

St Cyr, Lili 155
Salzman, Harry 270

Sanders of the River 24–6
Schiffman, Verne 208
Secombe, Harry 108, 124, 142,
    210, 288
The Secret Keepers 245
'Sex' 145
Shane, Cyril 251
Sharp, Clive 198, 201–4, 208–10,
    220
Shirley Bassey Entertains 279–80
Shirley Stops The Shows 274
Showboat 206
Simmonds, Leslie 284
Sinatra, Frank 152–3, 165–6
Sinclair, Neil 25
'Smoke Gets in Your Eyes' 87
Sondheim, Stephen 297
Spettie, Irene (Lorne Lesley) 48–9
Spinetti, Victor 91
Splott 3, 35, 41–4, 60
Start, David (grandfather) 11–12
Start, Doris (half-sister) 12, 13,
    133
Start, Eliza Jane (née Barber –
    grandmother) 11–12, 13
Start, Ella (half-sister) 13
Steele, Tommy 144
Stoddart, Sarah 199, 212
'Stormy Weather' 65, 76, 94–5,
    97, 111, 113, 123, 141
Stott, Wally 142–3, 189
striptease 326–8
Such Is Life 126–30, 134, 141
Sullivan, Juhni 105, 106, 107, 147,
    148

Sullivan, Mike 92–5, 97–130,
  135–7, 164, 168, 199,
  209
  Australia 177, 185
  Bassey homecoming 162–3,
  166
  Café de Paris 144–6
  Daily Sketch article 178–82
  death 246n
  films 198
  first bust-up 116
  illness 170, 171
  and Kenneth Hume 225–6,
  230
  Las Vegas 155–8
  leaves Juhni 148
  legal battle 220
  Los Angeles 160–1
  and Neville-Willing 144,
  148
  New York 151–4
  Night of a Hundred Stars
  187–8
  Paris 150
  and Pepe 136–8, 140, 147
  rift with Shirley 193, 197,
  201–2
  Shirley leaves 202, 204
  Shirley leaves again 235–6
  Shirley returns 221–3
  Shirley's marriage breakdown
  246
  Shirley's recording career
  143–4, 149
  vanishing stunt 186–7

*Sunday Night at the London
  Palladium* 191

The Talk of the Town 7, 117,
  118–19, 262, 295
Taylor, Weston 213–14
television 118, 140–1, 190–1,
  213
  Bing Crosby Christmas Special
  241
  Ed Sullivan Show 219
  The Heart of Show Business
  288–9
  Night of a Hundred Stars
  187–9
  Shirley's debut 119–22
Ternant, Billy 118
'There'll Never Be A Night' 190
Thomas, Dylan 61
Thomas, Jack 162, 169
Thompson, J. Lee 197–8
Thunderball 274–5
Tiger Bay 2, 17–31, 33–5, 58, 258,
  303–15
  Eliza Jane moves in 14
  Henry Bassey arrives 16
  Lily Volpert's murder 316–19
  war 40
Tiger Bay (film) 197–8, 199
Timothy, Al 190
'Tonight My Heart She Is Crying'
  164
Turner, Yolande 260–1, 262–3

United Artists 279

Vaughan, Sarah 59
Volpert, Lily 316–19

Wainwright, Rufus 298
Walker Brothers 203
'The Wall' 154
Wallis, Shani 125, 286–7
Walsh, Michael 279–80
Wardlaw, Bob 107, 109
Warwick, Dionne 275
Watson, Morna 205n
'The Wayward Wind' 143
'What Now My Love?' 243
'Who Can I Turn To?' 264
Wilcox, Bert 89

William Morris Agency 150, 154,
    160–1
Williams, Eddie 84, 85
Wilmer, Val 21, 60–1, 86
Winchell, Walter 160
Winn, Godfrey 200
Wiseman, Thomas 127
'With These Hands' 212–13
Woods, Charlie 83
World War II 35–40

'You'll Never Know' 235

Zahl, Sonny 113
Zec, Donald 207–8